25x ARTICLES | 25x GUIDED NOTE SETS
25x HIGH-LEVEL REFLECTION QUESTION SETS
25x VOCABULARY SETS
25x CROSSWORDS | 25x WORD SEARCHES

25x

25x: Physical Science

version 2.0 - October 1, 2024

For more information: 3andB.com | email: info@3andB.com

11/2024
RDM

Welcome & Instructions

Welcome to 3andB's *25x: Physical Science - HS* workbook. Our workbook is an ideal resource for parents and educators who are looking to introduce students to important concepts and terminology related to physical science.

As a parent or teacher, we suggest reviewing and familiarizing yourself with the workbook content to facilitate a more engaging learning experience. We recommend assigning a designated time each week for the student to complete the assigned reading, guided notes, reflection questions, and term definitions, followed by word search and crossword activities.

Our workbook is strategically structured with 25+ topics that offer a comprehensive overview of important physical science concepts, terminology, and best practices. Each section includes a short and engaging article followed by guided notes and thought-provoking reflection questions, allowing students to internalize the material and apply it to their daily lives.

To enhance the learning experience, we suggest discussing the concepts with the students and encouraging them to brainstorm real-life scenarios where they can apply the concepts learned. This approach brings theoretical concepts to life, leading to a more meaningful and engaging experience for the students.

The workbook also includes 14 terms per section that the students are encouraged to define. We recommend that educators reinforce the importance of finding the best answer when defining these terms, as it will aid the students in understanding and internalizing the concepts.

As a career-oriented and professional organization, 3andB recognizes the importance of a high-quality education that prepares students for future success. Our workbook seeks to introduce physical science concepts that empower students to navigate real-life situations with confidence and a greater understanding of their capabilities.

Finally, we encourage feedback from our users to better understand how we can improve our products and services. Thank you for choosing 3andB's *25x: Physical Science - HS* workbook. We believe our workbook offers a great foundation for a fulfilling, successful future for our youth.

Very truly yours,
The 3andB Team

TABLE OF CONTENTS
25x: Physical Science - HS

Aligned to Next Generation Science Standards (NGSS) HS-PS: High School Physical Science

Discover the World Around You:
Why Physical Science Matters

Have you ever wondered why the sky is blue, how your smartphone works, or what makes up the ground beneath your feet? Physical science is all about understanding the world around us, from the tiniest atoms to the vast expanse of space. It's a fascinating field that helps us make sense of our everyday lives and the universe we live in.

What is Physical Science?

Physical science is a branch of natural science that studies non-living systems. It's like putting on a pair of special glasses that let you see how things work at a deeper level. Physical science is divided into three main areas: chemistry, physics, and earth sciences. Each of these areas helps us understand different parts of our world.

Chemistry: The Science of Matter

Chemistry is all about studying matter, the stuff that makes up everything around us. It looks at how different substances interact, combine, and change. Think about baking cookies. When you mix flour, sugar, eggs, and other ingredients, then heat them in the oven, you're actually doing chemistry. The ingredients combine and change to create something new and delicious.
In your daily life, chemistry is everywhere.

Chemistry is the study of the composition, structure, and properties of matter.

It's in the soap you use to wash your hands, the medicines that help you feel better when you're sick, and even in the air you breathe. Understanding chemistry can help you make better choices about the products you use and how you interact with the world around you.

Physics: The Science of Energy and Motion

Physics focuses on energy, forces, and how things move. It helps us understand everything from why a ball falls when you drop it to how electricity powers your home. Physics explains the basic rules that govern our universe.

You use physics every day without even realizing it. When you ride a bicycle, throw a ball, or use a lever to open a soda can, you're applying principles of physics. Understanding physics can help you become better at sports, make smarter decisions about energy use, and even appreciate the beauty of natural phenomena like rainbows or the night sky.

Earth Sciences: Understanding Our Planet

Earth sciences study our planet and its systems. This includes geology (the study of rocks and the Earth's structure), meteorology (the study of weather and climate), and oceanography (the study of oceans). Earth sciences help us understand natural disasters, climate change, and how to find and use natural resources responsibly.

Knowing about earth sciences can help you make informed decisions about where to live (avoiding areas prone to earthquakes or floods), how to prepare for severe weather, and how your actions impact the environment. It can also lead to exciting careers in fields like environmental protection or natural resource management.

Why is Physical Science Important in Your Life?

You might be wondering, "Why should I care about physical science?" The truth is, physical science impacts almost every aspect of your daily life. Here are a few reasons why it's important:

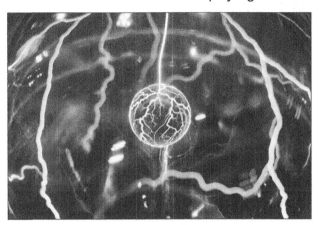

Physics is the study of matter, energy, and the interactions between them.

Problem-solving skills: Physical science teaches you how to think critically and solve problems. These skills are useful in any career or life situation.

Technology: From smartphones to electric cars, physical science is behind the technology we use every day. Understanding the basics can help you use technology more effectively and even inspire you to create new inventions.

Health and safety: Knowledge of physical science helps you make informed decisions about your health and safety. For example, understanding chemistry can help you choose safer cleaning products, while knowing about physics can make you a safer driver.

Environmental awareness: Physical science helps us understand environmental issues like climate change, pollution, and resource depletion. This knowledge empowers you to make eco-friendly choices and contribute to a sustainable future.

Career opportunities: Many exciting and well-paying careers are based on physical science, including engineering, medicine, environmental science, and technology development.

6. Appreciation of the world: Understanding physical science can increase your appreciation for the beauty and complexity of the world around you. It can make everyday phenomena, from sunsets to thunderstorms, even more awe-inspiring.

Physical science isn't just about memorizing facts or formulas. It's about developing a way of thinking that helps you understand and interact with the world around you. Whether you're deciding what products to buy, trying to save energy at home, or considering a career path, the knowledge and skills you gain from studying physical science will serve you well. Keep your mind open. You might just discover a passion that leads to an exciting career or a lifelong interest in understanding some part of our universe.

Introduction

1. Physical science helps us understand _____, from the tiniest _____ to the vast expanse of _____.

What is Physical Science?

2. Physical science is a branch of _____ science that studies _____ systems.

3. The three main areas of physical science are:

    a. _____   b. _____

    c. _____

Chemistry: The Science of Matter

4. Chemistry studies _____, which makes up everything around us.

5. Give an everyday example of chemistry in action: _____

6. List two ways chemistry affects your daily life:

    a. _____

    b. _____

Physics: The Science of Energy and Motion

7. Physics focuses on _____, _____, and how things _____.

8. List three everyday activities where you use physics:

    a. _____

    b. _____

    c. _____

Earth Sciences: Understanding Our Planet

9. Earth sciences include (fill in the blanks):

    a. _____: study of rocks and Earth's structure

    b. _____: study of weather and climate

    c. _____: study of oceans

10. How can knowledge of earth sciences help you in daily life?

_____

Importance of Physical Science in Your Life

11. List three reasons why physical science is important:

    a. _____

    b. _____

    c. _____

12. How can understanding physical science help you make better decisions about your health and safety? _____

_____

13. Name two career fields related to physical science:

    a. _____

    b. _____

Reflection

14. Which area of physical science interests you the most and why?

_____

15. Describe one way you can apply what you've learned about physical science in your daily life:

_____

_____

#1

How does physical science relate to your everyday life? Can you think of three examples?

Look around your room or think about your daily routine. What objects or activities involve chemistry, physics, or earth sciences?

#2

Which area of physical science (chemistry, physics, or earth sciences) interests you the most and why?

Think about what you enjoy learning or what fascinates you. Do you like experimenting with materials, understanding how things move, or learning about our planet?

#3

How might understanding physical science help you make better decisions about your health and the environment?

Think about the products you use, the food you eat, or how you travel. How could knowledge of physical science influence your choices?

#4

Can you describe a natural phenomenon you've observed that physical science helps explain?

Think about weather events, the changing seasons, or even simple things like why objects fall when you drop them.

#5

How do you think studying physical science could help prepare you for a future career?

What jobs or fields interest you? How might understanding the physical world be useful in those areas?

#6

In what ways does physical science contribute to technological advancements?

Think about a piece of technology you use often. How might principles of chemistry, physics, or earth sciences be involved in how it works?

TERM	DEFINITION
Physical science	
Chemistry	
Physics	
Earth sciences	
Matter	
Energy	
Force	

TERM	DEFINITION
Geology	
Meteorology	
Oceanography	
Natural disaster	
Climate change	
Natural resources	
Environmental protection	

What Is Physical Science?

```
V C R K N A T U R A L R E S O U R C E S A F Z N
H Z Z Q J K Q N H K D E N M E T E O R O L O G Y
Y Q W G O Q V N K T M M V U R L H M Y E B K E S
F I P H Y S I C A L S C I E N C E O C E Q U Q Y
J O D F T Z P H S H R G R O M J W E H I G W I M
F T R O P A T V J B W Y O S O Q C O P Z N G B V
Z S P R N P H Z I R H M N M A T T E R Y J M L G
I M H C N B W Q G C L I M A T E C H A N G E V G
N O Y E T G K S K N S O E Y K U T V V H I L H F
O V S M D E U D A T E K N G G D E F Q P C F H Y
V M I F S O M M Z Z E I T E L F G S V Y P U R R
C O C N L L E P A X C N A A I U U C J U Q M W K
B L S Z R O U T B N H R L R Y V L I V U K T F T
G E N E R G Y J E W E Z P T U D C K K U F W P I
W S V G A Y F Q X C M F R H R A U C P F Z H B I
N N B Y I R D P V V I H O S V J O O N P R B C S
F J U U E U F Q O X S S T C R B A Q M B O S Z A
Z G Z B Z W P K J A T W E I K I Z N L D W Q V Y
V D D Y W V I X K R R L C E D B U Y F M Z V P U
Q S Q B A I S T X F Y L T N P G H I P E Q S U B
O C E A N O G R A P H Y I C G N Y M A Z L U R B
X L R K T C G D L J Q Q O E J L H Z B N J Y S T
B B A M N X Q T Y X R Y N S T C C O A F T X L T
F P W J S A Z N A T U R A L D I S A S T E R U P
```

Environmental protection

Natural disaster

Meteorology

Energy

Chemistry

Natural resources

Earth sciences

Geology

Matter

Physical science

Climate change

Oceanography

Force

Physics

What Is Physical Science?

Across

7. Materials from the Earth that we use, like water, oil, or minerals. Natural _____

9. Long-term changes in temperature and weather patterns on Earth. _____ change

11. The study of our planet's systems, including geology, meteorology, and oceanography. _____ sciences

12. The study of weather patterns and climate.

13. The study of the Earth's structure and the rocks that make it up.

14. The study of energy, forces, and motion in the universe.

Down

1. The study of oceans and their systems.

2. The stuff that makes up everything around us.

3. A push or pull that can change the motion of an object.

4. The branch of science that studies non-living systems and matter. (Two words)

5. The study of matter, its properties, and how substances interact and change.

6. A sudden event in nature that causes damage or loss of life, like earthquakes or hurricanes. Natural ----

8. Actions taken to preserve and care for the natural world. Environmental _____

10. The ability to do work or cause change in the world.

The Power of Numbers in Everyday Life

Have you ever wondered how scientists can measure things as tiny as atoms or as huge as galaxies? Or why your phone's storage is measured in gigabytes instead of pounds? The answer can be found in the world of measurement, units, and scientific notation. These tools aren't just for scientists in lab coats – they're all around us, making our daily lives easier and more precise.

Why Measurement Matters

Imagine trying to bake a cake without measuring cups, or buying clothes without knowing your size. Measurements help us understand and describe the world around us. They let us compare things, make predictions, and solve problems. Whether you're checking the weather app, counting calories, or figuring out how much gas to put in your car, you're using measurements.

Speaking the Same Language: Units

Units are like the alphabet of measurement. They give meaning to numbers and help everyone understand exactly what's being measured.

Measurements and units help us to accurately describe different qualities of all kinds of substances.

Here are some common units you probably use every day:

Length: inches, feet, meters
Weight: ounces, pounds, kilograms
Time: seconds, minutes, hours
Temperature: Fahrenheit, Celsius

Using the right units is super important. In 1999, NASA lost a $125 million Mars orbiter because one team used metric units while another used imperial units. This mix-up caused the spacecraft to crash instead of orbiting Mars. Oops!

The Metric System: A Universal Language

Most countries use the metric system, which is based on powers of 10. This makes it easy to convert between units. For example:

1 kilometer = 1000 meters
1 meter = 100 centimeters
1 centimeter = 10 millimeters

The metric system uses prefixes to show how big or small something is:

Kilo means 1000 times bigger
Centi means 100 times smaller
Milli means 1000 times smaller

This system makes it easy to work with very large or very small numbers.

Scientific Notation: Taming Extreme Numbers

Sometimes, numbers get so big or so small that they're hard to write and read. That's where scientific notation comes in handy. It's a way of writing numbers using powers of 10.

For example, instead of writing 1,000,000,000 we can write 1×10^9. Both mean the same thing, but the second way is much easier to handle.

Here's how it works:
1. Write the number as a decimal between 1 and 10

2. Multiply it by 10 raised to a power

Some examples:
$5,000 = 5 \times 10^3$
$0.00025 = 2.5 \times 10^{-4}$

Scientists use this all the time. The mass of an electron is about 0.00000000000000000000000000000911 kg. In scientific notation, that's 9.11×10^{-31} kg. Much easier to write and understand!

Why This Matters to You

You might be thinking, "Okay, but why do I need to know this?" Here's why:

Better understanding of the world: Knowing about measurement and units helps you make sense of information you see every day, from news reports to product labels.

Making smart decisions: Understanding units and big numbers helps you compare things accurately. Is 200 mg of caffeine a lot? How does a gigabyte of data compare to a terabyte?

Preparing for the future: Many careers use these concepts daily, including healthcare, engineering, finance, and technology.

Avoiding mistakes: Remember the NASA story? Understanding units can help you avoid costly errors in school projects, at work, or in daily life.

Appreciating science: These tools let us describe and explore things too big, small, fast, or slow for us to experience directly. They're the key to unlocking the mysteries of the universe!

Precise measurements are important, especially in chemistry.

Bringing It All Together

Measurement, units, and scientific notation are powerful tools that help us understand and describe our world. They're not just for scientists – they're part of everyday life. From cooking the perfect meal to understanding how much storage your new phone has, these concepts are always at work.

As you continue your studies in physical science and beyond, keep an eye out for how these ideas pop up in your daily life. You might be surprised at how often you use them without even realizing it. The more comfortable you get with these concepts, the better equipped you'll be to understand the world around you and make informed decisions.

1: Measurement, Units, & Scientific Notation
GUIDED NOTES

Introduction

1. Measurement is important because it helps us:

   • Understand and _____ the world around us

   • _____ things

   • Make _____

   • Solve _____

2. List three everyday activities that involve measurement:

   a. _____   b. _____

   c. _____

Units of Measurement

3. Units are like the _____ of measurement. They give _____ to numbers.

4. Match the following quantities with their common units:

   • Length: _____, _____, _____

   • Weight: _____, _____, _____

   • Time: _____, _____, _____

   • Temperature: _____, _____

5. Why is using the correct units important? Provide an example from the text:

   _____

   _____

The Metric System

6. The metric system is based on powers of _____.

7. Complete the following metric conversions:

   • 1 kilometer =   _____ meters

   • 1 meter =   _____ centimeters

   • 1 centimeter =   _____ millimeters

8. Fill in the blanks for these metric prefixes:

   • Kilo means _____ times bigger

   • Centi means _____ times smaller

   • Milli means _____ times smaller

Scientific Notation

9. Scientific notation is used for numbers that are very _____ or very _____.

10. Steps to write a number in scientific notation:

   a. Write the number as a decimal between _____ and _____

   b. Multiply it by _____ raised to a power

11. Convert the following numbers to scientific notation:

   • 5,000 = _____ × 10^_____

   • 0.00025 = _____ × 10^_____

12. Why is scientific notation useful? Provide an example from the text:

   _____

   _____

Real-World Applications

13. List five reasons why understanding measurement, units, and scientific notation is important:

   a. _____

   b. _____

   c. _____

   d. _____

   e. _____

14. Think of an example from your own life where you've used measurement concepts:

   _____

   _____

Reflection

16. How might you use these concepts in your future studies or career?

   _____

   _____

#1

How do measurements help us in our daily lives?

Think about your typical day. When do you use measurements, even without realizing it?

#2

Why is it important to use the correct units when measuring?

Remember the NASA Mars orbiter story. What could happen if we mix up units in other situations?

#3

How does the metric system make it easier to work with very large or very small numbers?

Look at the prefixes (kilo-, centi-, milli-) and how they relate to powers of 10.

#4

When might scientific notation be more useful than writing out a full number?

Think about extremely large numbers, like the distance to stars, or very small numbers, like the size of atoms.

#5

How could understanding measurement, units, and scientific notation help you in a future career?

Which jobs or fields might rely heavily on precise measurements or dealing with very big or small numbers?

#6

Can you think of a time when you've seen or used scientific notation outside of your science class?

Look at product labels, news articles about scientific discoveries, or technology specifications. Where might you spot these concepts in the real world?

TERM	DEFINITION
Measurement	
Units	
Scientific notation	
Metric system	
Imperial units	
Conversion	
Prefix	

TERM	DEFINITION
Power of 10	
Kilogram	
Meter	
Celsius	
Fahrenheit	
Decimal	
Exponent	

Measurement, Units, & Scientific Notation

```
K M I Y O W P O W E R E H M 0 X A M I W E N C U
M G V P 0 Y S E M E H E I E K L N O M N A N U L
E F A 0 N 1 P F L C E I C T R P 1 L P 0 M Y M 0
A P O H U D N K 0 R W L E E G L T D E V A R F R
S Y D 0 U 0 D E C I M A L R S K D M R P H E W E
U C L A G F 0 1 C C R M S F E I 0 E I T P P Y X
R O 0 O R F F U T S M Y I X N O X T A H C X X E
E N Y 0 R E E F D N F T U P O P T R L A H F I X
M V O W T N S W S U O V S A Y M M I U P 1 R G A
E E N C P P E 0 1 O E L L X T D C C N W A L Y Y
N R Y X V K T T E X P O N E N T T S I O S K X H
T S C C S R R X E H E G U V K E Y Y T L A G N D
H I P R E F I X I I X X Y P T Y L S S R S R U L
1 O E G 0 V N H M V E P V G S K C T F P R 0 E H
F N N T D Y E 1 X M K G H A U D E E A H A K O G
W H 1 K E W 0 I T X M U H E X H H M H L N K X O
1 K I L O G R A M E Y L K R P O W E R O F 1 0 T
O K Y U D V L 0 D S E S W A G I A W E G F P C O
X Y O N R N N A C A N R P U V O A 0 N K R Y U Y
K H C I 0 M C R P A P O C R F F H D H P S U G M
E Y O T F F D M L E H O U V E Y G V E E R N U A
E H G S D X 0 S H S Y N W G W G N T I G F N H W
H Y 0 P T R R D T C C K U W C N S T T C G K V H
C K F S R S C I E N T I F I C N O T A T I O N A
```

Power of 10	Imperial units	Metric system
Scientific notation	Exponent	Decimal
Fahrenheit	Celsius	Meter
Kilogram	Prefix	Conversion
Units	Measurement	

Measurement, Units, & Scientific Notation

Across

3. The metric unit for measuring weight or mass.

4. The process of determining the size, amount, or degree of something using standard units.

7. The process of changing a measurement from one unit to another, like feet to meters.

9. The basic metric unit for measuring length or distance.

10. A number system based on 10, using a point to separate whole numbers from fractions.

11. A number that shows how many times a base number is multiplied by itself, often used in scientific notation.

13. A measurement system used in some countries, including the United States, with units like inches and pounds. _____ units

14. A temperature scale used in the metric system, where water freezes at 0° and boils at 100°.

Down

1. A temperature scale commonly used in the United States, where water freezes at 32° and boils at 212°.

2. Standard amounts used to express measurements, like inches for length or pounds for weight.

5. A measurement system based on powers of 10, used in most countries worldwide. _____ system

6. A number expressed as 10 multiplied by itself a certain number of times, used in scientific notation. _____ of 10

8. A way of writing very large or very small numbers using powers of 10. _____ notation

12. In the metric system, a word part added to the beginning of a unit to show size, such as "kilo-" or "milli-".

The Magic of Molecules:
Why Chemistry Matters in Your Life

Have you ever wondered why your soda fizzes, how soap cleans your hands, or what makes fireworks explode in colorful bursts? The answers to these questions and many more can be found in the subject of chemistry.

What is Chemistry?

Chemistry is the study of matter, the stuff that makes up everything around us. It explores how different substances interact, combine, and change. Think of chemistry as the science of building blocks. Just like you can create

Chemistry is the study of matter and its various interactions.

amazing things with Lego bricks, chemists work with the tiniest particles of matter to understand our world and create new materials.

The Basics: Atoms and Molecules

Everything is made up of tiny particles called atoms. These are like the Lego bricks of the universe. When atoms join together, they form molecules. Water, for example, is a molecule made of two hydrogen atoms and one oxygen atom (H_2O).

Why Should You Care About Chemistry?

You might be thinking, "That's cool, but why does it matter to me?" Great question!

Chemistry actually plays a huge role in your everyday life. Let's explore some ways:

Food and Cooking: Ever wonder why bread rises or why cut apples turn brown? It's all chemistry! Understanding basic chemical reactions can make you a better cook and help you appreciate the science behind your favorite snacks.

Personal Care and Cleaning: Shampoo, soap, toothpaste these all rely on chemistry to keep you clean and healthy. Knowing a bit about chemistry can help you choose the best products for your needs and understand how they work.

Medicine and Health: From pain relievers to life-saving drugs, chemistry is crucial in medicine. It helps us understand how our bodies work and how different substances affect us.

Technology: The smartphone in your pocket? The battery that powers it? The screen you're reading this on? All made possible by advances in chemistry. New materials discovered through chemistry lead to cooler, faster, and more efficient gadgets.

Environment: Chemistry helps us understand pollution, climate change, and how to protect our planet. It also leads to the development of cleaner energy sources and more eco-friendly products.

Chemistry in Action
Let's look at some everyday examples of chemistry:

Fizzy Drinks: When you open a can of soda, you release carbon dioxide gas that was dissolved in the liquid under pressure. This is why your drink fizzes and bubbles.

Mood Rings: These fun accessories change color based on your body temperature. The liquid crystals in the ring react to heat, changing their structure and the way they reflect light.

Glow Sticks: When you bend a glow stick, you break a small glass tube inside. This allows two chemicals to mix, creating a chemical reaction that produces light without heat!

Chemistry Careers
Interested in a future in chemistry? There are tons of exciting career paths:

Forensic Scientist: Use chemistry to solve crimes by analyzing evidence.

Environmental Chemist: Work on solutions to environmental problems.

Food Scientist: Develop new foods or improve food safety.

Pharmacist: Understand how medicines work and how to use them safely.

Materials Scientist: Create new materials for technology, construction, or fashion.

How to Learn More
Chemistry might seem complicated at first, but it's all about curiosity and observation. Here are some ways to explore further:

Do Simple Experiments: Try safe experiments at home, like making a volcano with baking soda and vinegar.

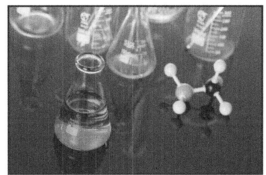

Chemistry is used in forensics, medicine, and making new materials.

Watch Online Videos: There are many great YouTube channels that explain chemistry concepts with cool visuals.

Read Science News: Keep an eye out for chemistry-related stories in the news.

Ask Questions: Don't be afraid to ask your teacher about chemistry topics that interest you.

Chemistry isn't just a subject in school, it's the science of everything around you. From the air you breathe to the latest technology in your home, chemistry plays a crucial role. Understanding even a little bit of chemistry can help you make sense of the world, make better decisions about products you use, and maybe even inspire you to solve some of the big challenges facing our planet.

What is Chemistry?

Chemistry is the study of _____, which makes up everything around us. It explores how different substances _____, _____, and _____.

Think of chemistry as the science of _____ _____. Like building with Lego bricks, chemists work with the _____ particles of matter to understand our world and create new materials.

The Basics: Atoms and Molecules

1. _____ are the tiny particles that make up everything.

2. When atoms join together, they form _____.

3. Example: Water is a molecule made of _____ hydrogen atoms and _____ oxygen atom, written as _____.

Why Chemistry Matters in Everyday Life

List five areas where chemistry plays a crucial role:

1. _____   2. _____

3. _____   4. _____

5. _____

Chemistry in Action

Explain the chemistry behind these everyday phenomena:

1. Fizzy Drinks: _____

_____

2. Mood Rings: _____

_____

3. Glow Sticks: _____

_____

Chemistry Careers

Match the chemistry career with its description:

____ Forensic Scientist   A. Develop new foods or improve food safety

____ Environmental Chemist   B. Create new materials for technology or fashion

____ Food Scientist   C. Use chemistry to solve crimes by analyzing evidence

____ Pharmacist   D. Work on solutions to environmental problems

____ Materials Scientist   E. Understand how medicines work and how to use them

How to Learn More About Chemistry

List four ways to explore chemistry further:

1. _____

2. _____

3. _____

4. _____

Reflection

In your own words, explain why understanding chemistry is important in our daily lives:

_____

_____

_____

_____

_____

#1

How does chemistry affect your daily life?

Think about three everyday activities you do and explain how chemistry might be involved in each.

#2

If you could become a chemist and solve one problem in the world, what would it be and why?

Think about issues you care about, like environmental problems, health challenges, or technological needs. How might chemistry help address these issues?

#3

Describe a chemical reaction you've seen in your own life.

What happened, and what do you think caused the change you observed? Remember, chemical reactions often involve changes in color, temperature, or the production of gas.

#4

How might understanding chemistry help you make better decisions about the products you use or the food you eat?

Chemistry can help you understand ingredients, how products work, and their potential effects on your health or the environment.

#5

Choose one of the chemistry careers mentioned in the article.

What interests you about this career, and what skills do you think you'd need to succeed in it?

#6

The article compares atoms to Lego bricks.

Can you think of another analogy to explain what atoms and molecules are?

TERM	DEFINITION
Chemistry	
Matter	
Atom	
Molecule	
Chemical reaction	
Compound	
Element	

TERM	DEFINITION
Solution	
Catalyst	
pH	
Polymer	
Combustion	
Oxidation	
Synthesis	

Chemistry

```
B I E T V X B C C O G W B K I Q E Y A M B X C N
M A T T E R Q T E X X G J S C Z M P G A I O I T
X Z P S Z X F M F I R L S D K H E K A N B B G X
M O L E C U L E E D E C Y C W O W F R Y R C A Y
X Q H U J V Y I G A J L U H H W C N X B W G Y V
K P Q Y K A U H E T E E C E R W R C B T A W Z G
F E I N L T G G R I D Q S M I L Z K H R O C X T
U L F E H P X M U O S L H I J V H L O P Y A N K
P E C F P Y V Q X N D D S S R P E T Y R D T J H
A M O R C D R F D L J Y Y T V A H D G P N A W R
V E M A A D J R D Y U U L R R H B D I V K L Y F
F N P T E D W E Q R S O J Y I N S N Y V C Y N H
C T O O G G D G I C Y Y F M W M W J B N W S K B
P F U M C F O U L Z N E L S Y W O D G A G T M M
Q N N J G O D X O I T L G P S O L U T I O N M X
F L D B M A E B E R H I L R Z A F A P C R C D N
O M K S Q K V A E I E H S F J L D D H U Z F I P
T X T L R K N R I J S S Z R N J S D G O D L U F
U G P D X O R A N D I X E T J D P T B M K M M H
X F Y H A U W Q X S X D C G Z X U U X T L W P
Z L Q T C H E M I C A L R E A C T I O N X O N S
F W L X Q U J J X U U K O F S M J M P N P W V N
L V S Y R D L Y L M R P D M D Y V Q B P E W M Y
S G K P O L Y M E R I Q Y J C O M B U S T I O N
```

Synthesis	Oxidation	Combustion
Polymer	pH	Catalyst
Solution	Element	Compound
Chemical reaction	Molecule	Atom
Matter	Chemistry	

Chemistry

Across

3. The smallest unit of matter, like a tiny building block of the universe.

5. A scale that measures how acidic or basic a substance is, from 0 (very acidic) to 14 (very basic)

8. The process of combining simpler substances to create a more complex substance.

9. When substances change into different substances through breaking and forming bonds. (Two words)

11. A mixture where one substance is dissolved evenly into another, like sugar in water.

12. The stuff that makes up everything around us, from tiny atoms to huge planets.

13. A substance made of two or more different elements chemically combined.

14. A large molecule made up of many repeated smaller units, like plastic or DNA.

Down

1. A substance that speeds up a chemical reaction without being used up itself.

2. A chemical reaction where a substance combines with oxygen, often producing heat and light.

4. The study of matter, its properties, and how substances interact and change.

6. A type of chemical reaction where a substance loses electrons, often when combining with oxygen.

7. A pure substance made of only one type of atom, like oxygen or gold.

10. Two or more atoms joined together, forming a specific substance.

A Universe Made of Matter: Matter Matters

Have you ever wondered what everything around you is made of? From the air you breathe to the phone in your hand, it's all matter! Let's explore the fascinating world of matter, its properties, and how it changes states. We'll also see why understanding matter is super important in our everyday lives.

What Is Matter?

Matter is simply anything that takes up space and has mass. That means pretty much everything you can see, touch, or feel is matter. The air, water, your desk, and even you are made up of matter.

Matter can change into different states when energy is added or removed.

Properties of Matter

Matter has two main types of properties: physical and chemical.

Physical properties are things you can observe or measure without changing what the matter is made of. Here are some examples:

Color: The way matter looks to our eyes.

Texture: How something feels when you touch it.

Hardness: How easily something can be scratched or dented.

Melting point: The temperature at which a solid turns into a liquid.

Boiling point: The temperature at which a liquid turns into a gas.

Density: How much mass is packed into a certain volume.

Chemical properties describe how matter reacts with other substances or changes into different substances. Some examples are:

Flammability: Whether something burns easily.

Reactivity: How quickly or easily a substance reacts with others.

Toxicity: How poisonous a substance is.

States of Matter

Matter can exist in different states, depending on temperature and pressure. The three main states are:

1. Solid: Particles are tightly packed and vibrate in place. Solids have a fixed shape and volume.
Example: Ice cube

2. Liquid: Particles are close together but can move around each other. Liquids have a fixed volume but take the shape of their container.
   Example: Water in a glass

3. Gas: Particles are far apart and move freely. Gasses have no fixed shape or volume and fill their container.
   Example: Steam from boiling water
There's also a fourth state called plasma, but it's less common in everyday life. You can see plasma in lightning or neon signs!

Changing States

Matter can change from one state to another when energy is added or removed. These changes are called phase changes. Here are some examples:

Melting: Solid to liquid (like ice cream on a hot day)

Freezing: Liquid to solid (like water turning into ice cubes)

Evaporation: Liquid to gas (like puddles drying up after rain)

Condensation: Gas to liquid (like water droplets forming on a cold drink)

Why Is This Important in Our Lives?

Understanding matter and its properties is crucial for many reasons:

Some substances have drastically different points at which they boil or melt than others.

Everyday decisions: Knowing about melting points helps you decide how to store food. Understanding density explains why oil floats on water.

Safety: Learning about flammability and toxicity keeps you safe around household chemicals.

Cooking: Phase changes are essential in cooking. You use evaporation to reduce sauces and melting to make chocolate fondue.

Technology: Smartphones use special materials that change properties when electricity flows through them.

Environment: Understanding states of matter helps us grasp concepts like the water cycle and climate change.

Health: Knowing how matter behaves helps doctors develop new medicines and treatments.

Fun science experiments: You can do cool tricks like making slime or creating a lava lamp using your knowledge of matter.

The world of matter is all around us, shaping every aspect of our lives. By understanding its properties and how it changes states, we gain a deeper appreciation for the stuff that makes up our universe. From making better ice cream to developing new technologies, the study of matter opens up endless possibilities.

Introduction

1. Matter is defined as anything that _____ _____
_____ and has _____.

2. List three examples of matter from your everyday life:

    a. _____   b. _____

    c. _____

Properties of Matter

Physical Properties

1. Physical properties can be observed or measured without _____
_____ the matter is made of.

2. Match the physical property with its description:

    a. Color   ____ How easily something can be scratched or dented

    b. Texture   ____ How much mass is packed into a certain volume

    c. Hardness   ____ The way matter looks to our eyes

    d. Melting point ____ How something feels when you touch it

    e. Boiling point   ____ The temperature at which a solid turns into a liquid

    f. Density   ____ The temperature at which a liquid turns into a gas

Chemical Properties

1. Chemical properties describe how matter _____ with other

substances or _____ into different substances.

2. List three examples of chemical properties:

    a. _____   b. _____

    c. _____

States of Matter

1. Fill in the table with the characteristics of each state of matter:

State	Particle Arrangement	Shape	Volume	Example
Solid				
Liquid				
Gas				

2. What is the fourth state of matter mentioned in the article? _____

   Where can you see it in everyday life? _____

Changing States

1. Match the phase change with its description:

   a. Melting   ____ Gas to liquid

   b. Freezing   ____ Liquid to gas

   c. Evaporation   ____ Solid to liquid

   d. Condensation   ____ Liquid to solid

2. Provide an example for each phase change:

   a. Melting: _____

   b. Freezing: _____

   c. Evaporation: _____

   d. Condensation: _____

Importance in Our Lives

Explain how understanding matter and its properties is important in each of the following areas:

1. Everyday decisions: _____

2. Safety: _____

3. Cooking: _____

4. Technology: _____

5. Environment: _____

6. Health: _____

7. Fun science experiments: _____

#1

How does understanding the properties of matter help you make decisions in your daily life?

Think about how you choose what to wear based on the weather, or how you store different foods.

#2

Can you describe a time when you observed matter changing states in your everyday life?

Remember instances of cooking, freezing water, or watching ice melt.

#3

How might knowing about chemical properties like flammability and toxicity keep you safer at home?

Think about household products you use and how you handle them.

#4

In what ways do you think scientists use their knowledge of matter's properties when developing new technologies?

Imagine creating a new material for a specific purpose, like a water-resistant fabric.

#5

How does understanding the states of matter help explain natural phenomena like the water cycle?

Think about how water exists as a solid, liquid, and gas in nature.

#6

Can you come up with an idea for a fun experiment that demonstrates a property or state change of matter?

Think about common household items and how they might react to heat, cold, or mixing with other substances.

TERM	DEFINITION
Matter	
Physical properties	
Chemical properties	
Melting point	
Boiling point	
Density	
Flammability	

TERM	DEFINITION
Reactivity	
Toxicity	
Solid	
Liquid	
Gas	
Plasma	
Phase change	

Properties & States Of Matter

```
U D E P Y Q W F F L A M M A B I L I T Y P F C K
J E M J N K N R E A C T I V I T Y A Z G E K A C
N N L M Y K N K U N N S O V F N V G K B Y D J P
Z S H B Z Y G W P V I I L X V I R A E S L N D H
N I F A R A J J H U S D P Z Z O M S Y P A U T Y
P T A P R O G R Y U O F O R C Z A D W H I W C S
D Y U G O G U H V S L D G M H Y P J X R N N B I
G U B J E O L X R A I X H I E O D M E V Q X Q C
T I U A G T Z R I H D Y Z P M V P E P K T A W A
T Z O Y V B O I L I N G P O I N T L J J G L D L
T R O A W X Y Y Q X C P C D C A Q T Y F Q U Y P
S F R I H S N P G Y D H E I A E Q I M A T T E R
Y Z W L F C P D H I M E E X L O M N I I V L G O
N B Z P B E O H D A R N Z J P C U G E H C L D P
W D L H Q X H W D P W I E C R I D P H C M G E E
F A Z A N T B O L G S C A P O N M O I I Q C U R
L T J S X O W P W D P X H R P P G I F W O E N T
Q N D E W X X T E I L M T C E Y S N F I X I X I
Z F J C W I F L H D W B Z E R V C T N B P H L E
S K A H L C G R P Z J P J X T G D C R Z H E X S
H R I A Q I K N M G K X C M I G L I Q U I D V L
Z J E N T T W S R I N F X O E X M L G Q Y X K R
H G R G F Y Y B R R M M M S Q L J G T G O R H
Y X I E Y E L I P L A S M A U S Q Q O Y M C T F
```

Phase change	Boiling point	Melting point
Chemical properties	Physical properties	Plasma
Gas	Liquid	Solid
Toxicity	Reactivity	Flammability
Density	Matter	

Properties & States Of Matter

Across

2. Characteristics that describe how a substance reacts with or changes into other substances. ____ properties

4. A state of matter where particles are close together but can move around, with a fixed volume but no fixed shape.

6. A state of matter where particles are tightly packed and have a fixed shape and volume.

7. The amount of mass packed into a certain volume of a substance.

10. How easily a substance catches fire and burns.

12. A state of matter where particles are far apart and move freely, with no fixed shape or volume.

13. The temperature at which a liquid turns into a gas. ____ point

14. The temperature at which a solid turns into a liquid. ____ point

Down

1. How quickly or easily a substance interacts with other substances.

3. The process of matter changing from one state to another when energy is added or removed. ____ change

5. How poisonous or harmful a substance is to living things.

8. Observable characteristics of a substance that don't change its chemical makeup. ____ properties

9. A fourth state of matter, less common in everyday life, seen in things like lightning or neon signs.

11. Anything that takes up space and has mass.

The Building Blocks of Everything

Have you ever wondered what makes up the world around us? From the air you breathe to the phone in your hand, everything is made of tiny particles called atoms. Understanding atomic structure is like having a secret key to unlock the mysteries of the universe. Let's learn what atoms are, how they're built, and why knowing about them is important.

What Is an Atom?

Imagine shrinking yourself down to the size of a dust speck. Now shrink even smaller, about a million times smaller. At this tiny scale, you'd be able to see atoms. These are the basic building blocks of all matter. Everything in the universe is made up of atoms – including you.

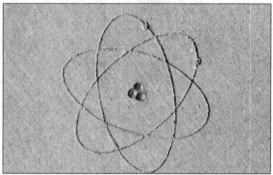
Atoms are made up of protons, electrons, and neutrons.

The Parts of an Atom

Atoms aren't just simple balls. They have different parts, each with its own job:

Nucleus: This is the center of the atom. It's super tiny but contains most of the atom's mass.

Protons: These are positively charged particles found in the nucleus. The number of protons determines what element the atom is.

Neutrons: Also found in the nucleus, neutrons have no electrical charge. They help keep the nucleus stable.

Electrons: These negatively charged particles zoom around the nucleus in areas called electron shells or energy levels.

The number of protons, neutrons, and electrons in an atom can change how it behaves and interacts with other atoms.

Why Atomic Structure Matters in Your Life

You might be thinking, "Okay, but why should I care about atoms?" Here's the thing: understanding atomic structure helps explain so much about the world we live in. Let's look at some examples:

Chemistry in the Kitchen

When you cook, you're actually doing chemistry! Mixing ingredients, heating food, and even the fizz in your soda are all about atoms interacting. For instance, when you bake a cake, heat causes atoms in the ingredients to move faster and form new bonds, changing the batter into a fluffy treat.

Electronics and Technology

Your smartphone, laptop, and video game consoles all work because of our knowledge of atoms. The chips inside these devices are made of carefully arranged atoms that control the flow of electricity. Without understanding how atoms behave, we wouldn't have any of this cool tech!

Medicine and Health

Many medicines work by interacting with atoms in your body. For example, antacids neutralize stomach acid by changing the atomic structure of the acid molecules. Doctors also use tools like X-rays and MRI machines, which work by interacting with the atoms in your body to create images.

Environmental Science

Understanding atoms helps us tackle big problems like pollution and climate change. For instance, we know that carbon dioxide traps heat in the atmosphere because of how its atoms are arranged. This knowledge helps scientists develop cleaner energy sources and ways to reduce harmful emissions.

Everyday Materials

The clothes you wear, the buildings you live and study in, and even the air you breathe are all made of atoms. Knowing about atomic structure helps us create stronger, lighter, and more useful materials for all kinds of purposes.

Atoms of different elements can combine in amazing in complex ways to create a variety of molecules and materials.

The Building Blocks of You

Here's something mind-blowing: the atoms in your body are constantly changing. Every year, almost all the atoms in your body are replaced with new ones. You're literally not the same person you were last year, at least on an atomic level. Yet, you're still you because of how these atoms are organized.

Atomic Energy: Power and Responsibility

Understanding atomic structure also led to the discovery of nuclear energy. This powerful source of electricity comes from splitting atoms (fission) or joining them together (fusion). While nuclear power can provide clean energy, it also comes with risks and responsibilities. That's why it's important for everyone to have a basic understanding of atomic science – it helps us make informed decisions about how we use this knowledge.

Looking to the Future

As we learn more about atoms, we unlock new possibilities. Scientists are working on incredible things like:

**Nanotechnology:
Building tiny machines
atom by atom**

New materials: Creating substances with amazing properties, like self-healing plastics
Clean energy: Developing better ways to harness the power of atoms without harming the environment

As you continue to learn about science, you'll discover even more ways that atomic structure shapes our world and our future. Remember, every time you look at something, touch an object, or even take a breath, you're interacting with countless atoms. By understanding these tiny building blocks, you gain a deeper appreciation for the complexity and wonder of the universe.

What Is an Atom?

1. Atoms are the basic _____ _____ of all matter.

2. Everything in the universe is made up of atoms, including _____.

Parts of an Atom

Fill in the table below with information about each part of an atom:

Part	Location	Charge	Function
Nucleus			
Protons			
Neutrons			
Electrons			

Why Atomic Structure Matters in Your Life

Match each application of atomic structure to its description:

1. ____ Chemistry in the Kitchen   2. ____ Electronics and Technology

3. ____ Medicine and Health   4. ____ Environmental Science

5. ____ Everyday Materials

A. Explains how carbon dioxide traps heat in the atmosphere

B. Allows for the creation of stronger, lighter, and more useful materials

C. Enables the function of smartphones and computers

D. Explains how cooking changes food at a molecular level

E. Helps in developing medicines and medical imaging techniques

The Building Blocks of You

True or False: The atoms in your body stay the same throughout your entire life.

Answer: _____

Explain your answer: _____

_____

Atomic Energy

1. Nuclear energy comes from two processes:

   a. _____: splitting atoms

   b. _____: joining atoms together

2. Why is it important for everyone to have a basic understanding of atomic science?

_____

_____

Looking to the Future

List three areas where our understanding of atomic structure is leading to new developments:

1. _____: Building tiny machines atom by atom

2. _____: Creating substances with amazing properties

3. _____: Developing better ways to harness the power of atoms

Reflection

In your own words, explain why understanding atomic structure is important in our daily lives:

_____

_____

_____

_____

#1

How might understanding atomic structure change the way you think about everyday objects around you?

Think about your favorite possessions or foods. How does knowing they're made of atoms affect your perspective?

#2

In what ways could learning about atoms help you make better decisions about environmental issues?

Reflect on how atomic structure relates to pollution and climate change mentioned in the article

#3

How do you think scientists' understanding of atoms might lead to new inventions in the future?

Look at the examples of nanotechnology and new materials in the "Looking to the Future" section.

#4

Why do you think it's important for everyone, not just scientists, to have a basic understanding of atomic science?

Think about how atomic knowledge affects areas like technology, medicine, and energy production.

#5

How does learning that your body's atoms are constantly changing affect your understanding of yourself?

Reflect on the idea that you're not the same person you were last year on an atomic level.

#6

In what ways do you think atomic science might be used to solve current global challenges?

Think about issues like energy needs, health problems, or environmental concerns that atomic knowledge might help address.

TERM	DEFINITION
Atom	
Nucleus	
Proton	
Neutron	
Electron	
Element	
Electron shell	

TERM	DEFINITION
Atomic structure	
Fission	
Fusion	
Nanotechnology	
Nuclear energy	
Matter	
Molecule	

Atomic Structure

```
R  B  U  N  V  R  K  F  N  Z  B  D  O  A  H  T  T  M  J  A  H  T  J  A
F  U  S  I  O  N  E  G  E  V  R  T  Y  L  O  L  Y  V  W  E  W  V  U  K
Y  C  A  E  B  J  O  N  V  F  X  U  W  P  C  N  T  P  T  B  S  G  W  G
X  Q  A  T  A  C  S  H  H  B  I  K  Z  U  M  L  F  E  M  N  O  L  B  K
L  C  T  Y  W  I  C  H  U  L  N  V  P  D  A  U  D  X  S  T  X  C  L  X
V  R  N  U  X  W  U  L  A  N  A  Q  A  D  A  F  U  V  Y  A  O  C  F  M
B  Z  J  I  H  T  D  C  F  L  N  B  M  O  F  F  N  V  Y  G  K  F  J  P
S  X  M  A  T  T  E  R  A  R  O  I  W  E  F  I  S  S  I  O  N  R  R  N
P  M  K  N  M  C  S  I  T  O  T  T  D  T  U  I  E  M  R  Z  O  L  M  U
W  A  Z  U  R  W  D  K  O  V  E  B  Y  O  L  E  V  U  X  E  M  J  S  C
C  S  M  C  Y  X  M  Y  M  S  C  S  M  N  X  L  M  Z  P  Q  L  H  N  L
E  S  O  L  W  C  V  K  I  E  H  H  O  Y  M  E  O  U  Z  Q  O  X  O  E
W  J  L  E  Z  Y  K  F  C  U  N  C  N  G  C  C  F  J  T  A  N  U  R  A
B  A  E  U  B  B  B  B  B  S  H  O  W  Q  H  B  T  B  E  V  A  S  Y  E  R
Y  T  C  S  X  P  V  S  T  D  L  T  H  L  E  R  A  J  Y  M  F  U  Q  E
A  O  U  F  T  X  W  A  R  J  O  I  A  Y  L  O  M  B  C  X  Y  E  W  N
W  M  L  Q  B  T  A  W  U  S  G  H  Z  Y  E  N  J  Q  C  P  O  W  L  E
B  X  E  Y  D  N  D  J  C  G  Y  Q  N  J  M  S  P  B  X  U  T  I  T  R
G  S  Z  T  D  E  D  X  T  R  S  O  M  D  E  H  P  N  E  R  P  H  Y  G
X  Z  O  U  K  U  Z  I  U  B  F  L  O  S  N  E  Y  R  X  Y  U  V  R  Y
K  G  B  J  Y  T  D  P  R  O  T  O  N  D  T  L  D  O  F  V  J  R  E  O
D  B  V  B  G  R  J  M  E  C  W  J  N  U  C  L  K  Z  C  A  K  N  Y  Y
K  J  W  M  J  O  R  M  D  A  E  C  S  H  T  E  L  E  C  T  R  O  N  E
E  S  H  L  V  N  E  Z  U  L  S  I  K  A  M  R  L  T  A  G  V  A  Y  M
```

Nuclear energy	Atomic structure	Electron shell
Molecule	Matter	Nanotechnology
Fusion	Fission	Element
Electron	Neutron	Proton
Nucleus	Atom	

Atomic Structure

Across

2. A positively charged particle found in the nucleus of an atom.

7. A group of atoms bonded together, forming the smallest unit of a compound.

8. Anything that takes up space and has mass, made up of atoms.

9. A negatively charged particle that moves around the nucleus of an atom.

10. The process of splitting atoms to release energy.

13. Power generated by changing the structure of atoms. _____ energy

14. The center part of an atom that contains most of its mass.

Down

1. The arrangement of parts within an atom. Atomic _____

3. The science of building extremely small machines at the atomic level.

4. A substance made up of atoms with the same number of protons.

5. The smallest unit of matter that makes up everything in the universe.

6. A particle with no electrical charge located in the nucleus of an atom.

11. An area around the nucleus where electrons move. Electron _____

12. The process of joining atoms together to create energy.

Your Guide to the Building Blocks: Organizing the Elements

Have you ever wondered what makes up the world around you? From the air you breathe to the phone in your pocket, everything is made of tiny particles called elements. These elements are the basic building blocks of all matter, and scientists have organized them into a handy chart called the periodic table.

What is the Periodic Table?

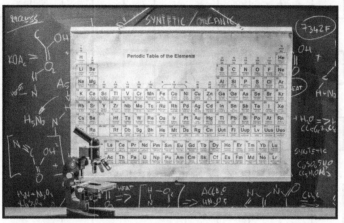

The framework for the modern periodic table has been around since 1869.

The periodic table is like a giant cheat sheet for chemists and students. It organizes all the known elements in a specific order based on their properties. Each element gets its own box, which includes important information like its name, symbol, and atomic number.

Imagine the periodic table as a big family tree of elements. Just like families have similar traits, elements in the same column (called a group) share common characteristics. For example, all the elements in the far-right column are called noble gasses, and they don't like to react with other elements.

Why is the Periodic Table Important?

It helps us understand the world: The periodic table gives us a map of the basic ingredients that make up everything around us. It's like having a recipe book for the entire universe!

It predicts how elements behave: By looking at where an element sits on the table, scientists can predict how it will interact with other elements. This is super useful for creating new materials or understanding chemical reactions.

It organizes a lot of information: Instead of memorizing facts about 118 different elements, the table helps us see patterns and relationships between them.

It guides scientific discoveries: The periodic table has helped scientists discover new elements and even predict their properties before finding them.

How Does the Periodic Table Affect Your Life?

You might think the periodic table is just something you see in your science classroom, but it actually plays a huge role in your everyday life. Here are some examples:

Technology: The silicon in your computer chips, the lithium in your phone battery, and the rare earth elements in your headphones are all found on the periodic table.

Health: Your body needs various elements to function properly. Iron helps your blood carry oxygen, calcium strengthens your bones, and sodium helps your nerves send signals.

The periodic table organizes the elements and their properties.

Food: The periodic table helps farmers and food scientists understand soil chemistry and create better fertilizers to grow healthier crops.

Environment: Understanding elements helps us tackle environmental issues like air and water pollution, and develop cleaner energy sources.

Consumer products: From the aluminum in soda cans to the fluorine in toothpaste, elements from the periodic table are in products you use every day.

Fun Facts About the Periodic Table

The lightest element is hydrogen (H), and the heaviest naturally occurring element is uranium (U).

Some elements, like gold (Au) and silver (Ag), have been known since ancient times. The most recently discovered element is oganesson (Og), named after a Russian physicist.

There's a helium shortage on Earth, even though it's the second most abundant element in the universe. Some elements, like francium (Fr), are so rare and unstable that only a few grams exist on Earth at any given time.

The periodic table might look complicated at first glance, but it's actually an amazing tool that helps us make sense of the world around us. From the air you breathe to the latest smartphone, everything is made up of elements found on this chart. As you continue studying science, the periodic table will become your trusty sidekick. It'll help you understand chemical reactions, and predict how materials behave.

5: The Periodic Table
GUIDED NOTES

Introduction

1. Everything in the world is made up of tiny particles called _____.

2. These particles are organized into a chart called the _____
_____.

What is the Periodic Table?

3. The periodic table organizes elements based on their _____.

4. Each element's box includes:

   a. _____

   b. _____

   c. _____

5. Elements in the same column (called a _____) share common

   characteristics.

6. The elements in the far-right column are called _____ _____.

Why is the Periodic Table Important?

List four reasons why the periodic table is important:

7. _____

8. _____

9. _____

10. _____

How Does the Periodic Table Affect Your Life?

Match the following areas with how the periodic table relates to them:

11. _____Technology

12. _____Health

13. _____Food

14. _____Environment

15. _____Consumer products

A. Helps understand soil chemistry and create better fertilizers

B. Helps tackle pollution and develop cleaner energy

C. Contains elements needed for computer chips and batteries

D. Provides information on elements the body needs to function

E. Includes elements used in everyday items like soda cans and toothpaste

Fun Facts About the Periodic Table

Fill in the blanks:

16. The lightest element is _____, and the heaviest naturally occurring element is _____.

17. _____ and _____ are elements that have been known since ancient times.

18. The most recently discovered element is _____, named after a Russian physicist.

19. There's a _____ shortage on Earth, even though it's the second most abundant element in the universe.

20. Some elements, like _____, are so rare and unstable that only a few grams exist on Earth at any given time.

Conclusion

21. The periodic table helps us make sense of the _____ around us.

22. It will help you understand _____ _____ and predict how _____ behave.

#1

How does the periodic table relate to your everyday life?

Think about the technology you use, the food you eat, and the products in your home.

#2

Why is it helpful to organize elements into groups on the periodic table?

How might grouping similar elements make it easier for scientists to study and use them?

#3

Can you think of an element that's important for your health? How does it help your body?

The article mentions iron, calcium, and sodium. What do these elements do for you?

#4

How might understanding the periodic table help solve environmental problems?

Think about pollution and the development of clean energy sources.

#5

If you could discover a new element, what properties would you want it to have? Why?

What problems could your new element solve, or what cool things could it do?

#6

How does the periodic table show that science is always changing and growing?

The article mentions recently discovered elements. What does this tell us about scientific knowledge?

TERM	DEFINITION
Elements	
Periodic Table	
Atomic Number	
Group	
Noble gasses	
Chemical Reactions	
Silicon	

TERM	DEFINITION
Lithium	
Rare Earth Elements	
Fertilizers	
Hydrogen	
Uranium	
Oganesson	
Francium	

The Periodic Table

```
R V M W E K E E X O G A N E S S O N W J Q U S M
B W E J C P Q W U B U H X N P I M H W N H L K D
C H E M I C A L R E A C T I O N S C Q M S U I P
N S R G V C J I C S K O R I M G L L Q H P S U X
T H Y D R O G E N W N Z A E G F U Y T A Z B Z V
N G S O W I X R N T W T R M T J V B N I J N P T
K C E H D A F R O E L P E K Q T F M Z Z Z P Z Z
V L F A L G I Q B G U J E V S C R Z Z T A D T R
P I P U K J E U L P K S A Y L B A W E N A D P W
D R E B F L H N E Y G B R J E Y N U R A N I U M
R O R J M D M D G D R J T M Z D C J L K T S V H
Y H I I G H O E A K R A H O O J I R P J J I Q G
M T O D R S L G S S B T E D C Z U G B F E C H Q
F L D W G U E A E O K O L D Q N M V F V S K S N
V E I H Z L V C S P M M E X O C G M X G I M L O
C V C F P I S Q F O U I M P X P V C G H L S I B
H F T N W J K R N K H C E Y W C I E Z X I U T L
F G A M Z H Y J L J O N N L Z O D G O J C X H E
V E B Z H J O E N M E U T C J K D N B B O B I G
C E L E M E N T S S C M S Q G G R O U P N U U A
F V E J D K A I S V K B P K K B Z Z M Y Q R M S
J H E F E R T I L I Z E R S R H F I R Z F M X S
X J D K V G B Q I O P R I H C Y Y A I G T C S E
T F U S A O E G W C P Y F Y M U Y E S L T V W S
```

Noble gasses

Atomic number

Uranium

Lithium

Periodic table

Rare earth elements

Francium

Hydrogen

Silicon

Elements

Chemical reactions

Oganesson

Fertilizers

Group

The Periodic Table

Across

2. An extremely rare and unstable element that exists in very small quantities on Earth.
5. A chart that organizes all known elements based on their properties. (Two words)
7. The basic building blocks of all matter in the universe.
9. Substances containing elements that help plants grow, used to improve soil quality.
10. The lightest element, found at the top left of the periodic table.
11. The most recently discovered element, named after a Russian physicist.
13. Elements in the far-right column of the periodic table that don't react easily with other elements. (Two words)
14. An element commonly used in computer chips and other electronic devices.

Down

1. A group of elements often used in technology, like headphones. ___ ___ elements
3. The heaviest naturally occurring element on Earth.
4. A light metal element used in rechargeable batteries.
6. Processes where elements or compounds interact to form new substances. Chemical ____
8. A column in the periodic table containing elements with similar characteristics.
12. A unique number assigned to each element, representing the number of protons in its nucleus. ____ number

Chemical Bonds:
The Glue of Our World

Have you ever wondered what holds everything together? From the air we breathe to the food we eat, chemical bonds are the invisible forces that shape our world. These tiny connections between atoms are like the glue that keeps molecules stuck together.

What Are Chemical Bonds?

Imagine you're building with LEGO bricks. Each brick represents an atom, and the way they snap together represents chemical bonds.

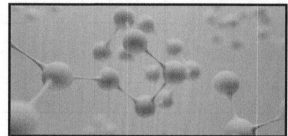

Bonds between atoms make molecules.

Just like LEGO bricks can join in different ways to make various structures, atoms can bond in different ways to form molecules and materials.

Chemical bonds form when atoms share or transfer electrons. Electrons are tiny particles that orbit around the center of an atom. When atoms bond, they become more stable, which is why they "like" to form these connections.

Types of Chemical Bonds

There are three main types of chemical bonds:

1. Covalent Bonds: These are like best friends sharing toys. Atoms share electrons to form these strong bonds. Water (H_2O) is a great example – hydrogen and oxygen atoms share electrons to stay together.

2. Ionic Bonds: Think of these as a game of catch with electrons. One atom gives up an electron, and another atom catches it. This creates oppositely charged ions that attract each other. Table salt (NaCl) is held together by ionic bonds between sodium and chlorine.

3. Hydrogen Bonds: These are weaker bonds, like a high-five between molecules. They're important in water and in our DNA.

Why Chemical Bonds Matter

You might wondering why chemical bonds are important. Well, they're actually incredibly important in our daily lives. Here's why:

The Air We Breathe

The oxygen we breathe is made of two oxygen atoms held together by a covalent bond ($O2$). Without this bond, oxygen wouldn't exist as a gas in our atmosphere.

The Water We Drink

Water molecules are held together by hydrogen bonds. These special bonds give water unique properties that make life possible. They're why ice floats and why water can climb up plant stems.

The Food We Eat
Chemical bonds determine the nutrients in our food. For example, the bonds in sugar molecules give us energy when they break during digestion.

Our Bodies
Proteins, which are essential for our bodies, are long chains of atoms held together by chemical bonds. These bonds determine the shape of proteins, which affects how they work in our bodies.

The Clothes We Wear
Many fabrics, like polyester, are made of long chains of molecules held together by chemical bonds. These bonds give clothes their strength and stretchiness.

Technology We Use
The silicon chips in our phones and computers rely on very specific arrangements of chemical bonds to work properly.

Chemical bonds can create different molecular geometries.

Chemical Bonds in Action: A Day in Your Life
Let's follow a typical day to see chemical bonds at work:

Morning: You wake up and stretch. The proteins in your muscles, held together by chemical bonds, allow you to move.

Breakfast: You eat cereal with milk. The bonds in the milk's proteins and fats give it its taste and texture.

School: In science class, you mix baking soda and vinegar. The fizzy reaction happens because new bonds form, creating carbon dioxide gas.

After School: You play sports. The rubber in your sneakers, made of long chains of molecules bonded together, gives you traction on the field.

Evening: You message friends on your phone. The screen lights up thanks to chemical bonds in special materials that produce light when electricity flows through them.

The Future of Chemical Bonds
Scientists are always finding new ways to use chemical bonds. They're working on:

• New materials that are stronger and lighter than ever before

• Better ways to store energy, like improved batteries

• Medicines that can target specific parts of our bodies

Understanding chemical bonds could help us solve big problems like climate change and disease.

Chemical bonds might be invisible, but they're everywhere. From the air we breathe to the latest technology, these tiny connections shape our world in amazing ways. The next time you drink a glass of water, send a text, or eat your favorite snack, remember the chemical bonds that make it all possible.

6: Chemical Bonds
GUIDED NOTES

Introduction

1. Chemical bonds are like _____ that keeps molecules stuck together.

What Are Chemical Bonds?

2. The LEGO brick analogy:

   • Each brick represents an _____

   • The way bricks snap together represents _____

3. Chemical bonds form when atoms _____ or _____ electrons.

Types of Chemical Bonds

4. Fill in the table:

Bond Type	Description	Example
Covalent		
Ionic		
Hydrogen		

Why Chemical Bonds Matter

5. List three areas where chemical bonds are important in our daily lives:

   a. _____   b. _____

   c. _____

6. Explain how chemical bonds are important in each of the following:

Air: _____

_____

Water: _____

_____

Food: _____

_____

Our bodies: _____

_____

Clothes: _____

_____

Technology: _____

_____

Chemical Bonds in Action: A Day in Your Life

7. Match the daily activity with the role of chemical bonds:

a. Waking up and stretching   ___ Bonds in rubber provide traction

b. Eating cereal with milk   ___ Screen lights up due to special materials

c. Science class experiment   ___ Proteins in muscles allow movement

d. Playing sports   ___ Bonds in milk proteins and fats affect taste

e. Messaging friends   ___ New bonds form, creating carbon ioxide

The Future of Chemical Bonds

8. List two areas where scientists are working to use chemical bonds in new ways:

a. _____

b. _____

9. How might understanding chemical bonds help solve big problems? Give an example.

_____

_____

Reflection

10. In your own words, explain why chemical bonds are important in our everyday lives.

_____

_____

#1

How do chemical bonds relate to the LEGO bricks you might play with at home?

Think about how LEGO bricks connect and how that might be similar to atoms joining together.

#2

Why do atoms form chemical bonds? What's in it for them?

Remember what the article says about stability and electrons.

#3

Can you think of an example from your daily life where you've seen or experienced the effects of chemical bonds?

Look around your room or think about activities you do every day. How might chemical bonds be involved?

#4

How do chemical bonds affect the food you eat?

Think about what happens to food when you digest it and how that relates to chemical bonds.

#5

Why are scientists interested in studying and working with chemical bonds?

What future possibilities did the article mention? How might these affect our lives?

#6

If you could design a new material using chemical bonds, what would it be and what properties would it have?

Think about materials we use every day. What could be improved, and how might chemical bonds help?

TERM	DEFINITION
Chemical bond	
Atom	
Molecule	
Electron	
Covalent bond	
Ionic bond	
Hydrogen bond	

TERM	DEFINITION
Element	
Compound	
Protein	
Silicon chip	
Polyester	
Carbon dioxide	
Nutrient	

Chemical Bonds

```
J  P  V  T  C  O  M  P  O  U  N  D  E  R  Q  N  Q  G  G  M  T  S  P  S
T  G  J  N  F  C  G  C  A  R  B  O  N  D  I  O  X  I  D  E  C  T  S  H
D  O  F  Z  W  Q  U  U  Y  Z  F  X  M  L  P  R  O  T  E  I  N  G  L  H
A  P  K  X  I  O  N  I  C  B  O  N  D  V  G  S  A  O  M  D  K  O  T  R
M  F  I  K  T  R  E  G  E  Q  O  H  N  Q  Z  D  X  U  G  Q  A  S  Y  Y
H  T  Z  C  O  P  M  T  C  U  E  C  U  Z  S  W  Y  D  A  S  Q  J  S  Z
S  Z  K  O  R  K  C  K  H  P  D  L  D  Z  M  J  H  Y  B  E  P  R  C
D  E  S  Q  I  V  U  F  C  P  W  Y  V  R  D  P  Z  U  N  K  G  U  U  I
G  Z  R  C  O  V  A  L  E  N  T  B  O  N  D  N  L  Q  O  M  E  N  G  O
I  E  U  P  O  R  O  C  B  C  H  E  M  I  C  A  L  B  O  N  D  U  D  S
T  Z  U  S  D  E  A  U  V  B  Y  A  R  J  Q  Z  D  Q  G  O  J  T  W  L
V  T  T  T  O  Q  J  P  L  P  R  E  Q  V  Y  I  X  E  O  M  A  R  E  Z
H  O  W  L  A  O  W  O  N  C  T  S  P  N  Y  A  K  T  U  O  N  I  W  N
A  E  P  F  B  T  E  L  E  C  T  R  O  N  U  Q  B  X  X  L  W  E  M  T
I  N  P  R  S  B  Q  Y  E  K  L  Y  R  C  B  X  K  S  Q  E  R  N  R  S
N  E  H  A  B  C  D  E  O  A  N  P  Z  D  J  Q  L  B  M  C  D  T  E  K
N  H  N  E  V  M  I  S  C  D  D  B  F  S  U  S  O  L  G  U  L  K  P  D
A  L  W  P  E  W  B  T  U  Y  T  R  Y  B  E  D  Z  J  G  L  D  J  V  A
F  X  G  V  A  Q  H  E  E  E  L  E  M  E  N  T  N  C  F  E  M  P  T  T
W  R  Y  Z  S  T  G  R  F  B  C  V  D  U  K  K  U  D  Z  E  R  K  X  O
E  N  S  R  R  F  L  I  N  M  J  B  E  X  P  U  O  K  B  G  Y  E  O  M
J  I  Z  D  K  M  O  V  U  Q  U  O  Q  T  E  J  G  P  O  R  T  N  V  J
H  Y  D  R  O  G  E  N  B  O  N  D  A  T  R  G  M  W  Z  I  G  R  R  W
F  T  H  O  O  Z  J  X  J  J  F  S  I  L  I  C  O  N  C  H  I  P  T  R
```

Silicon chip	Hydrogen bond	Ionic bond
Covalent bond	Nutrient	Carbon dioxide
Polyester	Protein	Compound
Element	Electron	Molecule
Atom	Chemical bond	

Chemical Bonds

Across

3. A type of fabric made from long chains of molecules held together by chemical bonds.

5. A chemical bond formed when one atom gives up an electron to another, creating oppositely charged ions that attract each other. ____ bond

6. A type of chemical bond where atoms share electrons. ____ bond

8. A weak type of chemical bond, often found between water molecules. ____ bond

10. A substance made up of two or more different elements chemically bonded together.

12. The smallest unit of matter that keeps the properties of an element.

13. A large molecule made up of chains of amino acids, held together by chemical bonds.

14. A group of atoms held together by chemical bonds.

Down

1. A force that holds atoms together in molecules or compounds. (Two words)

2. A tiny, negatively charged particle that orbits the center of an atom.

4. A gas created when new bonds form during certain chemical reactions, like mixing baking soda and vinegar. (Two words)

7. A small piece of silicon used in electronics, relying on specific arrangements of chemical bonds to work. Silicon ___

9. A substance in food that provides energy or helps build and repair body tissues, often determined by chemical bonds.

11. A weak type of chemical bond, often found between water molecules.

Transformative Power

Have you ever wondered why your bike rusts when left out in the rain? Or how a tiny seed grows into a tall tree? These everyday occurrences might seem ordinary, but they're actually examples of an amazing process that's happening all around us: chemical reactions. Let's get right into what chemical reactions are, why they're important, and how they affect our daily lives.

What Are Chemical Reactions?

At its core, a chemical reaction is a process where one or more substances change into different substances. It's like a magical transformation,

Rusting is a common oxidation reaction.

but instead of wands and spells, we have atoms and molecules rearranging themselves. When a chemical reaction occurs, the original substances (called reactants) are changed into new substances (called products).

Think of it like building with LEGO bricks. You start with a bunch of bricks connected in one way (the reactants), then take them apart and put them back together differently (the products). The bricks themselves don't change, but how they're arranged does.

Signs of a Chemical Reaction

How can you tell when a chemical reaction is happening? Look for these clues:

1. Color changes
2. Temperature changes (it gets hot or cold)
3. Bubbles forming (gas being released)
4. Light being produced
5. A new solid forming (called a precipitate)

For example, when you mix baking soda and vinegar, you'll see bubbles form as a gas is released. That's a clear sign of a chemical reaction.

Why Are Chemical Reactions Important?

Chemical reactions are the backbone of life and the world around us. They're happening constantly, both inside our bodies and in our environment. Here are some reasons why chemical reactions are super important:

Keeping Us Alive: Our bodies are like chemical factories. Digestion, breathing, and even thinking all involve chemical reactions. When you eat food, chemical reactions break it down into energy your body can use.

Growing Food: Plants use a chemical reaction called photosynthesis to turn sunlight, water, and carbon dioxide into food and oxygen. Without this reaction, we wouldn't have plants or the oxygen we breathe!

Making New Materials: From the clothes you wear to the phone in your pocket, many things we use every day are made possible by chemical reactions. For example, plastics are created through chemical reactions involving oil and other substances.

Cleaning and Cooking: When you wash your clothes or cook a meal, you're using chemical reactions. Soap works by chemical reactions that break down dirt and grease. Cooking changes the chemical structure of food, making it tastier and easier to digest.

Powering Our World: The gasoline in cars and the batteries in your devices rely on chemical reactions to produce energy. Even renewable energy sources like solar panels work because of chemical reactions.

Chemical Reactions in Everyday Life

Now that you know how important chemical reactions are, let's look at some examples you might see every day:

Rusting: When iron is exposed to oxygen and water, it forms rust. This is a chemical reaction called oxidation.

Baking a Cake: When you mix ingredients and put them in the oven, several chemical reactions occur, creating the fluffy texture and golden-brown color of a cake.

Fireworks: The bright colors and loud bangs of fireworks are all thanks to chemical reactions happening in the air.

Glowsticks: When you bend a glowstick, you're starting a chemical reaction that produces light.

Batteries: The power from batteries comes from chemical reactions between different materials inside the battery.

Why Study Chemical Reactions?

Understanding chemical reactions is crucial for many reasons:

Career Opportunities: Many exciting jobs involve chemical reactions, from being a chef to a doctor, or working in fields like environmental science or materials engineering.

Some chemical reactions release a large amount of energy.

Solving Global Challenges: Knowledge of chemical reactions is helping us develop cleaner energy sources, more effective medicines, and solutions to environmental problems.

Everyday Decision Making: Understanding basic chemistry can help you make informed choices about the products you use, the food you eat, and how you impact the environment.

Appreciating the World: Knowing about chemical reactions can give you a deeper appreciation for the complexity and wonder of the world around you.

Chemical reactions might seem like something that only happens in a lab, but they're actually all around us, shaping our world in countless ways. From the air we breathe to the food we eat, chemical reactions play an important role in our lives and environment. As you continue to learn about science, keep an eye out for chemical reactions happening in and outside of the classroom.

7: Chemical Reactions
GUIDED NOTES

What Are Chemical Reactions?

Definition: A chemical reaction is a process where _____ or more substances

change into _____ substances.

• Original substances are called: _____

• New substances formed are called: _____

Analogy: Chemical reactions are like building with _____ bricks. You start

with connected bricks (_____), then rearrange them (_____).

Signs of a Chemical Reaction

List five signs that indicate a chemical reaction is occurring:

1. _____

2. _____

3. _____

4. _____

5. _____

Example: When you mix baking soda and vinegar, you see _____ form,

which is a sign of a _____ being released.

Importance of Chemical Reactions

Complete the table with examples of why chemical reactions are important:

Area	Importance
Human Body	
Plants	
Manufacturing	
Household Activities	
Energy Production	

Chemical Reactions in Everyday Life

Match the following everyday phenomena with the type of chemical reaction:

1. ____ Rusting   2. ____ Baking a cake

3. ____ Fireworks   4. ____ Glowsticks

5. ____ Batteries

A. Produces light through chemical reaction
B. Oxidation reaction
C. Multiple reactions creating texture and color
D. Chemical reactions between different materials produce power
E. Reactions producing colors and sounds in the air

Why Study Chemical Reactions?

List four reasons why studying chemical reactions is important:

1. _____

_____

2. _____

_____

3. _____

_____

4. _____

_____

Reflection

1. Name one chemical reaction you've observed today: _____

_____

2. How might understanding chemical reactions help you in your future career or daily life?

_____

_____

#1

How do chemical reactions impact your daily life? Can you identify three examples from your own experiences?

Think about the activities you do every day, from eating breakfast to charging your phone. How might chemical reactions be involved in these activities?

#2

Why is it important for scientists to study chemical reactions? How could this knowledge benefit society in the future?

Reflect on some of the global challenges we face today, such as climate change or health issues.

#3

If you could design an experiment to observe a chemical reaction, what would it be and what signs of a reaction would you look for?

Remember the five signs of chemical reactions mentioned in the article. Which of these would be easiest or most interesting for you to observe?

#4

How does understanding chemical reactions help you appreciate the complexity of living things?

Think about how plants grow and provide food and oxygen for other organisms. How does the chemical reaction of photosynthesis make this possible?

#5

In what ways do chemical reactions contribute to both environmental problems and their solutions?

Think about issues like air pollution or plastic waste. How are chemical reactions involved in creating these problems, and how might they also help solve them?

#6

How might learning about chemical reactions influence your future career choices?

Think beyond obvious choices like chemist or scientist. How might understanding chemical reactions be useful in careers like cooking, engineering, or environmental conservation?

TERM	DEFINITION
Chemical reaction	
Reactants	
Products	
Precipitate	
Oxidation	
Photosynthesis	
Molecule	

TERM	DEFINITION
Atom	
Energy	
Catalyst	
Combustion	
Synthesis	
Decomposition	
pH	

Chemical Reactions

```
O H F Y S H O Y L D J O F Q W S P O T O U P T F
T N S D Y C Z B S R U I Z I X A O R S J S D D K
W Y R N N O M Y G S F V Z L P V S D G F G B D X
C K B K T P E E L S E N E R G Y U E S K Q Y F F
O T H W H N B B J P K Y P A V U N C Q H U A K I
M P T V E L F W I E Z J K T U I R O R U X B G P
B C R S S Q O X I D A T I O N V E M U F V G I C
U F C C I H B B V W N V J M J P H P Q I K O X R
S S R R S V D L H Z L K K M D C S O Z V L I U S
T K E I Z I B T R I A O C J C U K S Z V Z T O J
I F A B M S Z E J R X I G L O P Z I K X Q B N O
O Z C Y X Z Y F O K V M Q X S H U T K U I E L Z
N V T K N H K T P R O D U C T S G I E Q P C H Z
D N A P R E C I P I T A T E N J P O Z Z V H N H
P Y N T R S W I X O G A I H O F S N V Q H W M C
T Z T W U K R I Y V J K O R P D F Z N Q S E E C
F U S N F G Q V Q F D J C G D N K U G R K R S W
C H E M I C A L R E A C T I O N F H Q O N Z I H
Q L T P J N T C U T Q A Y O J R K U X M R I C E
F M I K M U P H O T O S Y N T H E S I S P I F A
G Q N A T W M O L E C U L E G W L A E Y B M B R
N S Y Z R C R F Q F H G Q D P R U C E E M U R S
Z T B U F E K C Q P U Z T S D N C A T A L Y S T
A Z R P G K K E A X S C S B Y M W P E L J W H Q
```

pH

Combustion

Atom

Oxidation

Reactants

Decomposition

Catalyst

Molecule

Precipitate

Chemical reaction

Synthesis

Energy

Photosynthesis

Products

Chemical Reactions

Across

2. A type of chemical reaction where a substance combines with oxygen, often resulting in rust formation on metals.

7. A process where one or more substances change into different substances. (Two words)

9. A chemical reaction used by plants to convert sunlight, water, and carbon dioxide into food and oxygen.

11. A substance that speeds up a chemical reaction without being consumed in the process.

12. The basic unit of matter, consisting of a dense nucleus surrounded by electrons.

13. A chemical reaction where a complex substance breaks down into simpler substances.

14. A chemical reaction where a substance combines with oxygen, often producing heat and light.

Down

1. A group of atoms bonded together, representing the smallest unit of a chemical compound.

3. The new substances formed as a result of a chemical reaction.

4. A new solid that forms and separates from a solution during a chemical reaction.

5. The original substances that undergo a change in a chemical reaction.

6. The capacity to do work or cause change, often released or absorbed during chemical reactions

8. A scale used to measure how acidic or basic a substance is, which can affect chemical reactions.

10. A type of chemical reaction where two or more simple substances combine to form a more complex substance.

Fizz, Clean, and Dissolve:
Incredibly Useful In Our Everyday

Have you ever wondered why soda fizzes, or how soap cleans your hands? You can find the answers in the topic of solutions, acids, and bases. These chemical concepts might sound complicated, but they're actually all around us, playing important roles in our everyday lives. Let's explore why understanding these topics are important to know about.

Acids and bases are used in cleaning products, health and medicine, and even in cooking.

What Are Solutions?

A solution is a mixture where one substance (called the solute) is dissolved in another substance (called the solvent). The most common example is sugar dissolved in water. When you stir sugar into your tea, it seems to disappear, right? That's because it has dissolved, forming a solution.

Solutions are everywhere: The air you breathe is a solution of gasses The ocean is a solution of salt and other minerals in water. Your blood is a complex solution that carries nutrients throughout your body

Understanding solutions helps us make better drinks, create medicines, and even clean our homes more effectively.

Acids: Not Just for Mad Scientists: When you hear "acid," you might think of bubbling beakers in a lab. But acids are much more common than that! An acid is a substance that can give away hydrogen ions (H+) when dissolved in water. This makes acids taste sour and feel slippery.

Some everyday acids include: Citric acid in lemons and oranges Acetic acid in vinegar Carbonic acid in sodas (which gives them their fizz)

Acids are crucial in digestion (your stomach uses hydrochloric acid to break down food), preserving foods, and even in batteries that power your devices.

Bases: The Opposite of Acids

Bases are like the yin to acids' yang. They accept hydrogen ions (H+) or give away hydroxide ions (OH-) in water. Bases feel slippery and taste bitter (though you should never taste chemicals in a lab!).

Common bases include:
• Sodium bicarbonate (baking soda)
• Ammonia (found in many cleaning products)
• Sodium hydroxide (used to make soap)

Bases are important in cleaning products because they can break down oils and grease. They're also used in antacids to neutralize stomach acid when you have heartburn.

Why This Matters to You
Understanding solutions, acids, and bases can help you in many ways:

Better cooking and baking: Knowing about solutions helps you mix ingredients properly. Understanding acids and bases can improve your baking (baking soda, a base, reacts with acidic ingredients to make cakes rise).

Safer cleaning: Many cleaning products are basic. Knowing this can help you use them safely and effectively. For example, never mix bleach (a base) with vinegar (an acid) – it creates dangerous fumes!

Health and medicine: Understanding pH (a measure of how acidic or basic a solution is) can help you make healthier choices. For instance, acid reflux occurs when your stomach acid (very acidic) backs up into your esophagus.

Eating less acidic foods or taking antacids (bases) can help.

Environmental awareness: Acid rain, caused by pollution, can harm plants and animals. Understanding this process can make you more environmentally conscious.

Future careers: Chemistry is crucial in many fields, from medicine and environmental science to food technology and engineering. This knowledge could spark your interest in an exciting career path!

Sodium hydroxide and hydrochloric acid react with each other and produce sodium chloride and water.

Everyday problem-solving: Knowing about solutions, acids, and bases gives you tools to understand and solve everyday problems. Got a clogged drain? A mixture of baking soda (a base) and vinegar (an acid) might do the trick!

Solutions, acids, and bases might seem like abstract chemistry concepts, but they're actually key players in your daily life. From the food you eat to the products you use to clean your home, these chemical principles are at work all around you. By understanding these basics, you're not just learning science – you're gaining knowledge that can help you make better decisions, stay safer, and maybe even inspire your future career.

Introduction

Solutions, acids, and bases are important chemical concepts that are present in our _____ lives. They help explain phenomena like:

- Why soda _____

- How _____ cleans your hands

What Are Solutions?

Definition: A solution is a mixture where one substance (called the _____) is dissolved in another substance (called the _____).

Common examples of solutions:

1. _____ dissolved in water

2. The air we breathe (a solution of _____)

3. The ocean (a solution of _____ and other minerals in water)

4. _____ (a complex solution carrying nutrients in our body)

Understanding solutions helps us:

• Make better _____

• Create _____

• Clean our homes more _____

Acids

Definition: An acid is a substance that can give away _____ ions (H+) when dissolved in water.

Characteristics of acids:

• Taste: _____

• Feel: _____

Everyday acids:

1. _____ acid in lemons and oranges

2. _____ acid in vinegar

3. _____ acid in sodas

Important roles of acids:

• In _____ (stomach uses hydrochloric acid)

• _____ foods

• In _____ that power our devices

Bases

Definition: Bases accept _____ ions (H+) or give away

_____ ions (OH-) in water.

Characteristics of bases:

• Feel: _____

• Taste: _____ (Note: Never taste chemicals in a lab!)

Common bases:

1. _____ (baking soda)

2. _____

3. _____ (used to make soap)

Important uses of bases:

• In _____ products (they break down oils and grease)

• In _____ to neutralize stomach acid

Why This Matters to You

Understanding solutions, acids, and bases can help you in many ways:

1. Better cooking and baking:
   • Helps with _____ ingredients properly
   • Understanding acids and bases improves _____ (e.g., baking soda reaction)

2. Safer cleaning:
   • Many cleaning products are _____
   • Never mix _____ (a base) with _____ (an acid) – it creates dangerous fumes!

3. Health and medicine:
   • Understanding _____ can help you make healthier choices
   • Example: Acid reflux and antacids

4. Environmental awareness:
   • Understanding _____ and its effects on plants and animals

5. Future careers:
   • Chemistry is crucial in fields like _____, _____, and _____

6. Everyday problem-solving:
   • Example: Unclogging a drain using a mixture of _____ (a base) and _____ (an acid)

#1

How might understanding solutions help you make better food or drinks at home?

Think about how you mix ingredients when cooking or making beverages.

#2

Can you name three acids you encounter in your daily life and explain how you use them?

Look in your kitchen or bathroom for common household items that might contain acids.

#3

Why is it important to be careful when mixing cleaning products containing acids and bases?

Remember the example in the article about mixing bleach and vinegar.

#4

How could learning about pH levels help you make healthier food choices?

Think about foods that might upset your stomach and why that happens.

#5

In what ways does understanding acids and bases contribute to environmental awareness?

Reflect on what you know about acid rain and its effects on the environment.

#6

How might knowledge of solutions, acids, and bases be useful in a future career you're interested in?

Think about jobs that involve chemistry, like cooking, healthcare, or environmental science.

TERM	DEFINITION
Solution	
Solute	
Solvent	
Acid	
Base	
pH	
Neutralize	

TERM	DEFINITION
Hydrogen ion	
Hydroxide ion	
Antacid	
Acid reflux	
Acid rain	
Citric acid	
Sodium bicarbonate	

Solutions, Acids & Bases

```
B Z T I Y B X I X L S O L U T I O N I F P D T W
W P R U K H L W A X Z X D U O Z F K K N V W S G
B Z L Y H C T R D V N R Y S H Z Y A P S F C O H
H Y D R O G E N I O N Y H U I R Y N U T O M L U
B E A J L V E E S W C A Y I U D N B G L A H U L
Z M G W V X M N X A K C D N C G F Z M O E H T W
R Z Z M A D Z F F U C B R B E B A X B H R O E Z
T V Z L C Z G J R C B A O Z W X H V Y Q Z N R M
K A H Q I Z B L O I X S X Y Y T P K G Q U I H K
A C U X D B U K L T F E I L R R H F B H H O S V
S I K O R T W O E I G R D E Y K F Y P I F H D U
W D O H A S Q B W R W A E Q M Z G M P L G Q U T
N B Y C I M L G Z C G F I D Z I Q L I I T N M H
S S J T N U B C M A U K O E I B B Y X Z W E H Z
V O N O T Y S X Y C O B N F Z K A N I D P U R J
J L O I R S X D T I Y N Z R U Y C K S J N T F X
E V Q I L F W H Q D C Y M H Y C M Z A P K R E A
C E U B R L Y Z P I O A W P E B V L D Z P A B I
V N B F P L D V A N T A C I D O S S N T Z L O Z
F T J M T F J J S C H Y R W T P Y B U O E I O P
F I P L H T R Q H N A C I D R E F L U X M Z G X
N O W O S S O D I U M B I C A R B O N A T E H Y
H D N X Q T V E C I X H Q W E J E Y D C V D P D
U C C N S M O Z Q W Z M I S O E F S Q L V K H H
```

Citirc acid	Hydroxide ion	Hydrogen ion
Sodium bicarbonate	Acid rain	Acid reflux
Antacid	Neutralize	pH
Base	Acid	Solvent
Solute	Solution	

Solutions, Acids & Bases

Across

2. A negatively charged particle (OH-) that bases release in water. _____ ion

3. Rainfall made acidic by pollution, which can harm plants and animals. (Two words)

9. A common acid found in citrus fruits like lemons and oranges. _____ acid

10. A positively charged particle (H+) that acids release in water. _____ ion

11. The substance that dissolves the solute in a solution.

12. A substance that accepts hydrogen ions (H+) or gives away hydroxide ions (OH-) in water, making it taste bitter.

13. A medicine that helps neutralize stomach acid to relieve heartburn.

14. To make an acid and base cancel each other out, resulting in a neutral solution.

Down

1. Another name for baking soda, a common base used in cooking and cleaning. (Two words)

4. A condition where stomach acid backs up into the esophagus, causing discomfort. (Two words)

5. A mixture where one substance (the solute) is dissolved in another substance (the solvent).

6. A substance that can give away hydrogen ions (H+) when dissolved in water, making it taste sour.

7. A measure of how acidic or basic a solution is.

8. The substance that is dissolved in a solution.

Building Life, Atom By Atom: The Stuff of Life

Have you ever wondered what makes up the food you eat, the clothes you wear, or even your own body? It's all thanks to organic chemistry. Don't let the word "chemistry" scare you – organic chemistry is actually all about the stuff that makes life possible.

What is Organic Chemistry?

Organic chemistry is the study of compounds that contain carbon. That might not sound exciting at first, but here's the cool part: carbon is the building block of life. Almost everything in living things, from the tiniest bacteria to the largest whale, is made up of carbon-based compounds.

But organic chemistry isn't just about living things. It also includes many substances we use every day, like plastic, gasoline, and even some medicines. In fact, there are millions of organic compounds out there, and scientists are discovering new ones all the time.

Why is Carbon So Special?

You might be wondering why is carbon special? Carbon has a unique ability to form strong bonds with other elements, especially hydrogen, oxygen, and nitrogen. It can also bond with itself to create long chains or rings. This flexibility allows carbon to form an incredible variety of molecules with different shapes and properties.

Think of carbon atoms like LEGO bricks. Just as you can build countless structures with LEGO, nature uses carbon to build an amazing array of molecules that make up living things and many useful materials.

Daily Organic Chemistry

You might not realize it, but organic chemistry plays a huge role in your everyday life. Here are some examples:

Food: The nutrients in your food – like carbohydrates, proteins, and fats – are all organic compounds. When you digest food, your body breaks down these compounds and uses them for energy and to build new cells.

Carbon, hydrogen, nitrogen, oxygen, phosphorus, and sulphur are the main elements that living things are made of.

Clothes: Many fabrics, including polyester and nylon, are made from organic compounds. Even natural fibers like cotton and wool are organic materials.

Medicine: Many drugs, from aspirin to antibiotics, are organic compounds. Understanding organic chemistry helps scientists develop new medicines to treat diseases.

Fuels: Gasoline, natural gas, and other fuels we use to power cars and heat homes are organic compounds derived from ancient plants and animals.

Plastics: From your phone case to food packaging, plastics are everywhere. They're made from organic compounds called polymers.

Cosmetics: Shampoos, lotions, and makeup often contain organic compounds that give them their special properties.

Why Should You Care About Organic Chemistry?

Understanding organic chemistry can help you make sense of the world around you. It can explain why certain foods are healthy, how medicines work, and even how living things grow and function. Here are a few reasons why organic chemistry matters:

Health and Nutrition: Knowing about organic compounds can help you understand why certain foods are good for you and how your body uses them.

Environmental Awareness: Many environmental issues, like plastic pollution and climate change, involve organic compounds. Understanding the chemistry can help you make informed decisions about protecting the environment.

Consumer Choices: From choosing cleaning products to deciding what fabrics to wear, knowledge of organic chemistry can help you make smarter choices as a consumer.

Hydrocarbons make many of our energy sources, like this coal.

Future Careers: Organic chemistry is crucial in many exciting fields, including medicine, pharmaceuticals, materials science, and environmental science. If you're interested in these areas, a solid understanding of organic chemistry is a great foundation.

Problem-Solving Skills: Studying organic chemistry can improve your critical thinking and problem-solving abilities, skills that are valuable in any career.

The Future of Organic Chemistry

Organic chemistry continues to be an exciting field with new discoveries happening all the time. Scientists are using organic chemistry to develop new materials, create more efficient renewable energy sources, and design better medicines. Keep an eye out for organic chemistry concepts. You'll be amazed at how often they pop up, from biology class to discussions about climate change.

9: Organic Chemistry
GUIDED NOTES

What is Organic Chemistry?

1. Organic chemistry is the study of compounds that contain _____.

2. Why is carbon important in organic chemistry?

   _____

   _____

3. List two examples of things that contain organic compounds:

   a. _____   b. _____

Why is Carbon Special?

4. Carbon can form strong bonds with which elements? (List 3)

   1. _____   2. _____

   3. _____

5. How is carbon similar to LEGO bricks?

   _____

   _____

Daily Organic Chemistry

6. Match the following areas of daily life with an example of organic chemistry:

Area of Life	Example of Organic Chemistry
Food	
Clothes	
Medicine	
Fuels	
Plastics	
Cosmetics	

Why Should You Care About Organic Chemistry?

7. List three reasons why organic chemistry matters:

a. _____

b. _____

c. _____

8. How can understanding organic chemistry help you make consumer choices?

_____

_____

9. Name two career fields where organic chemistry is crucial:

1. _____   2. _____

The Future of Organic Chemistry

10. List two areas where organic chemistry is being used for future developments:

_____

_____

_____

Reflection

11. What's one thing you learned about organic chemistry that surprised you?

_____

_____

_____

12. How do you think understanding organic chemistry could be useful in your daily life?

_____

_____

_____

#1

How does understanding organic chemistry help you make better choices about the food you eat?

Think about the nutrients mentioned in the article and how they relate to your daily diet.

#2

Can you name three everyday items in your home that are made from organic compounds?

Look around your room or kitchen. Remember that organic compounds are in many common materials, from fabrics to plastics.

#3

How might learning about organic chemistry help you understand environmental issues like plastic pollution?

Think about what plastics are made of and how this knowledge might affect your choices.

#4

If you had to explain to a friend why carbon is special in organic chemistry, what would you say?

Remember the LEGO brick comparison in the article. How does this help explain carbon's importance?

#5

How could knowing about organic chemistry be useful in a future career you're interested in?

The article mentions several fields that use organic chemistry. Can you think of how it might apply to a job you find interesting?

#6

Why do you think it's important for everyone, not just scientists, to have some understanding of organic chemistry?

Think about how organic chemistry affects your daily life, from the clothes you wear to the medicine you take when you're sick.

TERM	DEFINITION
Organic chemistry	
Carbon	
Compound	
Molecule	
Polymer	
Carbohydrate	
Protein	

TERM	DEFINITION
Fat	
Fossil fuel	
Antibiotic	
Fiber	
Cosmetic	
Environmental awareness	
Renewable energy	

Organic Chemistry

```
E A T D W U P D Y N E C A R B O H Y D R A T E U
N I C N R X R T Y Z N K R E Z K J T H G U F A T
V K R E V I O S T A Q J J N P E P Y J I W K W M
I M J J U N T M J H T R J H E H V L X A W N Y I S
R K K K Z L E U K U R P S W S D W R K O V G X B
O I F H N Y I Q W U S F S A Z L F L H W M A L A
N T E Y W R N R H O U W M B J W L P D N Q Y B B
M E D W V P A G X J Y Y O L V K F I B E R P G T
E J A H R D V I E C G V L E J V N I X T Q X P
N X N V H V K P B N S P E E S L Q V S L N A K V
T E M H Q O Q P W T Z K C N G Y G O H X C O W E
A W N C W O U K T C F F U E B Z M I C U O I I P
L O A A C T I U D N A J L R C I U S O E M M A R
A H H R D N X M S M Y A E G T T O M S R P J R Z
W B K B D V U D A K F Z C Y G G S U M Y O T O F
A F Z O C N V A N M W G E T W Y D E N U L Z R F
R T L N A F V P T V S Z V V W T P D T Q N D F X
E R D K B E O I I A G H X L H E X Q I P D E T L
N G E Z Q W S S B I Y Y P F G G T L C O O U S L
E I T N N V X V I F O S S I L F U E L L F Z R K
S V V I L C H I O R W S K U W B Q W T Q H
S U K E S K H I T A J J Y A C Z R J M C J O J
X A Q O R G A N I C C H E M I S T R Y E M E T C
G F L H M U V E C Y T F O V R F W J F R D L W I
```

Renewable energy

Cosmetic

Fat

Polymer

Carbon

Environmental awareness

Fiber

Protein

Molecule

Organic chemistry

Fossil fuel

Antibiotic

Carbohydrate

Compound

Organic Chemistry

Across

4. A type of organic compound essential for building and repairing body tissues.

6. A medicine made from organic compounds that fights bacterial infections.

7. A group of atoms bonded together, forming the smallest unit of a chemical compound.

8. The study of compounds that contain carbon. (Two words)

10. A substance made up of two or more different elements joined together.

12. A fuel, like gasoline or natural gas, made from the remains of ancient plants and animals. _____ fuel

13. An organic compound used by the body for energy storage and insulation.

14. A chemical element that is the main building block of life and can form many different compounds.

Down

1. A product used to enhance appearance, often containing various organic compounds.

2. An organic compound found in foods that provides energy, like sugar and starch.

3. Understanding how human actions affect the natural world, including issues related to organic compounds. _____ awareness

5. A thread-like structure in fabrics, which can be made from natural or synthetic organic materials.

9. Energy from sources that are naturally replenished, which organic chemistry can help develop more efficiently. _____ energy

11. A large molecule made up of many repeated smaller units, often used to make plastics.

The Power Within Atoms:
It's Radioactive, Radioactive

Have you ever wondered how the Sun gives us energy? Or how doctors can see inside our bodies without cutting us open? The answer to these questions and many more lies in the fascinating world of nuclear chemistry. This branch of science explores the tiniest parts of atoms and the incredible energy they can release.

What is Nuclear Chemistry?

Nuclear chemistry is all about the changes that happen in the core of atoms. This core is called the nucleus. It's super small if an atom were the size of a football field, the nucleus would be smaller than a pea! But don't let its size fool you. The nucleus packs a powerful punch.

Chernobyl is a famous example of what can happen after an accident at a nuclear power plant.

In nuclear chemistry, we study how these tiny nuclei can change. Sometimes they break apart, sometimes they join together, and sometimes they shoot out particles. These changes can release huge amounts of energy.

The Basics: Atoms and Elements

Before we go deeper, let's review some basics:

1. Atoms are the building blocks of everything around us.
2. The center of an atom is the nucleus, which contains protons and neutrons.
3. Different elements have different numbers of protons in their nuclei.
4. Isotopes are atoms of the same element with different numbers of neutrons.

Types of Nuclear Reactions

There are two main types of nuclear reactions:

1. Fission: This is when a big atom splits into smaller ones. It's like breaking a big rock into smaller pieces.

2. Fusion: This happens when small atoms join to make bigger ones. Think of it like sticking Lego blocks together.

Both of these reactions release a lot of energy!

Why Should You Care About Nuclear Chemistry?

Nuclear chemistry affects our lives in many ways:

Energy Production: Nuclear power plants use fission to generate electricity. This helps light up our homes and power our devices.

Medical Treatments: Doctors use radioactive materials to diagnose and treat diseases like cancer. This field is called nuclear medicine.

Food Safety: Nuclear techniques help keep our food safe by killing harmful bacteria without changing the food's taste or quality.

Archaeology: Scientists use a method called radiocarbon dating to figure out how old ancient objects are. This helps us understand our history better.

Space Exploration: Some spacecraft use nuclear power to travel far into space where solar panels wouldn't work well.

Environmental Studies: Nuclear chemistry helps scientists track pollutants in the air and water, keeping our planet cleaner.

The Good and the Bad

Like many powerful tools, nuclear chemistry has both positive and negative aspects:

Positives:
• Clean energy production (no greenhouse gasses)
• Advanced medical treatments
• Scientific research tools

Negatives:
• Potential for dangerous weapons
• Risk of accidents at nuclear plants
-Challenges in disposing of radioactive waste

It's important to understand both sides so we can make smart decisions about using nuclear technology.

Interesting Facts About Nuclear Chemistry

1. The Sun's energy comes from nuclear fusion of hydrogen atoms.
2. Bananas are slightly radioactive because of the potassium they contain!
3. Marie Curie, a famous scientist, discovered radioactivity and won two Nobel Prizes for her work.
4. Nuclear submarines can stay underwater for months without needing to refuel.

5. Some smoke detectors use a tiny bit of radioactive material to sense smoke particles.

Looking to the Future

As we face challenges like climate change and the need for clean energy, nuclear chemistry will play a big role in finding solutions. Scientists are working on safer, more efficient nuclear reactors. They're also exploring ways to use nuclear fusion for energy, which could provide almost limitless clean power.

In medicine, researchers are developing new treatments using radioactive materials to target cancer cells more precisely. This could lead to better outcomes for patients with fewer side effects.

Nuclear chemistry might seem complicated, but it's all around us. From the stars in the sky to the batteries in smoke detectors, the power of the atom shapes our world. As you continue your studies in physical science, remember that understanding nuclear chemistry can help you make sense of big issues like energy production, medical treatments, and environmental protection.

Nuclear power has the potential to produce a large amount of energy, but is not without its risks.

10: Nuclear Chemistry
GUIDED NOTES

Introduction

1. Nuclear chemistry explores changes in the _____ of atoms.

2. The nucleus of an atom is incredibly _____, but contains a lot of _____.

Basics of Atoms and Elements

3. List the four basic concepts mentioned in the article:

   a. _____

   b. _____

   c. _____

   d. _____

Types of Nuclear Reactions

4. The two main types of nuclear reactions are:

   a. _____: When a big atom _____ into smaller ones.

   b. _____: When small atoms _____ to make bigger ones.

5. Both types of reactions release a lot of _____.

Applications of Nuclear Chemistry

6. Match the application to its description:

   a. Energy Production _____ Helps determine the age of ancient objects

   b. Medical Treatments _____ Uses fission to generate electricity

   c. Food Safety _____ Diagnoses and treats diseases like cancer

   d. Archaeology _____ Kills harmful bacteria in food

   e. Space Exploration _____ Powers spacecraft for long-distance travel

   f. Environmental Studies _____ Tracks pollutants in air and water

Pros and Cons of Nuclear Chemistry

7. List two positive aspects of nuclear chemistry:

   a. _____

   b. _____

8. List two negative aspects of nuclear chemistry:

   a. _____

   b. _____

Interesting Facts

9. True or False: The Sun's energy comes from nuclear fission.

10. Why are bananas slightly radioactive? _____

_____

11. Who discovered radioactivity and won two Nobel Prizes for their work?

_____

Future of Nuclear Chemistry

12. Scientists are working on developing:

   a. Safer and more efficient nuclear _____.

   b. Ways to use nuclear _____ for energy production.

13. In medicine, researchers are exploring new treatments using radioactive materials to:

_____

Conclusion

14. In your own words, explain why understanding nuclear chemistry is important:

_____

_____

_____

#1

How might nuclear chemistry impact your daily life without you realizing it?

Think about the electricity in your home, medical treatments you've heard of, or even the food you eat. How might nuclear chemistry play a role in these areas?

#2

What are the main differences between nuclear fission and fusion? Why are both important?

Remember the analogy of breaking rocks versus sticking Lego blocks together. How do these processes relate to energy production on Earth and in stars?

#3

Nuclear chemistry has both benefits and risks. How would you weigh these to decide if nuclear power is good for society?

Look at the positives and negatives listed in the article. Which do you think are most important? Why?

#4

How could advancements in nuclear chemistry help address climate change?

Think about how nuclear energy is produced and its environmental impact compared to fossil fuels.

#5

If you could become a nuclear chemist, which area of research would you want to focus on and why?

Look at the different applications of nuclear chemistry mentioned in the article. Which excites you the most?

#6

How has learning about nuclear chemistry changed your view of the world around you?

Think about everyday objects or phenomena. Do you see them differently now that you know about the power within atoms?

TERM	DEFINITION
Nuclear chemistry	
Nucleus	
Proton	
Neutron	
Isotope	
Fission	
Fusion	

TERM	DEFINITION
Radioactive	
Nuclear power plant	
Nuclear medicine	
Radiocarbon dating	
Greenhouse gasses	
Radiation	
Element	

Nuclear Chemistry

```
H Q G J Z Z M P S W M F A A X Z Q Q T I T I W M
V W N U C L E A R C H E M I S T R Y H S N F D P
O L P Y M C Y Q L V E L J N G D U H H O P M A W
K R N U C L E A R P O W E R P L A N T T E V H J
V G R E E N H O U S E G A S S E S S A O N U P Z
H J K X T I I G E T W W W L T T J A K P U F E M
G N U C L E A R M E D I C I N E X B L E C K Q Z
R R G K Q N F E D C H H L R E I Y H E Z L Y G P
L A Y H C M I E X A D K N A T G X M A A E B F D
Q D G K I Q S N G X J G K D A Y H O H Q U Z D C
L I E D I J S H S S S S X I P H O V I P S U J Z
P A B L Z K I O A S L W R O F F U I N Q H C G B
Y T T H I B O U M U R K G C T H T L A Q N G B X
F I W V C P N S A H A I S A E M H X D N G Q M E
H O S G A R Y E O N D S J R S K F A A B U L T P
D N O F E O J G Y U I D N B A F M A H K E O N P
G S Z K C T N A M C O G S O W N P A S U B R Y G
X K F V X O E S G X A R Z N J Y Z O P T V W S P
L E Z B P N U E Y L C M E D E U J K V T A A M C
N C U S R Y T S J T T N P A C B N T L P J F K D
Q B E T C O R M L C I R Q T Y U Z U A T K Y F V
W L B P C M O S R J V C A I J A C A F X L W N I
D E W O S Q N K D B E A N N Y S L W I Y Q R A Z
F E L E M E N T X S S W Y G F U S I O N L N T Z
```

Greenhouse gasses	Radiocarbon dating	Nuclear medicine
Nuclear power plant	Element	Radiation
Radioactive	Fusion	Fission
Isotope	Neutron	Proton
Nucleus	Nuclear chemistry	

Nuclear Chemistry

Across
2. A particle with no electric charge found in the nucleus of an atom.
5. A nuclear reaction where a large atom splits into smaller ones, releasing energy.
8. Describing materials that give off energy in the form of particles or waves.
9. A facility that uses nuclear reactions to generate electricity. Nuclear ____ ____
11. A substance made up of atoms with the same number of protons in their nuclei.

12. A nuclear reaction where small atoms join to form bigger ones, releasing energy.
13. Gasses that trap heat in Earth's atmosphere, contributing to climate change. ____ gasses
14. A method used to determine the age of ancient objects using radioactive carbon. ____ dating

Down
1. The use of radioactive materials to diagnose and treat diseases. Nuclear ____

3. The study of changes in the core of atoms and the energy they release. (Two words)
4. Energy released from atoms in the form of particles or waves.
6. The center of an atom, containing protons and neutrons.
7. Atoms of the same element with different numbers of neutrons.
10. A positively charged particle found in the nucleus of an atom.

Matter, Energy, & Interactions:
Rules of the Universe

Have you ever wondered why the sky is blue, how your smartphone works, or why you can't walk through walls? While these questions might seem odd, they can be explained by physics. This topic of science can explain how our universe works, from the tiniest atoms to the largest galaxies.

What is Physics?

Physics is the study of matter, energy, and how they interact. It's like having a secret code that helps us understand everything around us. Physics explains the basic rules that govern our universe, from why objects fall to the ground to how light travels through space.

Why is Physics Important?

Physics is everywhere in your life. Here are some reasons why it's important:

It explains how things work: Physics helps us understand why things happen the way they do in nature and in the technology we use every day.

It solves problems: Understanding physics helps us find solutions to real-world problems, like creating clean energy or designing safer cars.

It leads to new inventions: Many of the gadgets you use, like smartphones and computers, were developed using principles of physics.

It prepares you for many careers: Physics is useful in fields like engineering, medicine, astronomy, and even sports science.

It helps you think critically: Studying physics improves your problem-solving skills and logical thinking.

Physics Concepts in Your Life

Let's look at some awesome physics ideas that are part of your world:

Gravity: The Force That Keeps Us Grounded

Gravity is the force that pulls everything towards the center of the Earth. It's why you don't float away when you jump and why planets orbit the Sun. Without gravity, life as we know it wouldn't exist!

A hydraulic press is capable of exerting a large amount of force.

Energy: The Power to Make Things Happen

Energy is the ability to do work or cause change. It comes in many forms, like heat, light, and motion. When you eat food, your body converts it into energy to help you move and think. The light from the Sun is energy that travels across space to warm our planet.

Motion: How Things Move

Physics explains how things move and why. When you ride a bike or throw a ball, you're using physics principles like speed, acceleration, and force. Understanding motion helps us design faster cars, more efficient airplanes, and even predict the paths of comets!

Electricity and Magnetism: Invisible Powers

These forces are behind many of the technologies we use daily. Electricity powers our homes and devices, while magnetism is used in everything from compasses to computer hard drives. Together, they form electromagnetism, which explains how light works and allows us to communicate wirelessly.

Matter: The Stuff Everything is Made Of

Physics helps us understand the properties of matter anything that takes up space and has mass. It explains why some materials are solid, liquid, or gas, and how they can change from one state to another.

Physics in Your Everyday Life

Let's see how physics shows up in a typical day:

Morning: The alarm on your phone uses electrical signals to wake you up. As you get out of bed, gravity pulls you down while the floor pushes back, keeping you balanced.

Breakfast: The toaster uses electrical energy to heat your bread. The heat causes a chemical reaction that turns the bread brown and crispy.

Travel to School: Whether you walk, bike, or ride in a car, you're using principles of motion, friction, and energy.

In Class: When you write, friction between your pencil and paper leaves marks. The light in the classroom travels in waves, allowing you to see.

Lunch: When you drink through a straw, you're creating a difference in air pressure that pushes the liquid up.

Sports Practice: Throwing a ball, running, or swimming all involve forces, energy transfer, and motion key concepts in physics.

Using Your Phone: Your smartphone is a marvel of physics, using electricity, light, and electromagnetic waves to function.

Evening: As the Sun sets, the Earth's rotation causes day to turn into night a perfect example of physics on a planetary scale.

Why Study Physics?

Learning physics helps you:
- Understand how the world around you works
- Develop problem-solving skills
- Prepare for careers in science, technology, engineering, and math (STEM)
- Appreciate the beauty and complexity of nature
- Make informed decisions about technology and environmental issues

Physics is the science that explains our entire universe From the screen you're reading this on to the stars in the night sky, physics is everywhere. By understanding physics, you gain an insight to the hidden rules that govern our world. Physics is more than formulas and equations. It's a way of thinking that can help you understand and appreciate the amazing world we live in.

Physics helps us understand topics such as energy and motion.

11: Physics
GUIDED NOTES

What is Physics?

Physics is the study of _____, _____, and how they _____.

It helps us understand:

1. _____

2. _____

Why is Physics Important?

List 5 reasons why physics is important:

1. _____

2. _____

3. _____

4. _____

5. _____

Key Physics Concepts

1. Gravity

Definition: _____

Example in everyday life: _____

2. Energy

Definition: _____

Two forms of energy mentioned:

1. _____   2. _____

3. Motion:

Physics explains _____ and _____.

Understanding motion helps us design:

1. _____

2. _____

3. _____

4. Electricity and Magnetism

These forces are behind many _____.

Together, they form _____, which explains:

a. _____

b. _____

5. Matter

Definition: _____

Physics explains:

• Why some materials are _____, _____, or _____

• How they can _____

Physics in Your Everyday Life

Match the daily activity with the physics concept it demonstrates:

_____ Alarm clock   a. Friction

_____ Getting out of bed   b. Chemical reaction and heat

_____ Toasting bread   c. Difference in air pressure

_____ Writing with a pencil   d. Electrical signals

_____ Drinking through a straw   e. Gravity and balanced forces

Benefits of Studying Physics

Complete the following statements:

1. You can understand how _____.

2. It helps you develop _____.

3. It prepares you for careers in _____.

4. You can appreciate the _____ and _____ of nature.

5. It helps you make _____ decisions about technology and

environmental issues.

Reflection

In your own words, explain why physics is considered "more than formulas and equations":

_____

_____

#1

How does physics impact your daily life? Can you give three examples?

Think about the activities you do from morning to night. How do concepts like gravity, energy, or motion play a role?

#2

Why is understanding physics important for solving real-world problems?

Remember the examples of clean energy and safer cars. How might physics knowledge help address other challenges we face?

#3

Which physics concept interests you the most and why?

Review the "Cool Physics Concepts" section. Which one seems most exciting or relevant to your own experiences?

#4

How might studying physics help you in a future career, even if it's not in science?

Think about how problem-solving and critical thinking skills from physics could apply to different jobs.

#5

Can you describe a situation where you've seen physics in action during sports or physical activities?

Recall the sports practice example. How do forces, energy, or motion apply to your favorite sport or activity?

#6

How does physics help us understand both very small things (like atoms) and very large things (like galaxies)?

Think about how the same basic rules of physics apply at different scales, from the tiniest particles to the largest structures in the universe.

TERM	DEFINITION
Physics	
Matter	
Energy	
Gravity	
Motion	
Acceleration	
Force	

TERM	DEFINITION
Friction	
Electricity	
Magnetism	
Electromagnetism	
Mass	
Wavelength	
Orbit	

Physics

```
L C Y J M Z D P G X O R B I T R V Z W T F Z P G
K D T D Z V W V G C S Y K N A A A M M M B K V C
W Z W M G W A G G L L N U A G K T A Z A Y E S E
H E D D E L J R T L F R O F I T M S A E A O Y B
E W T B N M A O O P F P J X J L H S O G W J D D
L G G G R A V I T Y Y I D S M C P Z H A D C G E
E M U E F T O T A L P F F Z J Q J X T S J A Y Z
C P P C W T F R X N W C W O V L S N R Y M X O M
T V Q A S E F K H M W R A J D H C U L Q R J H A
R Q U J Q R Y G N K U K V T S L D N P B K Y A G
I R B Z C X G Y S F P Z E B P F X F G A L J T N
C N N W T K D Z W T N C L L Z X O S F N F P P E
I D V J R U I F B R W M E K I Y W A R I W H A T
T M T S D U M O T I O N N B Z W W A I A V I K I
Y L U J K A C D H U P R G C A U I D C F B X F S
W V P K D A J K S M B I T B T W E X T S S D V M
S E B H P E H V J C V E H B F C Y V I R C D L D
T T L Y S J P E D Q E M O M X R H O N Z T N X
M R Z U H Y G U Q W Y N W B F T A V N H R T O X
H F D T X F M J V M U E P Z E G V N S N Q Y F
I T M N U P Z H A P Z R A C C E L E R A T I O N
K J B T V F S D A P U G M F O R C E S M U A M G
O N V P H Y S I C S M Y F H B Y C I K A S X Y S
C P M N K B E L E C T R O M A G N E T I S M E V
```

Orbit	Wavelength	Mass
Electromagnetism	Magnetism	Electricity
Friction	Force	Acceleration
Motion	Gravity	Energy
Matter	Physics	

Physics

Across

4. A force that can attract or repel certain materials, like iron.
6. A push or pull that can change an object's motion or shape.
8. The ability to do work or cause change, existing in various forms like heat, light, and motion.
10. Anything that takes up space and has mass.
11. The path an object takes as it moves around another object in space, like planets around the Sun.
12. The act of an object changing its position over time.
13. The resistance that occurs when two surfaces rub against each other.
14. The study of matter, energy, and how they interact in the universe.

Down

1. The rate at which an object's speed or direction changes.
2. The amount of matter in an object.
3. The distance between two peaks of a wave, such as in light or sound.
5. The combination of electricity and magnetism, explaining how light works and enabling wireless communication.
7. A form of energy resulting from the flow of electric charge.
9. The force that pulls objects towards the center of the Earth and keeps planets in orbit.

Push, Pull, and On the Move: Get Moving

Have you ever wondered why things move the way they do? Why does a car slow down when you hit the brakes? How does a rollercoaster stay on its track during loops? Understanding forces and motion can help us in answering those questions and others like them.

What are Forces and Motion?

At its core, motion is simply a change in position over time. When you walk to school, throw a ball, or even blink your eyes, you're creating motion. But what causes things to start moving, change direction, or stop? That's where forces come in.

Motion occurs when force is applied to an object.

A force is a push or pull acting on an object. Forces are all around us, even when we can't see them. Gravity pulling you towards the Earth, friction between your shoes and the ground, and the wind pushing against you on a breezy day are all examples of forces.

Newton's Laws: The Rules of the Game

To understand forces and motion, we need to talk about Isaac Newton. He was a brilliant scientist who lived over 300 years ago and came up with three important laws that explain how forces and motion work.

1. Newton's First Law: Objects at rest stay at rest, and objects in motion stay in motion, unless acted on by an outside force. This is also called the law of inertia. It's why you feel a jolt when a car starts moving or why you keep moving forward when a car suddenly stops.

2. Newton's Second Law: Force equals mass times acceleration ($F = ma$). This means that the more mass an object has, the more force you need to move it. It's why it's easier to push an empty shopping cart than a full one.

3. Newton's Third Law: For every action, there's an equal and opposite reaction. When you jump, you push down on the ground, and the ground pushes back up on you with the same force.

Why Forces and Motion Matter

Understanding forces and motion isn't just about passing a science test. This knowledge plays a huge role in our everyday lives:

Sports: Whether you're kicking a soccer ball, swinging a baseball bat, or doing a flip in gymnastics, forces and motion are at work. Athletes and coaches use this science to improve performance and reduce injuries.

Transportation: Cars, planes, and trains all rely on the principles of forces and motion. Engineers use this knowledge to design faster, safer, and more efficient vehicles.

Safety: Understanding forces helps us design better safety equipment. Seatbelts, airbags, and helmets all work by managing the forces involved in accidents.

Technology: From the way your smartphone's touchscreen works to how satellites stay in orbit, forces and motion are crucial in modern technology.

Nature: Forces explain natural phenomena like ocean tides, wind patterns, and even how plants grow towards sunlight.

Forces in Action: Everyday Examples

Let's look at some common situations where forces and motion come into play:

Riding a Bike: When you pedal, you create a force that moves the bike forward. Friction between the tires and the road helps you turn and stop. Air resistance (drag) is a force that works against your motion, which is why it's harder to bike into a strong wind.

Using a Seatbelt: When a car stops suddenly, your body wants to keep moving forward (remember Newton's First Law?). The seatbelt applies a force to keep you in your seat, preventing injury.

Jumping on a Trampoline: When you land on a trampoline, it stretches, storing energy. This energy is then released, pushing you back up. It's a perfect example of Newton's Third Law in action.

Playing Video Games: Many video games use realistic physics engines based on the laws of forces and motion. This is why objects in games fall, bounce, and collide in ways that look natural to us.

Newton's Laws help us understand forces and motion.

The Future of Forces and Motion

As we look to the future, understanding forces and motion becomes even more important. Scientists and engineers are using this knowledge to develop new technologies like:

• Magnetic levitation trains that float above the tracks, reducing friction

• Renewable energy sources like wind turbines that harness the force of moving air

• Space exploration technologies that can navigate the complex forces involved in traveling through the solar system

By learning about forces and motion now, you're preparing yourself to understand and perhaps even contribute to these exciting developments in the future.

Every time you move or see something move, forces are at work. By understanding these basic principles, you're unlocking the secrets of how our physical world operates. Whenever you're playing sports, riding in a car, or just walking down the street, take a moment to think about the amazing science of forces and motion happening.

12: Forces & Motion
GUIDED NOTES

Introduction

1. Motion is defined as: _____

2. A force is: _____

Newton's Laws

Fill in the blanks for Newton's three laws of motion:

1. Newton's First Law (Law of Inertia):

    Objects at _____ stay at _____, and objects in _____

stay in _____, unless acted on by an _____ _____.

2. Newton's Second Law:

    Force = _____ × _____

    Write the equation: _____ = _____ _____

3. Newton's Third Law:

    For every _____, there's an equal and _____ _____.

Importance of Forces and Motion

List five areas where understanding forces and motion is important:

1. _____   2. _____

3. _____   4. _____

5. _____

Everyday Examples

Explain how forces and motion apply in these situations:

1. Riding a Bike:

  - Force created by pedaling: _____

  - Role of friction: _____

  - Effect of air resistance: _____

2. Using a Seatbelt:

  Why do we move forward when a car stops suddenly? _____

  _____

  How does a seatbelt prevent injury? _____

  _____

3. Jumping on a Trampoline:

  Describe how this demonstrates Newton's Third Law:

  _____

  _____

Future Applications
Name three future technologies that rely on understanding forces and motion:

1. _____

2. _____

3. _____

Reflection
In your own words, explain why understanding forces and motion is important in everyday life:

_____

_____

_____

#1

How do Newton's three laws of motion apply to your favorite sport or physical activity?

Think about the different movements in your chosen activity, like throwing, jumping, or running. How do forces come into play?

#2

Can you describe a real-life situation where you've experienced Newton's First Law of Motion?

Remember, this law is about objects staying at rest or in motion unless acted upon by an outside force. Think about times when you've felt a sudden change in motion.

#3

How might understanding forces and motion help you design a safer car or bicycle helmet?

What forces are involved in accidents? How could you use this knowledge to reduce injuries?

#4

In what ways do you think knowledge of forces and motion might be important for future space exploration?

Space has different conditions than Earth. How might this affect the way objects and spacecraft move?

#5

Can you explain how forces and motion are involved in a simple machine you use every day?

Think about the pushes and pulls involved when you use these objects. How do they make tasks easier?

#6

How might video game designers use their understanding of forces and motion to create more realistic games?

What elements in video games try to mimic real-world physics? How do these make the game feel more realistic?

TERM	DEFINITION
Force	
Motion	
Gravity	
Friction	
Inertia	
Mass	
Acceleration	

TERM	DEFINITION
Newton's First Law	
Newton's Second Law	
Newton's Third Law	
Air resistance	
Momentum	
Energy	
Physics	

Forces & Motion

```
G J Q O N E W T O N S S E C O N D L A W O Y G G
N M A N C A J K A T S X K F D D X X Z W O M R O
G W U X O H N H A R R C J Y M N C A T W T O L L
D C F P H U W C Y H T J N T N I V C Y A Z M O N
G R A V I T Y Y K C O I P X G C R M S S O E V I
A C O L E F Z I A I R R E S I S T A N C E N Y K
T P F S K K N E W T O N S T H I R D L A W T P T
S L O F G B C I S G I I S G X C N X E R Z U H V
A L R L A Y M K T M K E N V R R Y W N K M E A
V N C I N E R T I A W A E A A S H B S E E A F I
Z T E V U R M W C P A M J K I X Z K I W R D G K
D Q Z S U Y O O K G D F P H Y S I C S T P V U Q
O F O F I V V Y J X R R W F N D G H B O P Q B E
S U U R H H K G B D Q I T M U A G M Q N L E M M
K K T Y C J B G I K O C Z U H S O Z I S F N A K
T Y V T J N W A B L H T E P A C S V J F I S S O
L F W V Q M O S A H K I C A U V H X P I O Q S P
R A Z R S O C P Q U F O Z X O R H F X R X R J B
G K K M R T N Y Z U M N P Q R Z G U X S K V M R
A P P S T I K E N Q R W W P F O M X Z T R O J P
Y P M E U O A C C E L E R A T I O N B L J H R J
N C H I S N U Y A W Z V A V Z J Y J A S C K M
V X O C E E N E R G Y O R O L A D A J W P G B H
N O A W B C W G S S B O F F V K D P P A P Z L F
```

Air resistance

Newton's First Law

Momentum

Inertia

Gravity

Newton's Third Law

Physics

Acceleration

Force

Motion

Newton's Second Law

Energy

Mass

Friction

Forces & Motion

Across

2. The force that pulls objects towards the center of the Earth.

3. The product of an object's mass and velocity.

5. The principle that for every action, there's an equal and opposite reaction. Newton's ___

7. The rate at which an object's speed or direction changes.

10. The principle that force equals mass times acceleration (F = ma). Newton's ___ ___

11. The force of air pushing against a moving object, also known as drag. Air ____

13. The tendency of an object to resist changes in its motion.

14. The scientific study of matter, energy, and their interactions.

Down

1. The principle that objects at rest stay at rest, and objects in motion stay in motion, unless acted on by an outside force. Newton's ___ ___

4. The force that resists motion between two surfaces in contact.

6. A change in position over time.

8. The amount of matter in an object.

9. A push or pull acting on an object.

12. The capacity to do work or cause change.

Doing Work Smarter Not Harder with Machines: Simplifying Work

Have you ever wondered how your smartphone charges so quickly? Or how a small car engine can move a whole vehicle? The answer can be found in the study of work, power, and machines. These concepts are not just for scientists, they play a big role in our daily lives.

What is Work?

In science, work has a specific meaning. It happens when a force moves an object. Imagine pushing a heavy box across the floor. You're using force, and the box is moving. That's work! The formula for work is simple:

Work = Force × Distance

So, the more force you use or the further you move something, the more work you do.

Understanding Power

Power is closely related to work, but it's not the same thing. Power measures how quickly work is done. If you and your friend both push boxes across a room, but you do it faster, you're using more power. The formula for power is:

Power = Work ÷ Time

This explains why we talk about car engines in terms of horsepower. A more powerful engine can do the same work in less time.

Machines are created to help us accomplish work far more easily.

Machines: Making Work Easier

Machines are devices that help us do work more easily. They can:
1. Increase the force we apply
2. Change the direction of a force
3. Increase the distance or speed of a motion

There are six types of simple machines:

- Lever
- Wheel and axle
- Pulley
- Inclined plane
- Wedge
- Screw

These simple machines are the building blocks for more complex machines we use every day.

Real-Life Examples

Smartphones: When you charge your phone, electrical energy is converted into chemical energy stored in the battery. This is work being done at the atomic level!

Cars: A car engine converts the chemical energy in gasoline into mechanical energy to move the car. The more powerful the engine, the faster it can accelerate.

Elevators: These use pulleys and counterweights to lift heavy loads with less effort.

Machines can increase the force applied, change the directions of a force, or increase the distance or speed of motion.

Bicycles: Bikes use wheels, axles, and gears (which are variations of the wheel and axle) to make it easier for you to travel long distances.

Can openers: These clever devices use the principles of the lever and the wedge to easily cut through metal.

Why This Matters to You

Understanding work, power, and machines can help you in many ways:

Better problem-solving: Knowing how machines work can help you figure out how to make tasks easier.

Energy awareness: Understanding power can help you make smarter choices about energy use at home.

Future careers: Many jobs use these concepts, from engineering and construction to healthcare and robotics.

Sports and fitness: These ideas apply to how your body moves and how exercise equipment works.

Everyday life: From using tools to understanding how household appliances work, this knowledge is always useful.

The Big Picture

Work, power, and machines are all around us. They're in the gadgets we use, the vehicles we ride, and even in our own bodies. By understanding these concepts, you're taking a big step in understanding how the world works. As you continue to learn about work, power, and machines, you'll start to see the world differently. You might look at a bicycle and appreciate the brilliant engineering behind it. Or you might think about how to use simple machines to make a difficult task easier.

13: Work, Power, & Machines
GUIDED NOTES

Introduction

1. What three concepts does this lesson focus on?

   a. _____   b. _____

   c. _____

2. How do these concepts relate to our daily lives? (List two examples)

   _____

   _____

What is Work?

3. In scientific terms, work occurs when:

   _____ moves an _____

4. Write the formula for work:

   Work = _____ × _____

5. According to this formula, how can you increase the amount of work done?

   _____

   _____

Understanding Power

6. How is power different from work?

   _____

7. Write the formula for power:

   Power = _____ ÷ _____

8. Why do we measure car engines in horsepower?

   _____

Machines: Making Work Easier

9. List three ways machines help us do work:

   a. _____

   b. _____

   c. _____

10. Name the six types of simple machines:

    1. _____   4. _____

    2. _____   5. _____

    3. _____   6. _____

Real-Life Examples

11. Match the device with the concept it best demonstrates:

    a. Smartphone   ____ Uses pulleys and counterweights

    b. Car engine   ____ Converts chemical energy to mechanical energy

    c. Elevator   ____ Converts electrical energy to chemical energy

    d. Bicycle   ____ Uses wheels, axles, and gears

    e. Can opener   ____ Uses principles of lever and wedge

Why This Matters to You

12. List three ways understanding work, power, and machines can benefit you:

    1. _____

    2. _____

    3. _____

The Big Picture

13. In your own words, explain why learning about work, power, and machines is important:

    _____

    _____

14. Describe one way you might look at the world differently after learning these concepts:

    _____

    _____

#1

How do you use work and power in your daily life?

Think about activities you do at home or school that involve moving objects or completing tasks quickly.

#2

Can you identify three simple machines you've used this week? How did they make your tasks easier?

Look around your home or classroom for tools or devices that help you do work with less effort.

#3

How might understanding work, power, and machines help you in a future career?

Think about jobs that involve building, fixing, or designing things, and how these concepts might apply.

#4

In what ways can learning about power help you make better choices about energy use at home?

Reflect on the appliances you use and how their power consumption might affect your home's energy bill.

#5

How do the concepts of work and power apply to sports or exercise you enjoy?

Think about how your body moves during physical activities and how equipment might help you perform better.

#6

Can you think of a task in your life that could be made easier by using a simple machine?

Identify a chore or activity you find challenging and brainstorm how one of the six simple machines could help. Which type of machine would you use and why?

TERM	DEFINITION
Work	
Power	
Force	
Machine	
Simple machine	
Lever	
Wheel and axle	

TERM	DEFINITION
Pulley	
Inclined plane	
Wedge	
Screw	
Mechanical energy	
Chemical energy	
Horsepower	

Work, Power, & Machines

```
S C R E W D A I X C O C J O M S J I U N T V Z M
H T A D P H P O B D U G I Q D V G K S F W A G U
P A M P N I X M E C H A N I C A L E N E R G Y R
F C A T B U Z Y X T Y Z C A N N J Z T C Z U Y B
G H C C A J I S R P B D L N K Y F W T T G T G P
Z M H B K M L G J I M H I R F I W E O R S P E N
T S I P U L L E Y K D C N D X Q H N D K V C F R
L I N X D S B A N F X D E S G V F S W K T V O E
K M E T K F Z D S T K J D A C H E M I C A L J E
Y P O W W M N B C Q T P P L U N Z H C V U Y C O
D L Z Z P U M H S Z P K L F J R M E K F M K Q N
C E Z F T Z K S A B J F A D Q K J U Q Q A Z H P
H M N P W E D G E O H O N H O Z X Q Z Z R H R T
Z A R U P A T W X J R R E R W O R K Q Z Y P B R
P C J J V C I N P I F C U U L L D B Z T Z M N J
X H Y X J P K I K O T E J Z A E C D S B E A Q L
O I R E G H O R S E P O W E R V Q P V E J T B T
H N L C A K Z L H Y Q O K Q G E J J W V V B E J
N E M D L Y E S B F Q G E N N R Z H W L T D Q O
L F N W H E E L A N D A X L E P T W V Z J F I J
I H F W K R R K H G U M F G S O A M G M V P U S
R T G W N G L Q J P M C R G K W J U W U B J I A
S K Z E L Q W Y B X B F K W Q E L V S X Q O D R
T C H E M I C A L E N E R G Y R C T N H U F H B
```

Chemical energy	Mechanical energy	Wheel and axle
Simple machine	Horsepower	Screw
Wedge	Inclined plane	Pulley
Lever	Machine	Force
Power	Work	

Work, Power, & Machines

Across
2. Energy associated with the motion or position of an object. ____ energy

3. Energy stored in the bonds between atoms in a substance. ____ energy

7. A unit of power, often used to measure the output of engines.

10. A basic mechanical device that changes the direction or magnitude of a force. ____ machine

12. A flat surface set at an angle to reduce the force needed to move an object upwards. (Two words)

13. An inclined plane wrapped around a central cylinder, used to lift objects or hold things together.

14. A simple machine consisting of a rigid object used with a fulcrum to lift or move heavy loads.

Down
1. A device that makes work easier by changing the size or direction of a force.

4. The transfer of energy that occurs when a force moves an object over a distance.

5. A push or pull acting on an object.

6. A triangular-shaped tool used to separate objects or hold them in place.

8. A simple machine made of a wheel attached to a central rod, used to reduce friction in motion. ____ and ____

9. The rate at which work is done, measuring how quickly energy is transferred.

11. A wheel with a grooved rim around which a cord passes, used to change the direction of a force.

Doing Work, Causing Change: Powering Our World

Energy is everywhere around us. It's in the food we eat, the cars we ride in, and even in our own bodies. But what exactly is energy, and why is it so important for all of us?

What is Energy?

Simply put, energy is the ability to do work or cause change. It's what makes things happen. When you kick a soccer ball, you're using energy to make it move. When you turn on a light, energy makes it glow. Energy comes in many forms, and it's constantly changing from one form to another.

Types of Energy

There are two main categories of energy:

Electricity can be generated through hydropower.

1. Potential Energy: This is stored energy. It's like having money in the bank, ready to be used when needed. *Examples include:*

A book on a high shelf (gravitational potential energy)

A stretched rubber band (elastic potential energy)

Food in your fridge (chemical potential energy)

2. Kinetic Energy: This is energy in motion. It's like spending the money you had in the bank. Examples include:

A car driving down the road
A ball rolling down a hill
Heat from a fire

Energy in Our Daily Lives

Now that we know what energy is, let's look at how it affects our everyday life:

At Home: Energy powers our lights, heats our homes, and runs our appliances. When you watch TV, play video games, or use your phone, you're using electrical energy.

Transportation: Cars, buses, and planes all need energy to move. Most vehicles use chemical energy from gasoline or diesel fuel, which is converted into kinetic energy to make the vehicle move.

Food: The energy in the food we eat keeps us alive and active. Our bodies convert the chemical energy in food into other forms of energy, like heat and motion.

Nature: The sun is a massive source of energy for our planet. It provides light and heat, helps plants grow through photosynthesis, and drives weather patterns.

Why is Energy Important?

Energy is crucial for several reasons:

It Keeps Us Alive: Our bodies need energy to function. We get this energy from the food we eat.

It Powers Our Modern World: Without energy, we wouldn't have electricity, transportation, or most of the technology we use every day.

It Drives Economic Growth: Industries need energy to produce goods and provide services. Energy production and management is also a major source of jobs.

It Affects Our Environment: How we produce and use energy has a big impact on our planet. Burning fossil fuels releases greenhouse gasses, which contribute to climate change.

The Energy Challenge
As our population grows and technology advances, we need more and more energy. But many of our current energy sources, like coal and oil, are non-renewable. This means they'll eventually run out. They also cause pollution and contribute to climate change.

This creates a big challenge: How can we produce enough energy to meet our needs without harming the environment? Scientists and engineers are working hard to solve this problem. They're developing cleaner, renewable energy sources like:

Solar power: Using the sun's energy to generate electricity

Wind power: Using wind to turn turbines and generate electricity

Hydropower: Using flowing water to generate electricity

Geothermal energy: Using heat from inside the Earth

What Can You Do?
Even as a high school student, you can make a difference when it comes to energy use:

Be Energy Efficient: Turn off lights and devices when you're not using them. Use energy-saving LED bulbs.

Solar power is a renewable energy source that harnesses sunlight.

Walk, Bike, or Use Public Transportation: When possible, choose transportation methods that use less energy.

Reduce, Reuse, Recycle: This helps save the energy used to make new products.

Learn More: The more you understand about energy, the better decisions you can make. Who knows? You might even become an energy scientist or engineer one day!

Energy is a fascinating and crucial part of our world. It powers our lives, drives our economy, and shapes our environment. As we face the challenges of the future, understanding and managing energy will be more important than ever. When you flip a light switch or bite into an apple, take a moment to appreciate the amazing energy that is needed for our way of life.

What is Energy?

Energy is defined as the ability to _____ _____ or cause

_____.

Types of Energy

There are two main categories of energy:

1. _____ Energy: This is stored energy.

   Examples:

   • A book on a high shelf (_____ potential energy)

   • A stretched rubber band (_____ potential energy)

   • Food in your fridge (_____ potential energy)

2. _____ Energy: This is energy in motion.

   Examples:

   1. _____   2. _____

   3. _____

Energy in Our Daily Lives

List four areas where we encounter energy in everyday life:

1. At Home: _____

2. Transportation: _____

3. Food: _____

4. Nature: _____

Why is Energy Important?

Complete the following reasons:

1. It keeps us _____

2. It powers our _____

3. It drives _____ growth

4. It affects our _____

The Energy Challenge

As our population grows, we need more energy. However, many current energy sources are:

• _____ (meaning they'll eventually run out)

• Cause _____ and contribute to _____

Renewable Energy Sources

List four clean, renewable energy sources:

1. _____: Using the sun's energy to generate electricity

2. _____: Using wind to turn turbines and generate electricity

3. _____: Using flowing water to generate electricity

4. _____: Using heat from inside the Earth

What Can You Do?

List four ways you can make a difference in energy use:

1. _____

2. _____

3. _____

4. _____

Reflection

In your own words, explain why understanding energy is important for our future:

_____

_____

_____

_____

#1

How does energy impact your daily life?

List at least 5 ways you use energy every day, from turning on lights to eating meals. Think about all the activities you do from the moment you wake up until you go to bed.

#2

What's the difference between potential and kinetic energy?

Think about objects at rest (potential energy) versus objects in motion (kinetic energy). Can you give an example of each from your own experiences?

#3

Why is it important to find renewable energy sources? What might happen if we don't?

How long will non-renewable resources last? What effects do they have on our environment?

#4

How could you personally contribute to energy conservation in your home or school?

What small changes in your daily routine could make a big difference in energy use?

#5

Why is energy important for economic growth?

Think about how different industries rely on energy and what might happen if that energy became scarce or too expensive. How might energy shortages affect businesses and jobs?

#6

How does the sun's energy affect life on Earth?

Beyond just providing light, how does the sun's energy influence weather, plant growth, and other natural processes? Describe the various ways solar energy is used directly and indirectly.

TERM	DEFINITION
Energy	
Potential energy	
Kinetic energy	
Renewable energy	
Non-renewable energy	
Fossil fuels	
Solar power	

TERM	DEFINITION
Wind power	
Hydropower	
Geothermal energy	
Greenhouse gasses	
Climate change	
Photosynthesis	
Energy efficiency	

Energy

```
F Q K J E Q K T K I N E T I C E N E R G Y M E H
P R K Q Z P N N S Q F M Y A B I M B P W H A N U
T L T F N K J C O U L O N S N X K Y X E Y B E E
Z R E N E W A B L E E N E R G Y G L H Z B J R H
N K U S X B V I A O Z K S M M K D T Y H Y K G V
F S K Y P D U L R Z Z K N Z P R B A D V U M Y I
S V D C Q H R T P E Z C Z G O C X X R U C M E H
N R X Z H F T Q O E I Q I R T K P E O X Z Q F G
D E O J X C J U W S Y L X E E L H F P L E F F E
Q Q P F I H U Z E S A C S E N X O Q O M S P I O
W P L H L W U Q R F N O L N T U T F W D W D C T
I L Y T I X Z P W W J R K H I W O X E O R S I H
N P P S B W T Z O P Q W V O A W S T R A N A E E
D D G P A O T D D W F M L U L N Y G J U X O N R
P H N H K O Y S D A K J O S E K N C T I C D C M
O N C E D L X X K M V Z O E N M T I L L H B Y A
W Y M X L X W G V X X K S G E O H W D C I D W L
E G O F C L K Z K R A F M A R Q E H B L W H G E
R W F O S S I L F U E L S S G T S W G W W W N N
J C D V F E N E R G Y J R S Y T I O P Z Z A S E
C L I M A T E C H A N G E E X E S H V X J V V R
Y Z G V N C G N W U D P L S K U B I Y F A L C G
V O I B K E R Q U U L G U W J B G Y S A S Z V Y
L X N O N R E N E W A B L E E N E R G Y Y E H O
```

Energy efficiency	Greenhouse gasses	Geothermal energy
Wind power	Solar power	Non-renewable energy
Renewable energy	Kinetic energy	Potential energy
Photosynthesis	Climate change	Hydropower
Fossil fuels	Energy	

Energy

Across

2. Energy sources that will eventually run out, such as coal or oil. ____ energy
7. Energy of motion; energy that an object has due to its movement. ____ energy
9. Stored energy that has the potential to do work. ____ energy
10. The process by which plants use sunlight to make food and grow.
12. The ability to do work or cause change.
13. Heat energy from within the Earth. ____ energy
14. Gasses in the atmosphere that trap heat and contribute to climate change. ___ gasses

Down

1. Energy sources that can be naturally replenished, like solar or wind power. ____ energy
3. Long-term changes in global or regional climate patterns. (Two words)
4. Using less energy to perform the same task or produce the same result. Energy ____
5. Energy generated by the movement of water, often using dams.
6. Energy generated by the movement of air, typically using wind turbines. ____ power
8. Non-renewable energy sources formed from the remains of ancient plants and animals, like coal and oil. (Two words)
11. Energy generated from the sun's rays. ____ power

Making Waves In Physical Science:
Music to Your Ears

Have you ever wondered how you can hear your favorite music through headphones? Or why you can feel the bass at a concert? This is all because of mechanical waves and sound. Let's learn about this topic and see why it's important.

What Are Mechanical Waves?

Imagine you're at a lake on a calm day. You toss a pebble into the water, and what happens? Ripples spread out from where the pebble hit. These ripples are a perfect example of mechanical waves.

Mechanical waves are disturbances that travel through a medium, like water, air, or even solid objects. They transfer energy from one place to another without moving the medium itself. Think about those ripples again. The water moves up and down, but it doesn't flow away from where the pebble landed.

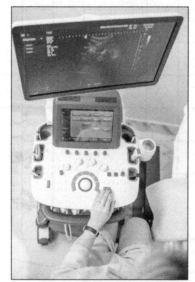

Ultrasound equipment uses high-frequency sound waves to create images.

There are different types of mechanical waves:

1. Transverse waves: The medium moves perpendicular to the direction of the wave. Example: waves on a string.

2. Longitudinal waves: The medium moves parallel to the direction of the wave. Example: sound waves in air.

3. Surface waves: A combination of transverse and longitudinal waves. Example: ocean waves.

Sound: The Wave We Can Hear

Next, let's focus on a special type of mechanical wave: sound. Sound waves are longitudinal waves that travel through air (or other mediums) and can be detected by our ears.

Here's how it works:
1. Something vibrates, like a guitar string or your vocal cords.
2. This vibration pushes air molecules together and apart.
3. These compressions and rarefactions of air molecules travel as a wave.
4. When the wave reaches your ear, it makes your eardrum vibrate.
5. Your brain interprets these vibrations as sound.

Why Mechanical Waves and Sound Matter

Mechanical waves and sound play a role in all of our lives:

Communication: We use sound waves to talk, sing, and express ourselves. Without understanding sound, we wouldn't have phones, music players, or even language as we know it.

Technology: Many devices use mechanical waves. Ultrasound machines in hospitals use high-frequency sound waves to create images. Sonar systems on ships use sound waves to navigate and detect objects underwater.

Music: Whether you're a musician or just love listening to tunes, understanding sound waves can help you appreciate how music works. It explains why different instruments sound unique and how we can record and play back music.

Safety: Mechanical waves help us detect dangers. Earthquakes produce seismic waves that scientists can measure to predict and prepare for disasters. Car horns use sound waves to alert us to potential accidents.

Nature: Many animals use sound waves for echolocation, like bats and dolphins. Understanding how they do this has inspired new technologies for the visually impaired.

Careers That Use Waves and Sounds

Mechanical waves and sound can lead to some cool job options. If you're into music, you could become an audio engineer and work on recording albums or mixing sound for concerts. Scientists who study earthquakes, called seismologists, use their knowledge of waves to predict and understand these natural events. Audiologists help people with hearing problems by using sound waves to test and improve hearing. In the world of tech, acoustic engineers design speakers, headphones, and even noise-canceling systems for cars and buildings. These careers mix science, creativity, and problem-solving to work with waves and sound in different ways.

Interesting Facts About Mechanical Waves and Sound

1. Sound can't travel in space because there's no air to carry the waves. That's why space battles in movies shouldn't have explosion sounds.

2. The speed of sound in air is about 343 meters per second (768 mph). That's why you see lightning before you hear thunder.

3. Whales can communicate over hundreds of miles using low-frequency sound waves that travel well in water.

4. The loudest sound ever recorded was the eruption of Krakatoa volcano in 1883. It was heard 3,000 miles away.

5. Dogs can hear higher-pitched sounds than humans, which is why dog whistles work.

Mechanical waves and sound are all around us, shaping how we experience the world. From the music we enjoy to the ways we communicate and stay safe, these invisible waves play an important role in our lives.

Waves are disturbances that travel through mediums like water, air, or solid objects.

15: Mechanical Waves & Sound
GUIDED NOTES

What Are Mechanical Waves?

Definition: Mechanical waves are _____ that travel through a _____, transferring _____ without moving the medium itself.

Example from the text: _____

_____

Types of mechanical waves:

1. _____ waves: Medium moves perpendicular to the wave direction

    Example: _____

2. _____ waves: Medium moves parallel to the wave direction

    Example: _____

3. _____ waves: Combination of the above two types

    Example: _____

Sound: The Wave We Can Hear

Sound waves are a type of _____ wave that travels

through _____.

How sound works:

1. Something _____, like _____

2. This pushes air molecules _____ and _____

3. These compressions and rarefactions travel as a _____

4. When the wave reaches your ear, it makes your _____ vibrate

5. Your _____ interprets these vibrations as sound

Why Mechanical Waves and Sound Matter
List five areas where mechanical waves and sound are important:

1. _____   2. _____

3. _____   4. _____

5. _____

Careers That Use Waves and Sound
Match the career with its description:

_____ Audio engineer   a. Studies earthquakes

_____ Seismologist   b. Helps people with hearing problems

_____ Audiologist   c. Designs speakers and noise-canceling systems

_____ Acoustic engineer   d. Works on recording albums and mixing sound

Interesting Facts
Fill in the blanks:

1. Sound can't travel in _____ because there's no _____ to carry the waves.

2. The speed of sound in air is about _____ meters per second or _____ mph.

3. _____ can communicate over hundreds of miles using low-frequency sound waves in water.

4. The loudest sound ever recorded was the eruption of _____ volcano in _____.

5. _____ can hear higher-pitched sounds than humans.

Reflection
1. What's one new thing you learned about mechanical waves or sound from this lesson?

_____

_____

2. How might understanding mechanical waves and sound be useful in your daily life?

_____

_____

_____

#1

How do mechanical waves transfer energy without moving the medium itself?

Think about the ripples on a lake what happens to a floating leaf?

#2

What's the main difference between transverse and longitudinal waves?

Picture a slinky toy how would it move for each type of wave?

#3

Why can't we hear sound in space?

What does sound need to travel that isn't present in space?

#4

How might understanding mechanical waves help in developing new technologies?

Think about how animals use sound waves and how we might copy this.

#5

Why do you see lightning before you hear thunder?

Compare the speed of light to the speed of sound mentioned in the article.

#6

How do mechanical waves and sound impact your daily life?

Think about your morning routine how many times do you encounter sound waves?

TERM	DEFINITION
Mechanical waves	
Medium	
Transverse waves	
Longitudinal waves	
Surface waves	
Sound waves	
Vibration	

TERM	DEFINITION
Compression	
Rarefaction	
Echolocation	
Ultrasound	
Sonar	
Seismic waves	
Frequency	

Mechanical Waves & Sound

```
L M L A E M I C M G L C O W I R U D Z E D W D D
O W Z W C R C O H Q K J W F R E Q U E N C Y Y I
N W I I H D A M M E C H A N I C A L W A V E S I
G E J Z O U M P D J V Y O P P N J H O F G S P G
I A R G L K S R K A K E H W G N Q G R H H M N K
T U O K O R K E Y S O U N D W A V E S F C X H O
U Q L T C B Y S W A A A U I D U Q U Y F H R F R
D U J P A G H S P H V F D T H V H R N P I U Z W
I E B A T W D I M I D R A R E F A C T I O N N J
N E S U I P E O V A G D K K N T S Z F C V H T F
A L V T O V D N J V Q N H L V I B R A T I O N M
L C B D N B T J B K B O W L X B U X S S Z F S E
W Y A E D U X B V U C B Y M I K X J Q X I J U D
A T A L R C T X C L R A B O G M H C M R A M R I
V X P N Z B G Q Z T K J N T K Q F M S F H Y F U
E Z T R A N S V E R S E W A V E S E B S W F A M
S G C Q B Q P G J A I V D Q P P M I Z F G P C W
K S P M J U X E C S L D L Y V T Q A B T L K E S
B K Y W F B I P D O A E K E D K V R E C Y T W Y
C D S L Q X I L H U U N F S O N A R E F X B A V
C B S F A W F S B E N U G O K C F J O O K A B V L
E E N K Q Y N M B D X A R T A A K Q X P M A E L
C C Y U L L M Q B D N S E I S M I C W A V E S G
U V S L L C O F X I I W J R H Z P K Y J H Q G W
```

Seismic waves

Longitudinal waves

Frequency

Echolocation

Vibration

Sound waves

Transverse waves

Sonar

Rarefaction

Medium

Surface waves

Mechanical waves

Ultrasound

Compression

Mechanical Waves & Sound

Across

2. High-frequency sound waves used in medical imaging and other technologies.

8. A combination of transverse and longitudinal waves, such as ocean waves. _____ waves

9. The substance or material through which a wave travels, such as water, air, or solid objects.

11. A rapid back-and-forth movement that creates sound waves.

12. A system that uses sound waves to navigate and detect objects underwater.

13. The part of a longitudinal wave where particles are pushed closer together.

Down

1. Waves where the medium moves parallel to the direction of the wave, like sound waves in air. _____ waves

3. Waves where the medium moves perpendicular to the direction of the wave, like waves on a string. _____ waves

4. The number of wave cycles that pass a fixed point in a given time, which determines the pitch of a sound.

5. Disturbances that travel through a medium, transferring energy without moving the medium itself. _____ waves

6. The use of sound waves to locate objects, as used by bats and dolphins.

7. The part of a longitudinal wave where particles are spread farther apart.

10. Mechanical waves that travel through the Earth, often caused by earthquakes. _____ waves

14. Longitudinal waves that travel through air or other mediums and can be detected by our ears. _____ waves

Surfing the Electromagnetic Spectrum: Let There Be Light

Have you ever wondered how your phone can send messages across the globe in seconds? Or how doctors can see inside your body without cutting you open? This is because of the electromagnetic spectrum and light. Let's explore how these invisible forces work and how they impact us.

What is the Electromagnetic Spectrum?

Imagine a giant rainbow that stretches far beyond the colors we can see. This is the electromagnetic spectrum. It's a fancy name for all the different types of energy that travel through space as waves. These waves come in various sizes, from tiny ripples to huge waves bigger than buildings.

The electromagnetic spectrum is used to create x-rays.

The electromagnetic spectrum includes:

1. Radio waves
2. Microwaves
3. Infrared light
4. Visible light (the rainbow we can see)
5. Ultraviolet light
6. X-rays
7. Gamma rays

Each type of wave has a different amount of energy and can do different things. Some can pass through solid objects, while others bounce off them. Some can heat things up, while others can take pictures of far-away stars.

Visible Light: The Star of the Show

Out of all these waves, visible light is the one we're most familiar with. It's the tiny slice of the spectrum that our eyes can detect. When you see the blue sky, the green grass, or your favorite red T-shirt, you're seeing visible light in action.

Visible light is made up of different colors, each with its own wavelength:

Red (longest wavelength)
Orange
Yellow
Green
Blue
Indigo
Violet (shortest wavelength)

Remember ROY G. BIV? That's a handy way to remember the colors of the rainbow.

Why is the Electromagnetic Spectrum Important?

The electromagnetic spectrum is like a Swiss Army knife of nature. It has a tool for almost everything. Let's look at some ways it affects your life:

Communication: Radio waves carry your favorite songs to your car radio and your text messages to your friends' phones.

Cooking: Microwaves heat up your leftover pizza by making water molecules in the food vibrate.

Remote Controls: Infrared light is used in TV remotes to change channels without getting up from the couch.

Seeing the World: Visible light allows us to see colors, read books, and enjoy beautiful sunsets.

Getting a Tan (or Sunburn): Ultraviolet light from the sun can give you a tan, but too much can cause sunburn and skin damage.

Medical Imaging: X-rays help doctors see inside your body to check for broken bones or cavities.

Studying Space: Gamma rays from distant stars and galaxies help scientists learn about the universe.

The Electromagnetic Spectrum in Action
Let's look at some everyday examples of how we use the electromagnetic spectrum:

Wi-Fi: Your internet connection at home uses radio waves to send data between your devices and the router.

Thermal Cameras: These use infrared light to "see" heat, helping firefighters find people in smoke-filled buildings.

Sunscreen: It protects your skin by blocking harmful ultraviolet light from the sun.

Night Vision Goggles: They work by detecting and amplifying infrared light that we can't normally see.

Airport Security: X-ray machines scan your luggage for prohibited items without opening your bags.

The Future of Light Technology
Scientists and engineers are constantly finding new ways to use the electromagnetic spectrum:

5G Networks: These use higher-frequency radio waves to transmit data faster than ever before.

Light-based Computers: Researchers are working on computers that use light instead of electricity to process information, potentially making them much faster.

Terahertz Waves: These sit between microwaves and infrared on the spectrum and could be used for super-accurate medical imaging or ultra-fast wireless communication.

The electromagnetic spectrum is like an invisible ocean of energy that surrounds us all the time. By learning to harness different parts of this spectrum, we've revolutionized communication, medicine, and our understanding of the universe. As you go about your day, take a moment to think about all the ways you're interacting with the electromagnetic spectrum. From the visible light that lets you read this article to the Wi-Fi signals carrying information to your devices, you're constantly using these invisible waves.

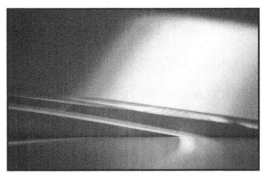

The colors of the visible light spectrum can be remembered through ROY G. BIV.

16: Electromagnetic Spectrum & Light
GUIDED NOTES

Introduction

1. What are two examples of how we use the electromagnetic spectrum in everyday life?

   a) _____

   b) _____

What is the Electromagnetic Spectrum?

2. The electromagnetic spectrum is all the different types of _____ that travel through space as _____.

3. List the seven types of waves in the electromagnetic spectrum:

   a) _____   b) _____

   c) _____   d) _____

   e) _____   f) _____

   g) _____

Visible Light

4. Visible light is the part of the spectrum that our _____ can detect.

5. List the colors of visible light in order from longest to shortest wavelength:

   _____, _____, _____, _____, _____, _____, _____

6. What mnemonic device can help you remember these colors? _____

_____

Importance of the Electromagnetic Spectrum

7. Match each type of wave with its application:

   a) Radio waves   ___ Heating food

   b) Microwaves   ___ TV remotes

   c) Infrared light   ___ X-ray imaging

   d) Ultraviolet light   ___ Carrying text messages

   e) X-rays   ___ Tanning (and sunburns)

8. How do gamma rays help scientists? _____

_____

The Electromagnetic Spectrum in Action

9. Fill in the blanks:

a) Wi-Fi uses _____ waves to send data.

b) Thermal cameras detect _____ light to see heat.

c) _____ protects your skin by blocking harmful ultraviolet light.

d) Night vision goggles amplify _____ light.

e) Airport security uses _____ to scan luggage.

The Future of Light Technology

10. Name three potential future applications of the electromagnetic spectrum:

a) _____

b) _____

c) _____

Reflection

11. In your own words, explain why the electromagnetic spectrum is important in our daily lives:

_____

_____

_____

_____

_____

#1

How does the electromagnetic spectrum impact your daily life?

Think about the devices you use every day and how they might rely on different parts of the spectrum.

#2

Why is visible light called "the star of the show" in the electromagnetic spectrum?

Reflect on how much you rely on your sense of sight and what life would be like without visible light.

#3

How has the discovery of different types of electromagnetic waves improved medical technology?

Think about X-rays and other medical imaging techniques mentioned in the article.

#4

What new technologies using the electromagnetic spectrum are you most excited about and why?

Look at the "Future of Light Technology" section and imagine how these advancements might change your life.

#5

How does understanding the electromagnetic spectrum help us learn about the universe?

Think about how we can study distant stars and galaxies using different types of electromagnetic waves.

#6

If you could invent a new technology using any part of the electromagnetic spectrum, what would it be and how would it work?

Be creative! Think about problems in the world that could be solved using different types of electromagnetic waves.

TERM	DEFINITION
Electromagnetic spectrum	
Wavelength	
Radio waves	
Microwaves	
Infrared light	
Visible light	
Ultraviolet light	

TERM	DEFINITION
X-rays	
Gamma rays	
ROY G. BIV	
Wi-Fi	
Thermal camera	
5G networks	
Terahertz waves	

Electromagnetic Spectrum & Light

```
A F G T 5 B F V O M M H A Y M H H V L E B 5 W C
E N H H W G Y K T E R A H E R T Z W A V E S H Z
L T P X D A S K 5 G N E T W O R K S O I 5 L K A
E U L T R A V I O L E T L I G H T Y S S G B R R
C W N N A N I K H I N R R U X S C P G I M A U
T B Y R P A O R O V H O H M Y W X R U B R U D F
R H E X X D P C X K 5 Y X X K T C B C L M P I K
O U U S G Z H P X 5 X G M F 5 T E X W E X E O O
M P O L G D S W R Y P B G U F G K W X L A C W A
A W Z T F G M N A Y O I H S Y R V A D I V R A S
G D P H C T 5 R Y T A V E T C G L V G G C Y V Z
N Y 5 B U F Y V S N E B T D D V Z E I H A F E A
E O Z T H E R M A L C A M E R A M L Y T N K S N
T F M O U W F G E B E N T P X S M E N K W X T I
I X Z B O O U B S R H E U 5 C S O N O K S T L A
C T B V G M R Z 5 E N D H E V K Z G A T A Y A Z
S I Z Y A H D S T F G O Z P S W X T Y E S I N P
P L R F M G N P B Z M E N A P Z X H U F I U Z D
E Z X E M N G P H R I N F R A R E D L I G H T U
C O W W A P R N D G F G Y X W U W D D V U R D P
T 5 I H R S U L W I F I R T G D F L Z B H Y V X
R F G P A U K V U F P Y M H Y B S T 5 5 E E N H
U U Y U Y D E G F D M N P H M I C R O W A V E S
M Z H F S I I I F U B I 5 5 S X K S G D M X M P
```

Terahertz waves	5G networks	Thermal camera
Ultraviolet light	Visible light	Infrared light
Radio waves	Electromagnetic spectrum	Wi-Fi
ROY G. BIV	Gamma rays	X-rays
Microwaves	Wavelength	

Electromagnetic Spectrum & Light

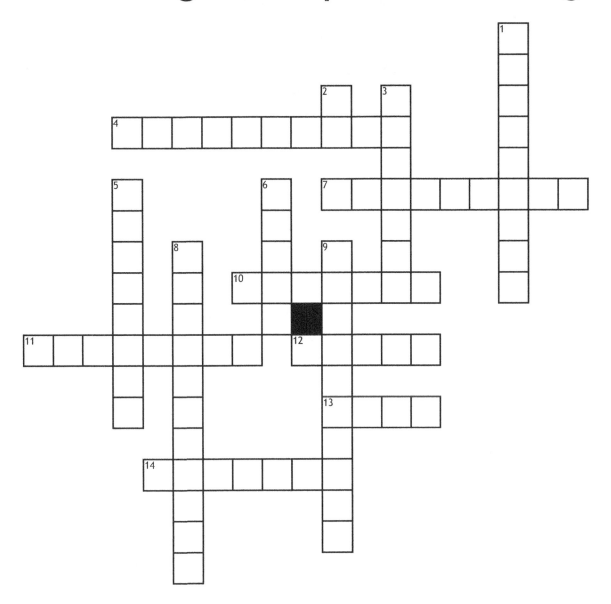

Across

4. The distance between two peaks of a wave in the electromagnetic spectrum.

7. Electromagnetic waves between microwaves and infrared, with potential uses in medicine and communication. ___ waves

10. The part of the electromagnetic spectrum that our eyes can see, including all the colors of the rainbow. ____ light

11. A type of electromagnetic radiation that we feel as heat, used in thermal imaging. ____ light

12. High-energy electromagnetic waves that can pass through soft tissue, used in medical imaging.

13. A technology that uses radio waves to connect devices to the internet wirelessly.

14. A memory aid for the colors of the visible light spectrum.

Down

1. The highest-energy waves in the electromagnetic spectrum, used to study space and in some medical treatments. (Two words)

2. The latest generation of cellular networks using high-frequency radio waves for faster data transmission. __ networks

3. A device that detects infrared radiation to create images of heat. ____ camera

5. The full range of all types of electromagnetic radiation, from radio waves to gamma rays. Electromagnetic ____

6. Long wavelength electromagnetic waves used for communication, like in cell phones and radios. ____ waves

8. Invisible electromagnetic waves from the sun that can cause sunburns and are blocked by sunscreen. ____ light

9. Electromagnetic waves that can heat food and are used in some communication devices.

The Spark of Knowledge:
The Power of Electricity

Imagine waking up one morning to find that nothing in your house works. Your alarm doesn't go off, your phone is dead, and when you flip the light switch nothing happens. This might sound like the start of a sci-fi movie, but it's what life would be like without electricity. Electricity is so woven into our daily lives that we often take it for granted. But what exactly is electricity, and why is it so important?

What is Electricity?

At its most basic, electricity is a form of energy caused by the movement of tiny particles called electrons. These electrons are part of atoms, which make up everything around us. When electrons move from one atom to another, they create an electric current. This current is what we harness to power our world.

Electricity has become a staple of our world. We are continuously trying to improve its production and storage.

Think of electricity like water flowing through a pipe. The electrons are like the water, and the wires in your walls are like the pipes. Just as water can power a water wheel, the flow of electrons can power all sorts of devices.

How Do We Make Electricity?

Most of the electricity we use comes from power plants. These plants use different methods to get those electrons moving:

1. Burning fossil fuels like coal or natural gas
2. Using nuclear reactions
3. Harnessing renewable sources like wind, solar, or hydroelectric power

Once the electricity is generated, it travels through a complex network of wires and transformers called the power grid. This grid delivers electricity to our homes, schools, and businesses.

Why is Electricity Important?

Electricity powers almost every aspect of our modern lives. Here are just a few ways it's important:

1. Lighting: From street lamps to the screen you're reading this on, electricity lights up our world.

2. Communication: Phones, computers, and the internet all run on electricity. Without it, staying in touch would be much harder.

3. Entertainment: Video games, TV, music players all powered by electricity.

4. Health Care: Many medical devices and machines in hospitals rely on electricity to save lives.

5. Education: Computers, projectors, and online learning platforms are all electric-powered tools that help us learn.

6. Transportation: While not all vehicles run on electricity, many systems that keep our roads safe (like traffic lights) do.

7. Food Storage: Refrigerators and freezers use electricity to keep our food fresh and safe to eat.

The Future of Electricity

As we become more aware of climate change, how we generate electricity is changing. Many countries are moving away from fossil fuels and towards renewable energy sources like solar and wind power. Electric cars are becoming more common, which could greatly reduce pollution from transportation.

Scientists are also working on new ways to store electricity, like advanced batteries. This could make renewable energy more reliable and help bring electricity to parts of the world that don't have it yet.

Electricity Safety

While electricity is incredibly useful, it can also be dangerous if not handled properly. Here are some important safety tips:

• Never put metal objects in electrical outlets

• Keep electrical devices away from water

• Don't overload outlets with too many plugs

• If you see a fallen power line, stay far away and call for help

Electricity is a fascinating and essential part of our world. It powers our homes, schools, and cities, making modern life possible. As you go through your day, take a moment to notice all the ways electricity is working for you. From charging your phone to keeping your food cold, electricity is truly lighting up our world. As we face challenges like climate change, our relationship with electricity will continue to evolve. By learning about it now, you're preparing yourself to be part of that exciting future.

Electricity is created by the movement of electrons.

17: Electricity
GUIDED NOTES

Introduction

1. Imagine a morning where nothing in your house _____.

2. Electricity is woven into our _____ _____.

What is Electricity?

3. Electricity is a form of _____ caused by the movement of tiny particles called _____.

4. When electrons move from one _____ to another, they create an _____ _____.

5. Analogy: Electricity is like _____ flowing through a _____.

   • Electrons are like the _____.

   • Wires are like the _____.

How Do We Make Electricity?

6. List three methods power plants use to generate electricity:

   a) _____

   b) _____

   c) _____

7. The complex network that delivers electricity is called the _____ _____.

Why is Electricity Important?

8. Match the following aspects of modern life with how electricity powers them:

   a) Lighting   ____ Keeps food fresh and safe

   b) Communication   ____ Powers medical devices

   c) Entertainment   ____ Enables online learning

   d) Health Care   ____ Runs traffic lights

   e) Education   ____ Connects phones and internet

   f) Transportation   ____ Illuminates streets and screens

   g) Food Storage   ____ Powers video games and TV

The Future of Electricity

9. Many countries are moving towards _____ energy sources like

_____ and _____ power.

10. _____ cars are becoming more common to reduce pollution.

11. Scientists are working on new ways to _____ electricity, like advanced

_____.

Electricity Safety

12. List four important safety tips related to electricity:

a) _____

b) _____

c) _____

d) _____

Reflection

13. In your own words, explain why electricity is essential in our modern world:

_____

_____

_____

14. Describe two ways you use electricity in your daily life that you might take for granted:

a) _____

b) _____

#1

How would your daily routine change if you suddenly had no electricity for a week?

Think about all the activities you do from morning to night that require electricity.

#2

Why do you think the article compares electricity to water flowing through pipes?

What similarities are there between how water and electricity move and are used?

#3

Of the three main ways to generate electricity mentioned in the article, which do you think is the most sustainable for the future?

What are the pros and cons of fossil fuels, nuclear power, and renewable energy sources?

#4

The article lists seven ways electricity is important in our lives. Can you think of an eighth way that wasn't mentioned?

Look around your home or school for things that use electricity but weren't listed in the article.

#5

How might advancements in electricity storage, like better batteries, change our use of renewable energy?

What are some current limitations of renewable energy sources like solar and wind power?

#6

Why do you think it's important for everyone to understand basic electrical safety?

What could happen if people don't follow the safety tips mentioned in the article?

TERM	DEFINITION
Electricity	
Electrons	
Electric current	
Power grid	
Fossil fuels	
Renewable energy	
Nuclear reactions	

TERM	DEFINITION
Climate change	
Electric cars	
Power plants	
Transformers	
Hydroelectric power	
Solar power	
Battery storage	

Electricity

```
V R I Y P P I V T Y X P E L E C T R O N S O K Y
H Y D R O E L E C T R I C P O W E R O R V D K V
O F N I Q B O H L A H L D N Q D X R T B U N J S
U V N R I E L E C T R I C I T Y H I D C G B B S
S O U W A F O S S I L F U E L S E B H L M H M U
P E C Y K U G I F N Q Z P A D K F A A I B U U V
E M L W L N O A D D L C N K K G Q T B M A L S G
H K E X U P A M C P L V R B U O V T D A R O V P
T R A N S F O R M E R S O Y E G C E G T G P I S
J L R Y N S A W Q O G L I C E U I R X E T N P C
Y B R O E K L Q L U L S I T S H U Y Y C O Y W K
E P E C P O W E R P L A N T S R N S G H G I P B
N J A D I J R E N I L P X T Z F S T S A U Q G I
J R C C Z U I Q B G O Z L F U F O O U N B R Z P
L Q T V Q L G K E A C N C J B Z L R S G P K Y O
H K I Y H Y V B C B V Y J U T J A A B E R D G W
O D O R R E N E W A B L E E N E R G Y C I R I E
S A N C S E Y V F P V L M U K B P E Y V R V I R
C L S Z T E O Q M O X T L P K B O F R W J O F G
S M S I E L E C T R I C C A R S W L S J T O E R
X M X G H U Q V L X R O B Y V E E A X V N A L I
S U A O O E L E C T R I C C U R R E N T O I X D
O T D I X V D X I Q D U X L V K U T D Z R O U J
H I G K G F W Q U W N I L R J O U S X Q S K F N
```

Battery storage

Power plants

Renewable energy

Electric cars

Electrons

Solar power

Climate change

Electric current

Fossil fuels

Electricity

Hydroelectric power

Nuclear reactions

Transformers

Power grid

Electricity

Across

3. Facilities where electricity is generated using various methods like burning fossil fuels or harnessing renewable sources. ___ plants

5. Vehicles that run on electricity stored in batteries instead of gasoline, helping to reduce pollution. (Two words)

9. A renewable energy source that converts sunlight into electricity using solar panels. ___ power

10. Sources of power that can be naturally replenished, such as wind, solar, or hydroelectric power. ___ energy

11. Devices in the power grid that change the voltage of electricity for safe transmission and use.

12. A process used in some power plants to generate electricity by splitting atoms. ___ reactions

13. Long-term changes in the Earth's weather patterns, often linked to human activities like burning fossil fuels. ___ change

14. Tiny particles that are part of atoms and create electric current when they move.

Down

1. Technology used to store electrical energy for later use, important for making renewable energy more reliable. ___ storage

2. Natural resources like coal and natural gas that are burned to generate electricity. (Two words)

4. The flow of electrons from one place to another, which creates electricity. Electric ___

6. A complex network of wires and transformers that delivers electricity to homes, schools, and businesses. (Two words)

7. A form of energy caused by the movement of electrons, used to power devices and machines.

8. A form of renewable energy that generates electricity using the force of flowing water. ___ power

Magnetic Fields: Attracting and Repelling

Magnetism is a force that can attract or repel certain materials. It's created by the movement of tiny particles called electrons inside atoms. When many atoms with their electrons lined up in the same direction come together, they create a magnetic field. This field is invisible, but it can interact with other magnetic materials.

Magnetism can attract or repel certain materials.

The most common magnetic material is iron, but nickel and cobalt are magnetic too. Materials that can be attracted to magnets are called ferromagnetic.

The Earth: Our Giant Magnet

Believe it or not, the Earth itself is like a huge magnet. The planet's core, made mostly of iron, creates a magnetic field that surrounds the Earth. This magnetic field is super important because it protects us from harmful radiation from space and helps some animals navigate.

Speaking of navigation, the Earth's magnetic field is what makes compasses work. A compass needle is a tiny magnet that aligns itself with the Earth's magnetic field, always pointing towards the magnetic north pole. Isn't that cool?

Electromagnetism: When Electricity and Magnetism Team Up

In the 1800s, scientists discovered that electricity and magnetism are closely related. They found that moving electric charges can create magnetic fields, and changing magnetic fields can create electric currents. This relationship is called electromagnetism.

Electromagnetism is the basis for many of the technologies we use every day. Here are some examples:

Electric motors: Found in everything from cars to blenders, these use electromagnets to convert electrical energy into motion.

Generators: These do the opposite of motors, using motion to create electricity. This is how we get most of our electric power!

Speakers and headphones: They use electromagnets to turn electrical signals into sound waves.

Computer hard drives: These store data using tiny magnetic regions on a spinning disk.

MRI machines: These use powerful electromagnets to create detailed images of the inside of our bodies.

Magnetism in Nature

Humans aren't the only ones who use magnetism. Many animals have a built-in magnetic sense that helps them navigate. For example:

-Birds use the Earth's magnetic field to find their way during long migrations.

-Sea turtles use magnetism to return to the beaches where they were born.

-Some bacteria contain tiny magnetic crystals that act like compasses, helping them find food.

The aurora's wavy patterns and curtains of light are caused by the Earth's magnetic field

The Future of Magnetism

Scientists and engineers are constantly finding new ways to use magnetism. Some exciting areas of research include:

Maglev trains: These super-fast trains use powerful magnets to float above the tracks, reducing friction and allowing for incredible speeds.

Fusion energy: Scientists are working on using powerful magnets to contain superheated plasma for clean, nearly limitless energy.

Quantum computing: Some types of quantum computers use magnetic fields to manipulate individual atoms, potentially leading to incredibly powerful computers.

Why Magnetism Matters to You

You might be thinking, "This is all interesting, but why should I care about magnetism?" Well, magnetism impacts your life in more ways than you might realize:

1. It powers many of the devices you use every day, from your smartphone to your video game console.

2. It helps doctors diagnose and treat illnesses using tools like MRI machines.

3. It's crucial for generating the electricity that lights up your home and charges your devices.

4. It could be the key to developing new, clean energy sources that will help fight climate change.

5. Understanding magnetism can help you make sense of the world around you, from how a simple compass works to how the aurora borealis (Northern Lights) forms.

Magnetism is an invisible but incredibly powerful force that shapes our world in countless ways. From the Earth's protective magnetic field to the tiny electromagnets in your headphones, this fundamental force of nature is all around us.

18: Magnetism
GUIDED NOTES

Magnetism

1. Magnetism is an invisible _____ that plays a huge role in our daily lives.

What is Magnetism?

2. Magnetism is created by the movement of _____ inside atoms.

3. A magnetic field is created when many atoms have their electrons lined up in the _____ direction.

4. Three common magnetic materials are:

    a. _____   b. _____

    c. _____

The Earth as a Magnet

5. The Earth's core is mostly made of _____, creating a magnetic field around the planet.

6. This magnetic field protects us from _____ from space.

7. A compass works because the needle aligns with the Earth's _____ _____.

Electromagnetism

8. Electromagnetism is the relationship between _____ and _____.

9. List three technologies that use electromagnetism:

    a. _____   b. _____

    c. _____

Magnetism in Nature

10. Name two animals that use the Earth's magnetic field for navigation:

    a. _____   b. _____

The Future of Magnetism

11. _____ trains use powerful magnets to float above the tracks.

12. Scientists are researching how to use magnetism for _____

    energy and _____ computing.

Why Magnetism Matters

13. List three ways magnetism impacts your daily life:

    a. _____

    b. _____

    c. _____

Reflection

14. What did you find most interesting about magnetism? Why?

    _____

    _____

15. Can you think of any other examples of magnetism in your everyday life not mentioned in the article?

    • _____

    • _____

    • _____

    • _____

    • _____

#1

How does the Earth's magnetic field benefit life on our planet?

Think about the harmful effects of space radiation and how animals use the magnetic field for navigation.

#2

In what ways do you interact with electromagnetic devices in your daily life?

Look around your home or classroom. How many items use electric motors, speakers, or store data?

#3

How might advances in magnetic technology, like maglev trains or fusion energy, change our future?

Think about current transportation and energy challenges. How could these magnetic technologies address them?

#4

Why is it important for scientists to understand the relationship between electricity and magnetism?

Reflect on how many modern technologies rely on both electricity and magnetism working together.

#5

How do animals use magnetism differently from humans?

Compare how animals use their natural magnetic sense to how humans use artificial magnetic devices like compasses.

#6

If you could invent a new technology using magnetism, what would it be and how would it work?

Think about current problems in the world and how a magnetic solution might help solve them.

TERM	DEFINITION
Magnetism	
Electrons	
Magnetic field	
Ferromagnetic	
Electromagnetism	
Electric motor	
Generator	

TERM	DEFINITION
MRI	
Maglev train	
Fusion energy	
Quantum computing	
Aurora borealis	
Compass	
Electromagnetic radiation	

Magnetism

```
Q F L X L B M E V W F Q C G R N X O F J K C R Z
I R X F H B L X Q R A Y P J E V Y N E P O O Y
T G R V O L N E C O M P A S S A I L I H M R T J
M J H M B U U C H C D Q W M Z W O G X F J W A N
M T Z Y Q Q N T W R E L E C T R O N S U U P U O
M A G L E V T R A I N S H I C K W W H S L G R L
Q E L E C T R O M A G N E T I S M U N I R Q O K
A K F E R R O M A G N E T I C L B P I O A F R O
S K L U M R I A N P O Q X F W H G A N V U A Y
K C N S W M N G I R E Y U A J H E P W E Z G B E
W R E X W H M N C F Q V S B W U L F F N Q R O A
X L P M A G N E T I C F I E L D E E L E P V R U
T G K X X V M T K U M Y E Y U T C P X R B F E R
F J O H I I A I Q I Z X V P X U T O E G J K A F
F F W V D F G C J G E M Y X S D R I J Y R K L F
S T N V Z D R T E A Z K B P I P X V Y Q I K
E Z N K Q S E A Z N E Q F O Y A C L N T M K S S
B U C G E A T D H E W F G G W A M K X R S H Q S
T B J B P R I I S R J T M Q N S O V T J Q P Q A
Y Q C H L C S A T A I T W Y N S T Y Y H M W P C
W E L J U K M T B T N K E B B T O R G U V I T Q
D L D J X D P I B O R A M O L F R T X N E T X O
A T E U B I S O G R D B F U B P V N T R N S Q E
E X K R Q U A N T U M C O M P U T I N G M H N X
```

Electromagnetic radiation

Fusion energy

Compass

Electromagnetism

Electrons

Aurora borealis

Maglev train

MRI

Ferromagnetic

Magnetism

Quantum computing

Electric motor

Generator

Magnetic field

Magnetism

Across

5. The relationship between electricity and magnetism, where moving electric charges create magnetic fields and changing magnetic fields create electric currents.

6. A force that can attract or repel certain materials.

9. A type of advanced computing that sometimes uses magnetic fields to manipulate individual atoms. _____ computing

10. Tiny particles inside atoms that create magnetism when they move.

11. A super-fast train that uses strong magnets to float above the

12. A potential future energy source that uses powerful magnets to contain superheated plasma. _____ energy

14. Energy that travels through space as waves, including harmful types that the Earth's magnetic field protects us from. Electromagnetic _____

Down

1. Also known as the Northern Lights, a natural light display in the sky caused by the Earth's magnetic field. _____ borealis

2. A navigation tool with a magnetic needle that always points toward the Earth's magnetic north pole.

3. aterials that can be attracted to magnets, like iron, nickel, and cobalt.

4. An invisible area around a magnet where its force can be felt. (Two words)

7. A medical imaging tool that uses powerful electromagnets to create detailed pictures of the inside of the body.

8. A machine that converts motion into electricity, the opposite of an electric motor.

13. A device that uses electromagnets to convert electrical energy into motion. Electric _____

Studying Our Planet:
A Look Into Earth's Systems

Have you ever wondered why earthquakes happen? Or how mountains form? Maybe you're curious about where our drinking water comes from or why the weather changes. If these questions interest you, then you're already thinking like an Earth scientist. Earth Sciences is a fascinating field that helps us understand the world around us. It's all about studying our planet from the rocks beneath our feet to the air we breathe.

What Are Earth Sciences?

Earth Sciences, sometimes called geosciences, is the study of our planet Earth. It's like putting together a giant puzzle to figure out how our world works. Earth scientists look at many different parts of our planet:

Earth sciences can help us predict and lessen the impact of natural disasters.

1. *The solid Earth (rocks, soil, mountains)*
2. *The water on Earth (oceans, rivers, glaciers)*
3. *The air around us (atmosphere)*
4. *Living things on Earth (plants, animals, humans)*

Earth Sciences combines knowledge from other subjects like physics, chemistry, and biology to help us understand Earth's systems.

Major Areas of Earth Sciences

Earth Sciences covers a lot of ground (pun intended!). Here are some of the main areas:

Geology: The study of rocks, minerals, and the processes that shape the Earth's surface.

Meteorology: The study of the atmosphere and weather patterns.

Oceanography: The study of the oceans and their processes.

Environmental Science: The study of how living things interact with their environment.

Climate Science: The study of long-term weather patterns and how they change over time.

Why Earth Sciences Matter in Our Lives

You might be thinking, "This all sounds interesting, but why should I care?" Well, Earth Sciences affects our daily lives in many ways:

Natural Disasters: Earth scientists help predict and prepare for natural disasters like earthquakes, volcanic eruptions, and hurricanes. Their work saves lives by giving us early warnings and helping us build safer buildings and cities.

Water Resources: Where does your drinking water come from? Earth scientists study groundwater and help us find and manage clean water sources. This is becoming more important as many places face water shortages.

Energy Resources: The gas that powers cars or the electricity in your home often comes from Earth's resources like oil, natural gas, or coal. Earth scientists help find these resources and also work on developing cleaner energy sources like geothermal power.

Climate Change: You've probably heard about climate change in the news. Earth scientists study how our planet's climate is changing and what effects this might have on our lives. Their research helps us understand what we can do to protect our environment.

Weather Forecasting: Ever check the weather before deciding what to wear? Thank an Earth scientist! Meteorologists use their knowledge of Earth's systems to predict the weather, which helps us plan our daily activities and prepare for severe weather.

It has been helpful for us to know about the different climates and weather patterns.

Agriculture: Farmers rely on Earth Sciences to understand soil types, weather patterns, and water availability. This knowledge helps them grow the food we eat every day.

Building and Construction: Before we build houses, roads, or bridges, Earth scientists study the ground to make sure it's safe and stable. Their work helps engineers design structures that can withstand earthquakes and other natural events.

Earth Sciences and Your Future

As you think about your future career, consider how Earth Sciences might play a role. The skills you learn in Earth Science classes can be useful in many jobs:

- Environmental consultant
- Meteorologist
- Geologist
- Oceanographer
- Urban planner
- Science teacher
- Natural resource manager

Even if you don't become an Earth scientist, understanding how our planet works can help you make informed decisions about important issues like energy use, water conservation, and climate change.

Earth Sciences helps us understand the amazing planet we call home. By studying the Earth, we can better protect ourselves from natural disasters, manage our resources wisely, and take care of our environment. As you continue your studies in Physical Science, remember that the Earth is a complex, interconnected system. The more we learn about it, the better equipped we are to face the challenges of the future.

Introduction

Earth Sciences, also known as _____, is the study of our planet Earth. It helps us understand:

1. _____

2. _____

3. _____

4. _____

What are Earth Sciences?

Earth Sciences is like putting together a giant _____ to figure out how our world works.

Earth scientists study four main parts of our planet:

1. The solid Earth: _____

2. The water on Earth: _____

3. The air around us: _____

4. Living things on Earth: _____

Earth Sciences combines knowledge from other subjects like _____, _____, and _____.

Major Areas of Earth Sciences

Fill in the definition for each area:

1. Geology: _____

_____

2. Meteorology: _____

_____

3. Oceanography: _____

_____

4. Environmental Science: _____

_____

5. Climate Science: _____

_____

Why Earth Sciences Matter in Our Lives

For each area, briefly explain how Earth Sciences impacts our daily lives:

1. Natural Disasters: _____

_____

2. Water Resources: _____

_____

3. Energy Resources: _____

_____

4. Climate Change: _____

_____

5. Weather Forecasting: _____

_____

6. Agriculture: _____

_____

7. Building and Construction: _____

_____

Earth Sciences and Your Future

List three potential career paths related to Earth Sciences:

1. _____   2. _____

3. _____

Reflection

In 2-3 sentences, explain why understanding Earth Sciences is important for everyone, even if they don't become Earth scientists:

_____

_____

_____

#1

How does Earth Sciences connect to your daily life?

Think about your activities today. Did you check the weather, drink water, or use electricity? How might Earth Sciences be involved in these actions?

#2

Which area of Earth Sciences interests you the most and why?

Look at the five main areas mentioned in the article. Which one sounds the most exciting or important to you? What about it catches your attention?

#3

How might understanding Earth Sciences help us prepare for natural disasters?

Think about different types of natural disasters. How could knowing more about the Earth help us predict or respond to these events?

#4

In what ways do Earth scientists contribute to solving environmental problems?

Look at the examples in the article about water resources, energy, and climate change. How do Earth scientists help with these issues?

#5

If you became an Earth scientist, what kind of questions would you want to investigate?

What mysteries about the Earth fascinate you? Is there something about our planet you've always wondered about?

#6

How might learning about Earth Sciences influence the decisions you make in the future?

Think about choices you might face as an adult, like where to live or what products to buy. How could knowledge of Earth Sciences affect these decisions?

TERM	DEFINITION
Earth sciences	
Geosciences	
Geology	
Meteorology	
Oceanography	
Environmental science	
Climate science	

TERM	DEFINITION
Natural disasters	
Groundwater	
Geothermal power	
Climate change	
Weather forecasting	
Natural resources	
Interconnected system	

Earth Sciences

```
H J Q G B J V S P T R Q X M C Z L V C X N R S G
T W P O U N V Z X Q H X B A Y Q H N S J U G W R
T I D C G T Q H K C Z I I B F U J U X G U R F E
V N P E W A S P D J U C Y U S P O B D Q T E U N
G T N A T U R A L R E S O U R C E S Q K G O E V
E E I N E C E T L L H T A F M D L Q W Z B A M I
O R D O L Q C L E A D L F Y Q T E F G R Q O S R
T C J G L R H C L I M A T E C H A N G E R E Z O
H O W R A X M Y J I A E V L F I B F H P W K T N
E N C A L B E P V U I A W U H H P P I J R W S M
R N L P S K T E Q P H N U B B R H Y E V F A Z E
M E I H D W E A T H E R F O R E C A S T I N G N
A C M Y F G O B Q X Q R T R C Z G O N G H E P T
L T A M Z W R U P B T I E N C X Y Q A H J L T A
P E T A I Z O Z K G E O S C I E N C E S J J A L
O D E C S U L T M U P A R A G M D R X H L X V S
W S S X E J O J Z V B O L T E X S T D O T A U C
E Y C W M L G H I O V G O H U B A I F Y G A N I
R S I B D B Y F D J M A H H T L G B K C E R S E
T T E R N A T U R A L D I S A S T E R S O A W N
G E N K G R O U N D W A T E R H L R S K L J P C
L M C T N C D W K J Y O I O T P U E X O O Q I E
L R E A F F R P D I Y X O Z Y E I Q L K G E B L
E A R T H S C I E N C E S F O D Z U D C Y R H W
```

Climate change	Interconnected system	Natural resources
Weather forecasting	Geothermal power	Natural disasters
Climate science	Environmental science	Groundwater
Oceanography	Meteorology	Geology
Geosciences	Earth sciences	

Earth Sciences

Across

2. The study of oceans and their processes.
3. The study of rocks, minerals, and the processes that shape Earth's surface.
8. Another name for Earth Sciences.
10. Predicting what the weather will be like in the near future. Weather ____
11. Long-term changes in Earth's weather patterns and average temperatures. ____ change

13. Water found underground in spaces between rocks and soil.
14. The study of our planet, including its rocks, water, air, and living things. (Two words)

Down

1. Materials found in nature that are useful to humans, like water, oil, or minerals. Natural ____
4. A group of parts that work together and affect each other, like Earth's different environments. ____ system

5. The study of how living things interact with their surroundings. ____ science
6. The science of studying the atmosphere and weather patterns.
7. A clean energy source that uses heat from inside the Earth. ____ power
9. Dangerous events caused by nature, like earthquakes, hurricanes, or volcanic eruptions. Natural ____
12. The study of long-term weather patterns and how they change over time. ____ science

The Hidden World Beneath Our Feet: Home Sweet Home

Have you ever wondered what's under your feet? Not just the grass, soil, or concrete, but deep, deep down? Our planet Earth is like a giant onion, made up of different layers. Each layer has its own special features and plays a crucial role in making our world work. Let's take a journey to the center of the Earth and discover why these layers matter to us.

Rocky layers on a slice of mountain.

The Crust: Our Home Sweet Home

The crust is the outermost layer of the Earth. It's where we live, build our cities, and grow our food. Think of it as Earth's skin. The crust is pretty thin compared to the other layers only about 5 to 70 kilometers thick. That might sound like a lot, but it's actually less than 1% of Earth's total radius!

The crust is made up of rocks and minerals. There are two types of crust:

1. Continental crust: This is the land we live on. It's thicker and lighter.
2. Oceanic crust: This is under the oceans. It's thinner and heavier.

Why it matters: The crust is our home. It provides the resources we need to survive, like soil for growing food and materials for building. Understanding the crust helps us find important minerals and manage natural disasters like earthquakes.

The Mantle: Earth's Muscle

Just below the crust is the mantle. It's the largest layer of the Earth, making up about 84% of the planet's volume. The mantle is mostly solid rock, but it's so hot that it can flow very slowly over long periods of time.

The mantle is divided into two parts:
1. Upper mantle: This part is rigid and forms the bottom of tectonic plates.

2. Lower mantle: This part is hotter and can flow, driving plate tectonics.

Why it matters: The mantle's slow movement causes plate tectonics, which shapes our planet's surface. This process creates mountains, volcanoes, and earthquakes. Understanding the mantle helps us predict these events and prepare for them.

The Core: Earth's Powerhouse

At the center of our planet is the core. It's split into two parts:

1. Outer core: This layer is liquid metal, mostly iron and nickel. It spins as the Earth rotates.

2. Inner core: This is a solid ball of metal at the very center of the Earth. It's incredibly hot about as hot as the surface of the Sun!

Why it matters:

The spinning outer core creates Earth's magnetic field. This invisible force protects us from harmful radiation from space and helps animals navigate. Without it, life as we know it wouldn't be possible!

Why Earth's Layers Matter

Natural resources: Many of the materials we use daily, like metals and fossil fuels, come from different layers of the Earth. Understanding these layers helps us find and use these resources responsibly.

Natural disasters: Earthquakes, volcanoes, and tsunamis all originate from processes happening in Earth's layers. Studying these layers helps scientists predict and prepare for these events, potentially saving lives.

Climate: The movement of Earth's layers affects our climate over long periods. For example, volcanic eruptions can release gasses that impact global temperatures.

Navigation: The Earth's magnetic field, generated by the core, makes compasses work. This has been crucial for exploration and is still used in modern GPS systems.

Understanding the layers of the Earth can give use insights into the past and help us find important resources.

Life itself: The Earth's layers work together to create the conditions necessary for life. They regulate temperature, create a breathable atmosphere, and provide the raw materials for living things.

Earth's layers might seem far removed from our daily lives, but they're actually vital to our existence. From the ground we walk on to the air we breathe, every aspect of our lives is influenced by these hidden layers. Understanding our planet's structure not only satisfies our curiosity but also helps us become better caretakers of our world. By learning about Earth's layers, we can make smarter decisions about how we use resources, prepare for natural disasters, and protect our environment for future generations.

20: Earth's Layers
GUIDED NOTES

Introduction

What's deep under our feet? Earth is like a giant _____, made up of

different _____.

The Crust: Our Home Sweet Home

1. The crust is the _____ layer of the Earth.

2. Thickness of the crust: _____ to _____ kilometers

3. The crust makes up less than _____% of Earth's total radius.

4. Two types of crust:

   a) _____: This is the land we live on. It's thicker and
                                        lighter.

   b) _____: This is under the oceans. It's thinner and eavier.

5. Why the crust matters: (List two reasons)

   • _____

   • _____

The Mantle: Earth's Muscle

1. The mantle is located just below the _____.

2. It makes up about _____% of the planet's volume.

3. The mantle is divided into two parts:

   a) _____: This part is rigid and forms the bottom of
                                          tectonic plates.

   b) _____: This part is hotter and can flow, driving plate
                                          tectonics.

4. Why the mantle matters: _____

_____

The Core: Earth's Powerhouse

1. The core is split into two parts:

   a) _____: This layer is liquid metal, mostly iron and nickel.

   b) _____: This is a solid ball of metal at the very center of the Earth.

2. Temperature of the inner core: _____

_____

3. Why the core matters: _____

_____

Why Earth's Layers Matter

Match each aspect to its importance:

1. Natural resources   _____

2. Natural disasters   _____

3. Climate   _____

4. Navigation   _____

5. Life itself   _____

a) Helps predict and prepare for events like earthquakes and tsunamis
b) Provides materials we use daily, like metals and fossil fuels
c) Creates conditions necessary for life, including temperature regulation
d) Affects global temperatures through processes like volcanic eruptions
e) Makes compasses work through the Earth's magnetic field

Reflection

In your own words, explain why understanding Earth's layers is important for our daily lives:

_____

_____

_____

_____

#1

How does the Earth's crust directly impact your daily life?

Think about the food you eat, the buildings you use, and the ground you walk on.

#2

Why is the mantle often called "Earth's muscle"? How does its movement affect the world we see?

Remember how the mantle causes plate tectonics and shapes Earth's surface over time.

#3

How does the Earth's core protect life on our planet?

Think about the magnetic field created by the outer core and what it does for us

#4

Can you explain how understanding Earth's layers might help us prepare for natural disasters?

Reflect on where earthquakes and volcanoes originate and how knowing this could be useful.

#5

How do Earth's layers work together to create conditions suitable for life?

Think about things like temperature regulation, atmosphere, and the materials needed for life.

#6

Why is it important for us to learn about Earth's structure, even though we can't see most of it?

How does this knowledge help us become better caretakers of our planet?

TERM	DEFINITION
Crust	
Mantle	
Core	
Continental crust	
Oceanic crust	
Plate tectonics	
Upper mantle	

TERM	DEFINITION
Lower mantle	
Outer core	
Inner core	
Magnetic field	
Natural resources	
Climate	
Atmosphere	

Earth's Layers

```
L G Q Y J B Z N H R M T O O Y J M Y S O J X M A
P T B D J A T M O S P H E R E I T M N U U G B R
J D E P L P O I U G N N R N F E H K D T L K U L
R K C U C R P N W F Q C D B O S Z U C E Z A K Z
E Z P Z I T D F I Z M A N T L E C Y R R Z N W X
V L L Y T J B H T Q G H V Q X G V H U C N A V O
N Y A T P L U U J M E Z A Z W C O A S O A U I M
I K T X B G P R F V A U W R C M N Q T R T G W R
J Z E F I S P G F Y T I B Z C K N R U E U E P L
S N T I K L E V C O N T I N E N T A L C R U S T
W J E E W H R Z J X X B X O D J O L T A A Y W B
A V C V A E M P C C L O T L X M F O F R L Q L O
Y O T G F G A Q T Y Z K Q E K O S W Y J R T I K
Q W O M K F N I Y W B V J X Z C R E K O E B B G
O X N X A D T N J H J G O V U L H R B E S K K Y
V H I Y P G L N O J J S Y E N Y O M B H O K K Y
C P C X U U E E G L P P N F K C I A B T U I D I
L M S H H E W R A A K E L L X J X N D A R O K K
I E K C L D P C N W M E K K J L A T H B C W C J
M P H Y C L O O U S I S H N K P U L X X E W Q K
A U P O Z K E R C O R E Z S P E K E P O S I T H
T U G N O Z C E L R L M A G N E T I C F I E L D
E O C E A N I C C R U S T L V B P P K C T D Z Z
M K C L I M A T E C H A N G E K D R O F P W K M
```

Climate change	Natural resources	Magnetic field
Inner core	Outer core	Lower mantle
Upper mantle	Oceanic crust	Continental crust
Atmosphere	Plate tectonics	Core
Mantle	Crust	

Earth's Layers

Across

3. The typical weather patterns in an area over a long period of time.

5. The hotter, flowing part of the mantle that drives plate tectonics. _____ mantle

7. The layer of gasses surrounding the Earth, providing air for us to breathe.

9. The solid metal center of the Earth, extremely hot and dense. _____ core

10. The thinner, heavier part of the Earth's crust found under the oceans. _____ crust

12. Materials from the Earth, like metals and fossil fuels, that we use in daily life. _____ resources

13. The outermost layer of the Earth where we live and build our cities.

14. The rigid top part of the mantle that forms the bottom of tectonic plates. _____ mantle

Down

1. The largest layer of the Earth, located between the crust and the core.

2. The movement of large sections of the Earth's crust, driven by the mantle. (Two words)

4. The thicker, lighter part of the Earth's crust that forms land masses. _____ crust

6. The center part of the Earth, divided into outer and inner sections.

8. An invisible force created by the Earth's spinning outer core that protects us from harmful space radiation. _____ field

11. The liquid metal layer of the Earth's core, mostly made of iron and nickel. _____ core

Earth's Structures and Processes:
This Subject Rocks

Have you ever picked up a cool-looking rock and wondered where it came from? Or felt the ground shake during an earthquake and asked yourself what's happening deep beneath your feet? These questions are at the heart of geology, the science that studies the Earth, its structure, and the processes that shape it.

What is Geology?

Geology is like being a detective for the Earth. Geologists use clues from rocks, mountains, volcanoes, and earthquakes to understand our planet's history and how it works today. They study everything from tiny crystals you can only see with a microscope to entire continents and ocean basins.

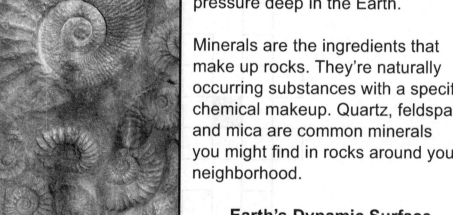

Fossils are found in sedimentary rocks.

The Building Blocks: Rocks and Minerals

Rocks are the Earth's storytellers. Each type of rock igneous, sedimentary, and metamorphic has its own tale to tell:

1. Igneous rocks form when hot, molten rock (magma or lava) cools and hardens. Volcanoes create igneous rocks!

2. Sedimentary rocks form when bits of other rocks, plants, or animals get squeezed and cemented together over time.

3. Metamorphic rocks start as other rocks but change when they're exposed to extreme heat or pressure deep in the Earth.

Minerals are the ingredients that make up rocks. They're naturally occurring substances with a specific chemical makeup. Quartz, feldspar, and mica are common minerals you might find in rocks around your neighborhood.

Earth's Dynamic Surface

The Earth isn't just a static ball of rock it's constantly changing! Geology helps us understand processes like:

Plate tectonics: The theory that explains how pieces of the Earth's crust move around, causing earthquakes, forming mountains, and creating volcanoes.

Erosion: How wind, water, and ice wear away rocks and land over time, shaping landscapes.

Deposition: When eroded materials get dropped off in new places, forming new landforms.

Why Geology Matters in Your Life

You might be thinking, "Okay, rocks are cool, but why should I care about geology?" Here are some reasons why geology is super important:

Natural Hazards: Geologists help predict and prepare for earthquakes, volcanic eruptions, landslides, and tsunamis. This knowledge saves lives!

Resources: The phone or computer you're reading this on? Many of its parts come from minerals mined from the Earth. Geologists help find the resources we use every day, from metals to the oil that makes plastic.

Environmental Protection: Understanding how pollutants move through soil and rock helps keep our water clean and our environment healthy.

Climate Change: Rocks and sediments hold clues about past climate changes. This info helps scientists understand and predict future climate patterns.

Building and Construction: Geologists make sure the ground is safe before big buildings or bridges are built.

Cool Careers: Studying geology can lead to awesome jobs like volcanologist, oceanographer, or even an astronaut studying rocks on other planets!

Geology in Your Backyard

You don't need fancy equipment to start thinking like a geologist. Here are some ways to explore geology in your everyday life:

• Look at the rocks in your yard or a nearby park. Can you spot different colors, shapes, or patterns?

• Notice how water flows when it rains. Where does it collect? Is it changing the land?

• If you live near mountains or a beach, observe how the landscape changes over time.

• Check out buildings in your town. What are they made of? Those materials came from somewhere!

The Big Picture

Geology reminds us that the Earth has an incredible, 4.6-billion-year history. Studying this history helps us understand our place in the world and how to take care of our planet for the future.

Obsidian is an igneous rock that forms when molten rock cools and hardens.

Next time you're outside, take a moment to look at the ground beneath your feet. You're standing on layers of rock that tell the story of our planet. Those ordinary pebbles or that hillside? They're full of secrets waiting to be discovered. Geology gives us the tools to unlock those secrets and more to understand the amazing world around us.

21: Geology
GUIDED NOTES

Introduction

1. Geology is the science that studies:

• The _____

• Its _____

• The _____ that shape it

What is Geology?

2. Geologists are like _____ for the Earth. They use clues from:

1. _____   2. _____

3. _____   4. _____

The Building Blocks: Rocks and Minerals

3. Complete the table about the three main types of rocks:

Rock Type	How It Forms
Igneous	
Sedimentary	
Metamorphic	

4. Minerals are:

• Naturally occurring _____

• With a specific _____ _____

5. List three common minerals mentioned in the text:

1. _____   2. _____

3. _____

Earth's Dynamic Surface

6. Define the following terms:

Plate tectonics: _____

_____

Erosion: _____

_____

Deposition: _____

_____

Why Geology Matters in Your Life

7. Match each application of geology to its description:

a) Natural Hazards   ____ Helps find resources for electronics

b) Resources   ____ Ensures ground stability for construction

c) Environmental Protection   ____ Predicts earthquakes and volcanic eruptions

d) Climate Change   ____ Studies past climate patterns

e) Building and Construction   ____ Tracks pollutant movement in soil and rock

Geology in Your Backyard

8. List three ways you can explore geology in your everyday life:

1. _____

2. _____

3. _____

The Big Picture

9. How old is the Earth? _____ years

10. Why is studying geology important for our future? (Write 2-3 sentences)

_____

_____

_____

#1

How does geology affect your daily life?

Think about the materials in your electronic devices, the buildings you use, and the natural landscapes around you.

#2

What type of rock do you think is most common in your area, and why?

Look at the landforms and buildings around you for clues about the local geology.

#3

How might understanding plate tectonics help people prepare for natural disasters?

Think about the connection between plate movements and events like earthquakes or volcanic eruptions.

#4

If you could choose a career in geology, which one would interest you most and why?

Reflect on your interests and how they might align with different geological fields, from studying volcanoes to exploring other planets.

#5

How can studying rocks and minerals help us understand climate change?

Think about how rocks and sediments can preserve information about past environments and climates.

#6

What geological features or processes have you noticed in your own neighborhood or nearby areas?

Pay attention to things like erosion from rainfall, the types of stones used in buildings, or any hills or valleys in your area.

TERM	DEFINITION
Geology	
Geologist	
Igneous rocks	
Sedimentary rocks	
Metamorphic rocks	
Minerals	
Plate tectonics	

TERM	DEFINITION
Erosion	
Deposition	
Magma	
Lava	
Volcanologist	
Oceanographer	
Natural hazards	

Geology

```
K V E J N G G R M Y O D E F W N A I H O B M I S
J H E A A K G Y W C K H M A K C V B X R H C K W
S E D I M E N T A R Y R O C K S I L R L S R Q V
P N Y U P O Q L L W F O Q V Q L G T T X S X D O
F L F O J B Y J G L I I T T S J N M C S U S Y T
B B Q Y Y E R O S I O N X Y P E E E V V U Z M N
D M Z G A C P K K I O H P D L E O T Z B W B I N
P Y I H I Z A W P I I R T F V L U A L G T D N A
L J A M G A N I Y R D Z D V V H S M J G Q E E T
A U P D Z F L R B X X G L U G O R O G N G P R U
T S Z I G M O W F D K L B D E I O R G Z U O A R
E A Q O E K C W E D C I H W O O C P K Z F S L A
T R L L E V X A E I X Q S K L A K H Y D M I S L
E Y E J Z F T Y B Q E D Z H O F S I E H S T I H
C Z U W B U U G U B E V J O G B P C I I R I R A
T C F M V O L C A N O L O G I S T R X T A O V Z
O O C E A N O G R A P H E R S U E O M L J N M A
N M B L K K P M U I P D W T T O L C D F J X E R
I M A G M A W S W Y R M L O L X M K A R X U O D
C E N Y Z D G M L M M I Z X N Y S N W I Z K S
S E G F Y U R Y Z T E E C V Q P T W A I K W M N
N C X U X M G E O L O G Y W O L E E Y S H G Y K
B T C E A B T Y L A V A G T Z O C F U O G B N G
O J G R V F H Y A I W Q N U J J B C D R Y X U L
```

Natural hazards

Igneous rocks

Lava

Erosion

Geologist

Metamorphic rocks

Oceanographer

Magma

Plate tectonics

Geology

Sedimentary rocks

Volcanologist

Deposition

Minerals

Geology

Across

3. The theory that explains how pieces of the Earth's crust move around, causing earthquakes, forming mountains, and creating volcanoes. (Two words)

5. Hot, molten rock beneath the Earth's surface.

8. The science that studies the Earth, its structure, and the processes that shape it.

9. Hot, molten rock that has erupted onto the Earth's surface.

10. Rocks formed when hot, molten rock (magma or lava) cools and hardens. _____ rocks

12. The process of wind, water, and ice wearing away rocks and land over time, shaping landscapes.

13. Rocks formed when bits of other rocks, plants, or animals get squeezed and cemented together over time. _____ rocks

14. A scientist who studies the Earth's structure and processes.

Down

1. A scientist who studies volcanoes and their behavior.

2. A scientist who studies the oceans and their processes.

4. Dangerous natural events like earthquakes, volcanic eruptions, landslides, and tsunamis that geologists help predict and prepare for. Natural _____

6. When eroded materials get dropped off in new places, forming new landforms.

7. Rocks that start as other types of rocks but change when exposed to extreme heat or pressure deep in the Earth. _____ rocks

11. Naturally occurring substances with a specific chemical makeup that make up rocks.

Diving into Earth's Waters:
A Water World

Have you ever wondered why the ocean is salty? Or why some rivers flow faster than others? These are just a few of the questions that scientists in oceanography and hydrology try to answer. But what exactly are these fields of study, and why should you care about them? Let's dive in head first and find out.

What are Oceanography and Hydrology?

Oceanography is the study of the world's oceans. It looks at everything from tiny sea creatures to massive underwater mountains. Oceanographers study how water moves in the oceans, how it affects weather and climate, and how it supports life.

Properly managing water as a resource is important for the environment and ourselves.

Hydrology, on the other hand, is all about fresh water on land. Hydrologists study rivers, lakes, and even the water underground. They look at how water moves through the earth and how it shapes the land around us.

Together, oceanography and hydrology help us understand Earth's water systems. This is important because water covers about 71% of our planet's surface.

Why Should You Care?

The oceans and freshwater play a huge role in our daily lives, even if we don't realize it. Here are some reasons why:

Weather and Climate: The oceans have a big impact on our weather. They store heat from the sun and move it around the planet. This affects everything from daily temperatures to long-term climate patterns. Understanding the oceans helps us predict weather and prepare for climate change.

Food: Many people around the world rely on fish and other sea creatures for food. Oceanographers help us understand how to protect these important food sources. Hydrologists help farmers use water wisely to grow the crops we eat.

Transportation: Ships carry goods all over the world through the oceans. Understanding ocean currents and weather patterns makes shipping safer and more efficient.

Clean Water: Hydrologists help make sure we have clean water to drink. They study how pollutants move through water systems and how to clean them up.

Natural Disasters: Both oceanographers and hydrologists help us predict and prepare for natural disasters like floods, tsunamis, and hurricanes.

Fun and Recreation: Whether you like swimming, boating, or just hanging out at the beach, understanding water systems can make these activities safer and more enjoyable.

The ocean plays a huge role in weather, climate, and supporting life.

Facts About Earth's Waters

Now that you know why oceanography and hydrology are important, check out these awesome water facts:

• The deepest part of the ocean is the Challenger Deep in the Mariana Trench. It's about 36,200 feet deep – that's almost 7 miles!

• The longest river in the world is the Nile River in Africa. It's about 4,132 miles long.

• There are underwater waterfalls in the ocean. The largest one is in the Denmark Strait between Greenland and Iceland.

• The Great Lakes in North America contain about 20% of the world's fresh surface water.

• The color of the ocean isn't really blue. It just looks that way because of how sunlight interacts with the water.

How You Can Get Involved

You don't have to be a scientist to help protect our water systems. Here are some simple things you can do:

1. Use less plastic. A lot of plastic ends up in the oceans, harming sea life.
2. Don't waste water. Turn off the tap when brushing your teeth or take shorter showers.
3. Learn more about your local water sources. Where does your drinking water come from?
4. Participate in beach or river clean-ups in your area.
5. Share what you learn with friends and family. The more people who understand the importance of water, the better.

Oceanography and hydrology might seem like big, complicated subjects, but they're really about understanding the water all around us. From the vast oceans to the rivers in your backyard, water shapes our world in countless ways. By learning about these fields, you're taking the first step in becoming a better steward of our planet's most precious resource.

22: Oceanography & Hydrology
GUIDED NOTES

Introduction

1. What percentage of Earth's surface is covered by water? _____%

Definitions

2. Oceanography is the study of _____.

3. Hydrology is the study of _____.

Importance of Oceanography and Hydrology

List four reasons why these fields are important:

4. _____

5. _____

6. _____

7. _____

Impact on Daily Life

Explain how oceanography and hydrology affect each area:

8. Weather and Climate: _____

_____

9. Food: _____

_____

10. Transportation: _____

_____

11. Clean Water: _____

_____

Fascinating Facts

Fill in the blanks:

12. The deepest part of the ocean is called _____ and it's approximately _____ miles deep.

13. The world's longest river is the _____ River, measuring about _____ miles long.

14. The Great Lakes contain approximately _____% of the world's fresh surface water.

15. True or False: The ocean's blue color is due to the water itself. _____

Getting Involved

List three ways you can help protect water systems:

16. _____

17. _____

18. _____

Reflection

19. Why do you think it's important for everyone, not just scientists, to understand oceanography and hydrology?

_____

_____

_____

20. What's one new thing you learned from this lesson that surprised you?

_____

_____

_____

#1

How do oceanography and hydrology affect your daily life?

Think about the water you drink, the weather you experience, and the food you eat.

#2

Why is it important to understand how ocean currents impact climate change?

How might changes in ocean temperature affect weather patterns in your area?

#3

Can you think of a way that understanding hydrology might help your community?

Does your area ever face water shortages or flooding issues?

#4

How might studying oceanography or hydrology lead to new job opportunities in the future?

What kinds of problems might need solving as our climate changes?

#5

What's one thing you learned about Earth's waters that surprised you, and why?

How does this new information change the way you think about water on our planet?

#6

What's one action you can take to help protect water systems in your area?

Look at the "How You Can Get Involved" section for ideas, but also think about specific issues in your community.

TERM	DEFINITION
Oceanography	
Hydrology	
Climate	
Current	
Pollutant	
Tsunami	
Steward	

TERM	DEFINITION
Underwater mountain	
Fresh water	
Sea creature	
Weather pattern	
Natural disaster	
Water system	
Trench	

Oceanography & Hydrology

```
M V N I R W J S G L L H P O L L U T A N T M K M
I H I C J C K T V N D C N T U S Z Q K L L L F N X
J I D S F R E S H W A T E R D U F E M X K N W J
M Z A S P K N A Q R E I N E R D J D S R H N L X
T S U N A M I U S Y Q U F S K J J C Y S J C W F
J A N L B N T B U Y U A I J C W T Q H T T M M S
B T D S U A D T N C U R R E N T Z O N G G D Y Z
D S E N W T I B A T E M W Y M H H P E T H G N L
O E R L C U O I J B N W S N Q S K R L Z V K G K
U A W Q X R E J L O S E O V O D C L G P N W R B
R C A R Q A N P T Z M A W A T E R S Y S T E M E
X R T T E L S N S F V T J M X G H N K C P D G
J E E I J D S W Q T I H V A R H W F O X A W D D
J A R B Y I M H C R M E C S E K N J C V Y B R I
F T M M E S V S L D W R I X N S W Z E A U P N K
P U O W B A O I I D D P R T C D Q Z A H N S M O
E R U Z I S Q E M B R A I H Q W P N P V U W M
M E N Y G T V H A M H T F N J B D J O O R I W G
S V T W Z E K B T N G T J M D E K E G L O A M Y
L R A M U R E U E A Y E I O Q G M O R F O V G A
U R I H D K S T E W A R D B V K J G A I K H O Q
B E N B M A W V K K A N T P O T R M P I U H Q H
P Y E T H Y D R O L O G Y G H Y A V H U M S P N
R W O G E X C Y U V V H I M W C D C Y W M F X
```

Water system	Natural disaster	Weather pattern
Fresh water	Underwater mountain	Trench
Sea creature	Steward	Tsunami
Pollutant	Current	Climate
Hydrology	Oceanography	

Oceanography & Hydrology

Across

3. A substance that contaminates water, air, or soil, making it harmful to living things.

5. The typical way weather behaves in a specific area. Weather ____

7. A major event caused by nature that can harm people and damage property. Natural ____

11. Any animal that lives in the ocean. (Two words)

13. The study of fresh water on land, including rivers, lakes, and underground water.

14. A steady flow of water in a particular direction within a larger body of water.

Down

1. The typical weather patterns in an area over a long period of time.

2. A large raised area on the ocean floor, also known as a seamount. ____ mountain

4. The study of the world's oceans, including their physical and biological features.

6. A giant ocean wave usually caused by an underwater earthquake or volcanic eruption.

8. Water that contains little or no salt, like in rivers and lakes. ____ water

9. Someone who takes care of and protects something, like the environment.

10. A long, narrow, deep depression in the ocean floor.

12. The network of water sources and how they connect and interact with each other. Water ____

The Planet's Protective Shield: Making Life Possible

Have you ever wondered why we can breathe on Earth but not on the Moon? Or why we don't get burned by the Sun's rays every time we step outside? This all thanks to Earth's atmosphere – a layer of gasses that surrounds our planet and makes life possible. Let's learn what the atmosphere is, how it works, and why it's so important in our daily lives.

Greenhouse gasses and air pollutants can contribute to global warming and harm air quality.

What is the Atmosphere?

Earth's atmosphere is like a blanket of air wrapped around our planet. It's made up of different gasses, with nitrogen (78%) and oxygen (21%) being the most common. The remaining 1% includes gasses like argon, carbon dioxide, and water vapor. This mix of gasses extends from the Earth's surface up into space for hundreds of miles, getting thinner as it goes higher.

Layers of the Atmosphere

The atmosphere is divided into five main layers:

1. Troposphere: The lowest layer where we live and breathe. It's where most weather happens.

2. Stratosphere: Above the troposphere, it contains the ozone layer that protects us from harmful UV rays.

3. Mesosphere: This is where most meteors burn up when entering Earth's atmosphere.

4. Thermosphere: A very thin layer where auroras (like the Northern Lights) occur.

5. Exosphere: The outermost layer that gradually fades into space.

Why is the Atmosphere Important?

The atmosphere plays several crucial roles that make life on Earth possible:

It Provides the Air We Breathe

The oxygen in our atmosphere is essential for most life on Earth. Plants and some bacteria produce this oxygen through photosynthesis, and animals (including us) use it to survive.

It Regulates Temperature

The atmosphere acts like a greenhouse, trapping heat from the Sun and keeping Earth warm. Without it, our planet would be much colder – too cold for most life to exist. Gasses like carbon dioxide play a big role in this process.

It Protects Us from Harmful Radiation

The ozone layer in the stratosphere blocks most of the Sun's harmful ultraviolet (UV) radiation. This protection is crucial because too much UV exposure can cause skin cancer and damage plants.

It Creates Weather and Climate

The atmosphere is where weather happens. As the Sun heats the Earth unevenly, it creates air currents, which lead to wind, clouds, and precipitation. These processes distribute heat and moisture around the planet, creating different climates.

It Shields Us from Space Debris

Meteors and other small objects from space often enter Earth's atmosphere. Most of them burn up due to friction with the air, protecting us from impacts.

The Atmosphere in Our Daily Lives

Even though we can't see it, the atmosphere affects us every day:

• When you check the weather forecast, you're looking at predictions about atmospheric conditions.

• The blue sky you see is caused by sunlight scattering in the atmosphere.

• Air pollution, which can affect our health, occurs when harmful substances enter the atmosphere.

• Climate change, a major global concern, is largely due to changes in the atmosphere's composition.

Caring for Our Atmosphere

Human activities have a big impact on the atmosphere. Burning fossil fuels releases greenhouse gasses like carbon dioxide, which trap more heat and contribute to global warming. Other pollutants can harm air quality and damage the ozone layer.

To help protect our atmosphere, we can:

• Use energy-efficient appliances and vehicles

• Reduce, reuse, and recycle to lower our carbon footprint

• Support clean energy sources like solar and wind power

• Plant trees and protect forests, which absorb carbon dioxide

Earth's atmosphere is an amazing and complex system that makes our planet habitable. It provides the air we breathe, protects us from harmful radiation and space debris, regulates our climate, and creates the weather we experience every day. Understanding the atmosphere helps us appreciate its importance and motivates us to take better care of our planet.

The atmosphere is where weather occurs, which impacts us daily.

23: Earth's Atmosphere
GUIDED NOTES

Introduction

1. We can breathe on Earth but not on the Moon because of Earth's

    _____.

2. The atmosphere protects us from getting burned by the _____'s rays.

What is the Atmosphere?

3. The atmosphere is like a _____ of air wrapped around our planet.

4. Complete the table about the composition of Earth's atmosphere:

Gas	Percentage
Nitrogen	
Oxygen	
Other gases (e.g., argon, carbon dioxide, water vapor)	

5. As the atmosphere extends into space, it gets _____.

Layers of the Atmosphere

6. Match each layer with its correct description:

   a) Troposphere   _____ Where auroras occur

   b) Stratosphere   _____ Where we live and breathe

   c) Mesosphere   _____ Contains the ozone layer

   d) Thermosphere   _____ Outermost layer

   e) Exosphere   _____ Where meteors burn up

Why is the Atmosphere Important?

7. List five crucial roles of the atmosphere:

a) _____

b) _____

c) _____

d) _____

e) _____

8. Which gas is essential for most life on Earth? _____

9. How does the atmosphere regulate temperature? _____

_____

10. What does the ozone layer protect us from? _____

_____

11. Explain how the atmosphere creates weather: _____

_____

The Atmosphere in Our Daily Lives

12. Give four examples of how the atmosphere affects our daily lives:

a) _____

b) _____

c) _____

d) _____

Caring for Our Atmosphere

13. What human activity releases greenhouse gases?

_____

14. List three ways we can help protect our atmosphere:

a) _____

b) _____

c) _____

#1

How does Earth's atmosphere differ from the Moon's?

Think about what the atmosphere provides that's necessary for life. How would the lack of an atmosphere affect living things? Why is this difference important for life?

#2

Explain how the atmosphere acts like a blanket for Earth.

What might happen if this "blanket" became too thick or too thin? Remember how the atmosphere traps heat. How might changes in its thickness affect Earth's temperature?

#3

Which layer of the atmosphere do you think is most important for human life?

Explain your reasoning. Review the functions of each layer. Which one provides the most direct benefits to our daily lives?

#4

How does the atmosphere influence the weather we experience every day?

Think about the connection between air currents, temperature, and moisture. How do these factors combine to create weather?

#5

What are some ways that human activities affect the atmosphere?

Reflect on the effects of pollution and greenhouse gasses. How might these alter the atmosphere's ability to protect and sustain life?

#6

If you could design an experiment to learn more about one aspect of the atmosphere, what would you choose to study and why?

Think about which part of the atmosphere interests you most. What questions do you have that aren't answered in the article?

TERM	DEFINITION
Atmosphere	
Nitrogen	
Oxygen	
Troposphere	
Stratosphere	
Ozone layer	
Mesosphere	

TERM	DEFINITION
Thermosphere	
Exosphere	
Greenhouse effect	
Climate	
Carbon footprint	
Fossil fuels	
Photosynthesis	

Earth's Atmosphere

```
Q D Z D V H M L F S T R A T O S P H E R E R X O
Z R N N I T R O G E N M H I P P F P W T Y T Q W
J X Z J D V E G Z D C L I M A T E E L F Q C O Y
V K C R T R O P O S P H E R E D Q N I B C N U U
B F K H R D O V G B Y U G E V Z U Q O G G Q I O
M M E I L S Z Y E X O S P H E R E Q A R Y C B E
V N K Q P K O M R S S N Q R Y K C D W E W P Z G
T X V C V W N O A M E S O S P H E R E E G T C Y
I R Z O U U E A V O D F F A F C C E P N G Z A Z
Z B L Z U U L D F M D G O X Y G E N I H F J R H
D A B N S M A T Z L W H S L M L A P V O L S B L
P K G M S X Y K I J R G S N J U H Z W U U C O A
S X Y W O B E N I F A D I Q G C F D N S T O N B
B P O V B M R J Q G T G L V T H Z B Q E T W F H
S I O R E O V W F C M E F A V P Y J L E M T O T
K A A F I J M O R S O M U A M V H L J F Q R O I
L Z F P V Y R A J T S M E O I E F P T F A F T S
V O V A B J U F C G P Y L L N B H W O E Y K P M
X S I T B I E I E E H X S R S R E V D C P Y R T
S B B K J O H Y V H E A I F X D U B S T D V I G
K W J C Z Y A C S A R X J I K Z V X P X Y D N R
Y U A Z C I L W V U E W F S O N K D D Y I C T D
W P W P O D P H O T O S Y N T H E S I S M P S V
Y C A G H M E E V T T H E R M O S P H E R E N U
```

Fossil fuels

Photosynthesis

Thermosphere

Stratosphere

Nitrogen

Carbon footprint

Climate

Mesosphere

Troposphere

Atmosphere

Greenhouse effect

Exosphere

Ozone layer

Oxygen

Earth's Atmosphere

Across

4. The amount of carbon dioxide released into the atmosphere as a result of human activities. Carbon ____

10. The typical weather patterns in an area over a long period of time.

11. The fourth layer of the atmosphere where auroras (like the Northern Lights) happen.

12. The lowest layer of the atmosphere where we live and most weather occurs.

14. The third layer of the atmosphere where most meteors burn up.

Down

1. The process by which plants and some bacteria produce oxygen using sunlight, water, and carbon dioxide.

2. A part of the stratosphere that blocks most of the Sun's harmful ultraviolet radiation.

3. The second layer of the atmosphere, containing the ozone layer that protects us from harmful UV rays.

5. Energy sources like coal, oil, and natural gas that release greenhouse gasses when burned. ____ fuels

6. The process by which the atmosphere traps heat from the Sun, keeping Earth warm. ____ effect

7. The most abundant gas in Earth's atmosphere, making up 78% of its composition.

8. The layer of gasses surrounding Earth that makes life possible.

9. The outermost layer of the atmosphere that gradually fades into space.

13. The second most common gas in the atmosphere, essential for breathing and making up 21% of its composition.

Understanding Our Place In Space:
A Final Frontier

Have you ever gazed up at the night sky and felt a sense of wonder? That feeling is at the heart of astronomy, the science that studies everything in space. From twinkling stars to massive galaxies, astronomy explores the universe beyond our planet. But why should you care about astronomy? Let's discover how this fascinating field connects to your everyday life.

The Sun is the center of our solar system and provides the energy for all life on our planet.

What is Astronomy?

Astronomy is the study of objects and events outside of Earth's atmosphere. It looks at planets, stars, galaxies, and other celestial bodies. Astronomers use telescopes, satellites, and computers to observe and understand the cosmos.

The Building Blocks of It All

Believe it or not, astronomy helps us understand what we're made of. The elements that make up our bodies like carbon, oxygen, and iron were created inside stars billions of years ago. When those stars exploded, they scattered these elements across space. Eventually, some of that stardust became part of Earth and everything on it, including you.

Pushing Technology Forward

Many technologies we use daily have roots in astronomy. For example:

1. Wireless internet: Radio astronomy techniques helped develop Wi-Fi.

2. GPS: Understanding how gravity affects satellite orbits makes GPS possible.

3. Digital cameras: The same technology in your phone camera was first used in space telescopes.

Solving Earth's Challenges

Studying other planets helps us better understand and protect our own. For instance:

Climate change: By observing Venus's runaway greenhouse effect, we learn about Earth's changing climate.

Weather prediction: Satellite technology developed for astronomy improves weather forecasting.

Energy solutions: Research into how stars produce energy could lead to better clean energy on Earth.

Inspiring Curiosity and Innovation

Astronomy sparks curiosity and drives innovation. It pushes us to ask big questions and solve complex problems. This mindset is valuable in many careers, not just science.

Your Place in the Universe

Astronomy gives us perspective on our place in the cosmos. Earth is just one small planet in a vast universe. This view can make our daily problems seem smaller and remind us of our shared humanity.

Astronomy in Your Life

You might not realize it, but astronomy touches your life in many ways:

• The phases of the Moon affect ocean tides.

• Seasons are caused by Earth's tilt and orbit around the Sun.

• Northern lights (aurora borealis) are created by particles from the Sun interacting with Earth's magnetic field.

• Meteorites (space rocks that land on Earth) teach us about the early solar system.

Looking to the Future

Space exploration: We're planning missions to Mars and beyond.

Finding other habitable planets: Astronomers are searching for worlds that could support life.

Protecting Earth: We're developing ways to detect and deflect asteroids that could hit our planet.

New discoveries: Powerful telescopes and missions will reveal more about dark matter, black holes, and the early universe.

How You Can Explore Astronomy

You don't need expensive equipment to start exploring astronomy:

1. Stargazing: On a clear night, find a dark spot and look up. Can you spot constellations or planets?

2. Apps: Download free astronomy apps that help identify stars and planets.

The universe is vast. There is plenty to explore and understand.

3. Local events: Many towns have astronomy clubs or stargazing events.

4. Online resources: NASA and other space agencies offer free videos, images, and learning materials.

5. School projects: Choose astronomy topics for science fairs or reports.

Astronomy may seem distant, but it connects to your life in surprising ways. It pushes technology forward, helps solve Earth's problems, and gives us a new perspective on our place in the universe. As you continue living and learning, keep looking up and wondering about the cosmos.

24: Astronomy
GUIDED NOTES

Introduction

1. Astronomy is the science that studies _____ in space.

2. Why should we care about astronomy? _____

_____

What is Astronomy?

3. Definition: _____

_____

4. Tools astronomers use:

1. _____   2. _____

3. _____

The Building Blocks of Life

5. The elements in our bodies were created _____

_____

6. How did these elements reach Earth? _____

_____

Astronomy's Impact on Technology

7. List three technologies influenced by astronomy and explain their connection:

a. _____ : _____

_____

b. _____ : _____

_____

c. _____ : _____

_____

Solving Earth's Challenges

8. How does studying Venus help us understand _____

_____?

9. Astronomy contributes to better _____ prediction on Earth.

10. Research on stars could lead to improvements in _____.

Inspiration and Perspective

11. How does astronomy inspire innovation? _____

_____

12. Explain how astronomy gives us perspective on our place in the universe:

_____

_____

Astronomy in Everyday Life

13. List four ways astronomy affects our daily lives:

a. _____

b. _____

c. _____

d. _____

The Future of Astronomy

14. Four areas of future exploration in astronomy:

a. _____

b. _____

c. _____

d. _____

Getting Involved in Astronomy

15. List five ways you can explore astronomy without expensive equipment:

a. _____

b. _____

c. _____

d. _____

e. _____

#1

How does astronomy connect to your daily life in ways you might not have realized before?

Think about the technologies you use every day and how they might be linked to space research.

#2

Why is understanding our place in the universe important for our perspective on life?

How might viewing Earth as just one small planet in a vast universe change how we think about our problems or our relationship with others?

#3

How could studying astronomy help address some of Earth's current challenges?

What can we learn from other planets that might help us understand and solve issues on Earth?

#4

In what ways does astronomy inspire innovation and problem-solving skills?

How might the process of exploring space and solving complex cosmic puzzles apply to other areas of life or careers?

#5

How do you think future discoveries in astronomy might affect humanity?

What impact could finding habitable planets or developing new space technologies have on our society?

#6

What steps could you take to explore astronomy further on your own?

What resources are available in your community or online that you could use to learn more about space?

TERM	DEFINITION
Astronomy	
Cosmos	
Celestial bodies	
Elements	
Greenhouse effect	
Satellite	
Constellation	

TERM	DEFINITION
Aurora borealis	
Meteorite	
Dark matter	
Black hole	
Habitable planet	
Asteroid	
Galaxy	

Astronomy

```
I  A  T  G  R  E  E  N  H  O  U  S  E  E  F  F  E  C  T  T  Y  Y  W  G
A  K  G  N  D  H  D  P  O  Z  X  C  B  D  G  H  P  N  R  F  R  R  J  Z
I  O  B  T  O  E  I  A  P  Y  T  W  M  E  T  E  O  R  I  T  E  Q  N  C
C  X  Z  W  G  B  S  S  C  O  W  G  G  L  P  H  O  A  A  Y  D  H  X  W
S  U  T  T  B  V  P  T  A  F  R  Q  D  C  D  V  L  B  Z  O  Q  S  Z  K
N  Y  R  X  S  P  F  E  X  Z  O  H  A  E  I  E  L  Y  E  J  S  K  Q  I
I  A  Y  V  E  E  O  R  N  S  A  T  E  L  L  I  T  E  L  H  C  L  X  A
D  F  X  U  K  W  G  O  J  V  E  X  T  E  W  V  D  R  E  A  X  D  B  B
W  V  H  N  N  V  A  I  C  O  M  A  J  S  R  I  A  E  L  E  M  E  N  T  S  B  Z  Z  I  O
E  K  B  J  N  J  L  D  Q  Y  W  U  G  T  J  G  S  R  E  I  R  W  H  T
O  B  K  C  C  H  A  O  W  M  B  R  E  I  E  H  W  C  N  T  J  B  Z  D
E  C  D  D  S  X  X  A  X  J  L  O  X  A  E  Y  C  O  T  A  L  X  W  M
I  Q  G  X  O  Q  Y  S  W  M  A  R  X  L  Q  B  L  N  S  B  Z  R  W  Q
E  L  C  M  R  B  A  V  V  B  C  A  H  B  J  F  Z  S  X  L  U  N  B  L
J  E  D  A  W  Z  V  I  V  Y  K  B  T  O  T  H  U  T  V  E  O  N  J  J
J  X  A  G  N  E  V  P  G  B  H  O  W  D  S  M  M  E  L  P  E  V  B  R
U  W  R  N  T  L  H  T  L  K  O  R  U  I  H  X  H  L  H  L  A  Q  J  R
C  U  K  Q  N  I  W  M  O  B  L  E  Y  E  M  H  P  L  F  A  K  B  U  R
G  C  M  G  P  X  Z  K  O  W  E  A  Y  S  C  B  Y  A  A  N  T  S  U  O
C  O  A  J  S  A  Z  C  G  T  A  L  V  F  D  A  J  T  X  E  O  T  L  U
K  S  T  O  V  U  M  J  B  D  F  I  O  Z  Q  X  B  I  K  T  Y  X  K  E
R  M  T  M  F  H  X  W  R  E  R  S  T  D  W  W  T  O  K  Z  P  Y  G  E
B  O  E  X  P  U  B  K  V  F  Z  O  Y  P  H  O  C  N  J  J  F  P  K  R
B  S  R  Z  R  P  C  P  E  Q  A  S  T  R  O  N  O  M  Y  E  F  R  P  S
```

Habitable planet

Greenhouse effect

Asteroid

Constellation

Cosmos

Dark matter

Celestial bodies

Black hole

Satellite

Astronomy

Aurora borealis

Galaxy

Meteorite

Elements

Astronomy

Across

4. The warming of a planet's surface due to gasses in its atmosphere trapping heat. _____ effect

8. An object that orbits around a planet or star, either natural (like moons) or artificial (made by humans).

11. A group of stars that form a pattern in the night sky.

12. A mysterious substance in space that can't be seen directly but affects the motion of visible matter. _____ matter

13. A vast collection of stars, gas, dust, and dark matter held together by gravity, like our Milky Way.

14. A piece of rock from space that survives falling through Earth's atmosphere and lands on the surface.

Down

1. An extremely dense region of space with gravity so strong that nothing, not even light, can escape it. (Two words)

2. A small, rocky object that orbits the Sun, typically found between Mars and Jupiter.

3. Also called the Northern Lights; colorful light displays in the sky caused by solar particles interacting with Earth's magnetic field. _____ borealis

5. The basic building blocks of matter, like carbon, oxygen, and iron.

6. The scientific study of objects and events beyond Earth's atmosphere.

7. Natural objects visible in the sky, such as stars, planets, and moons. _____ bodies

9. Another word for the universe, including all of space and everything in it.

10. A world with conditions that could potentially support life as we know it. _____ planet

Living, Non-living, & Their Interactions: A Whole Picture Using Lots of Sciences

Have you ever wondered how the world around us works? From the air we breathe to the water we drink, everything in our environment is connected. This is where environmental sciences come in. Time to learn what this field is all about and why it's so important for you and your future.

What are Environmental Sciences?

Environmental sciences is a field that looks at how living things interact with the world around

Environmental sciences aims to understand the affect we have on the environment and how those changes affect us.

them. It's like putting together a giant puzzle, where each piece represents a different part of nature. Scientists in this field study things like:

- The air we breathe
- The water in our rivers and oceans
- The soil where our food grows
- The plants and animals in our ecosystems
- The weather and climate patterns

By studying these pieces, environmental scientists try to understand how our planet works as a whole. They also look at how humans affect the environment and how changes in the environment affect us.

Why Should You Care?

Here are some reasons why environmental sciences are super important for your life:

It affects your health: The quality of the air you breathe and the water you drink directly impacts your health. Environmental scientists work to keep these resources clean and safe.

It shapes your future: Climate change, pollution, and loss of biodiversity are big challenges we face. Understanding these issues helps us find solutions and create a better future.

It creates job opportunities: As we focus more on protecting our planet, there's a growing need for people who understand environmental sciences. This could lead to exciting career paths for you!

It helps you make informed choices: Knowing about environmental issues helps you make better decisions in your daily life, like choosing eco-friendly products or conserving energy.

It connects you to the world: Learning about the environment helps you appreciate the natural world and understand your place in it.

Real-Life Examples
Let's look at some ways environmental sciences touch your life every day:

Weather forecasts: Environmental scientists study weather patterns to predict storms, heatwaves, and other events that affect your daily activities.

Food production: Understanding soil science and ecosystems helps farmers grow the food you eat.

Clean energy: Environmental scientists work on developing renewable energy sources like solar and wind power, which could power your home in the future.

Wildlife conservation: Efforts to protect endangered species and their habitats are based on environmental research.

Urban planning: Cities use environmental data to design parks, manage waste, and create sustainable communities.

How You Can Get Involved
You don't have to wait until college to start exploring environmental sciences. Here are some ways you can get involved now:

Join environmental clubs: Many schools have clubs focused on nature or conservation. These are great places to learn and take action.

Start recycling: If you're not already recycling at home or school, start now! It's a simple way to help the environment.

Do a science fair project: Choose an environmental topic for your next science project. You could study local water quality or track bird populations in your area.

Volunteer: Many organizations need help with beach cleanups, tree planting, or other environmental activities.

Stay informed: Keep up with environmental news and share what you learn with friends and family.

Environmental science uses many branches of science to tackle issues like energy use, waste management, and wildlife conservation.

Looking to the Future
As you continue your studies, you'll learn more about how different parts of science connect to the environment. Your physical science class is a great starting point! Concepts like energy, matter, and chemical reactions are key to understanding environmental processes.

Environmental sciences offer a chance to make a real difference in the world. Whether you're interested in technology, biology, chemistry, or even social studies, there's a place for you in this field. By understanding our environment, we can work together to protect our planet and create a sustainable future for all. Remember, every small action counts. Your choices and actions today can help shape a healthier planet for tomorrow.

25: Environmental Sciences
GUIDED NOTES

What are Environmental Sciences?

Environmental sciences is a field that studies how _____
_____ interact with the world around them.

Environmental scientists study:

1. _____

2. _____

3. _____

4. _____

5. _____

Why Should You Care?

List five reasons why environmental sciences are important for your life:

1. It affects your _____:

   Explanation: _____
   _____

2. It shapes your _____:

   Explanation: _____
   _____

3. It creates _____ opportunities:

   Explanation: _____
   _____

4. It helps you make _____ choices:

   Explanation: _____
   _____

5. It connects you to the _____:

   Explanation: _____
   _____

Real-Life Examples

Match the environmental science application to its description:

_____Weather forecasts   A. Helps farmers grow food

_____Food production   B. Predicts storms and heatwaves

_____Clean energy   C. Protects endangered species

_____Wildlife conservation   D. Develops solar and wind power

_____Urban planning   E. Designs parks and manages waste

How You Can Get Involved

List five ways you can get involved in environmental sciences now:

1. _____

2. _____

3. _____

4. _____

5. _____

Looking to the Future

How does your physical science class connect to environmental sciences?

_____

_____

_____

Name three areas of study that can connect to environmental sciences:

1. _____

2. _____

3. _____

Reflection

Write two sentences about why you think environmental sciences are important for your future:

_____

_____

_____

25: Environmental Sciences

#1

How does environmental science connect to your daily life?

> Think about the air you breathe, the water you drink, and the food you eat. How might environmental scientists be involved in keeping these things safe and healthy?

#2

What environmental issue do you think is most important for your community, and why?

> Look around your neighborhood or town. Are there any environmental problems you notice, like pollution, lack of green spaces, or wildlife issues?

#3

How might learning about environmental science help you make better choices in the future?

> Think about decisions you might make as an adult, like what car to drive or how to power your home. How could environmental knowledge influence these choices?

#4

Which career in environmental science sounds most interesting to you, and why?

The article mentions several areas where environmental scientists work, such as weather forecasting, food production, and urban planning. Which of these appeals to you most?

#5

What's one small action you could take right now to help the environment?

Remember, the article suggests things like recycling, joining environmental clubs, or doing environmentally-focused science projects. What's something realistic you could start doing today?

#6

How do you think environmental science might change or become more important in the next 10 years?

Think about current environmental issues like climate change or pollution. How might these problems evolve, and what role could environmental science play in addressing them?

TERM	DEFINITION
Environmental sciences	
Ecosystem	
Biodiversity	
Climate change	
Renewable energy	
Conservation	
Sustainability	

TERM	DEFINITION
Pollution	
Urban planning	
Recycling	
Habitat	
Weather patterns	
Soil science	
Environmental impact	

Environmental Sciences

```
T E N V I R O N M E N T A L S C I E N C E S A J
C E N V I R O N M E N T A L I M P A C T K U H K
W P W S J Z R F T Y L L D V E N K Z R Q H T I A
L R W U J F G X I M P A C T K L G Q E A A A O K K
N H D S W E A T H E R P A T T E R N S A B U R Y
T V L T E X L N C M K B D F K P M X E O I Q S E
W Z E A I M L I B L B D J H Q S M O I D T C O I
R I J I Y V Q S B X U Q N J X K R Y F O A B I K
Z C T N O T F W U N N V K O C R W Q X B T B L H
W V V A Z U R B A N P L A N N I N G C C D F S M
C W O B D W J D Y P W D B Q Q G C A O J V Y C U
N Y G I B I O D I V E R S I T Y G E V P S E I R
U P L L Z F L M U E T G U O R C H P M E C U E C
Q O H I M R E C Y C L I N G P U C R J Q M U N O
C L A T W Z R T G D U P C Q W A V G D N X D C N
Q L E Y Z K I H N V G U N P W J W Q I A Z E E S
X U X T R L B I F H J Z M P R Z H V H I E F W E
N T P P H Z J J M S D Z C X I M Q Q B V V M D R
Y I H U R T N V L E C O S Y S T E M N W A D J V
V O Y R T O L B T B Z U M F S X E L Q M W Y O A
X N I D T O B P V U K G S N T W M C H H L R Y T
Q E T W B A H Y P A H M A I D I X L H H L P G I
L C L I M A T E C H A N G E P Z Z K H M P C Q O
R W Z T H Q R E N E W A B L E E N E R G Y P O N
```

Environmental impact	Soil science	Weather patterns
Renewable energy	Environmental sciences	Habitat
Recycling	Urban planning	Pollution
Sustainability	Conservation	Climate change
Biodiversity	Ecosystem	

Environmental Sciences

Across
2. Energy from sources that are naturally replenished, like sunlight or wind. ____ energy

3. The effect of human activities on the natural environment. Environmental ____

7. A community of living things and their environment, working together as a system.

8. The process of designing and organizing cities and towns for efficient and sustainable living. (Two words)

9. The recurring characteristics of weather in a particular area. Weather ____

12. The study of the mixture of minerals and organic matter as a natural resource, including its formation, classification, and mapping. ____ science

13. Meeting our current needs without compromising the ability of future generations to meet their needs.

14. Long-term changes in temperature and weather patterns on Earth. (Two words)

Down
1. The study of how living things interact with the world around them. ____ sciences

4. The protection and careful management of natural resources and the environment.

5. The variety of plant and animal life in a particular habitat or on Earth as a whole.

6. The introduction of harmful substances into the environment.

10. The process of converting waste materials into new materials and objects.

11. The natural home or environment of an animal, plant, or other organism.

Your greatest superpower is your ability to choose one thought over another.

Choose positive thoughts over negative to live your very best life.

Answer Keys

Introduction

1. Physical science helps us understand the world around us, from the tiniest atoms to the vast expanse of space.

What is Physical Science?

2. Physical science is a branch of natural science that studies non-living systems.

3. The three main areas of physical science are:
   a. Chemistry
   b. Physics
   c. Earth sciences

Chemistry: The Science of Matter

4. Chemistry studies matter, which makes up everything around us.

5. Give an everyday example of chemistry in action:
   Possible answers: Baking cookies, soap cleaning dishes, rusting of metal, etc.

6. List two ways chemistry affects your daily life:
   Possible answers:
   a. In the soap you use to wash your hands
   b. In the medicines that help you feel better when you're sick

Physics: The Science of Energy and Motion

7. Physics focuses on energy, forces, and how things move.

8. List three everyday activities where you use physics:
   Possible answers:
   a. Riding a bicycle
   b. Throwing a ball
   c. Opening a soda can with a lever

Earth Sciences: Understanding Our Planet

9. Earth sciences include (fill in the blanks):
   a. Geology: study of rocks and Earth's structure
   b. Meteorology: study of weather and climate
   c. Oceanography: study of oceans

10. How can knowledge of earth sciences help you in daily life?
   Possible answer: It can help you make informed decisions about where to live (avoiding areas prone to natural disasters), how to prepare for severe weather, and how your actions impact the environment.

Importance of Physical Science in Your Life

11. List three reasons why physical science is important:
   Possible answers:
   a. Develops problem-solving skills
   b. Helps understand and use technology effectively
   c. Increases environmental awareness

12. How can understanding physical science help you make better decisions about your health and safety?
   Possible answer: Understanding chemistry can help you choose safer cleaning products, while knowing about physics can make you a safer driver.

13. Name two career fields related to physical science:
   Possible answers:
   a. Engineering
   b. Medicine

Reflection

14. Which area of physical science interests you the most and why?
   (Answers will vary based on student's personal interests)

15. Describe one way you can apply what you've learned about physical science in your daily life:
   (Answers will vary, but should relate to concepts discussed in the article)

What Is Physical Science?

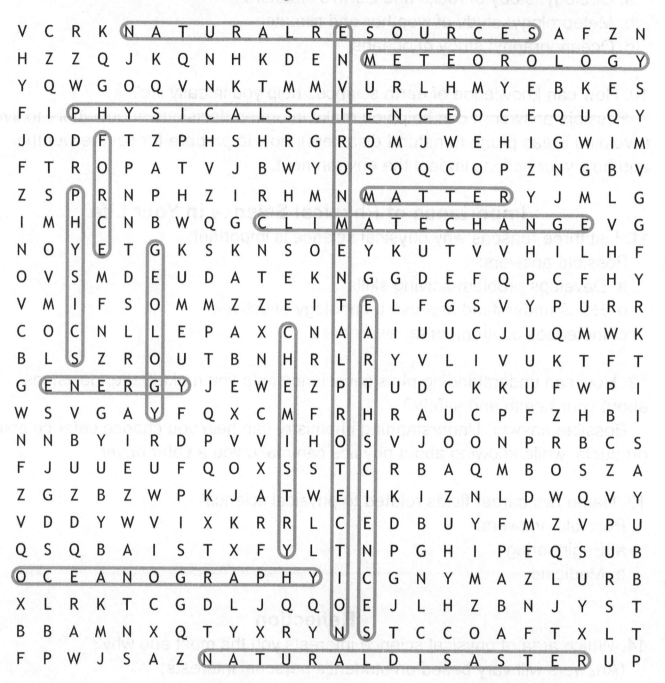

Environmental protection   Natural resources   Climate change

Natural disaster   Earth sciences   Oceanography

Meteorology   Geology   Force

Energy   Matter   Physics

Chemistry   Physical science

What Is Physical Science?

Across

7. Materials from the Earth that we use, like water, oil, or minerals. Natural _____

9. Long-term changes in temperature and weather patterns on Earth. _____ change

11. The study of our planet's systems, including geology, meteorology, and oceanography. _____ sciences

12. The study of weather patterns and climate.

13. The study of the Earth's structure and the rocks that make it up.

14. The study of energy, forces, and motion in the universe.

Down

1. The study of oceans and their systems.

2. The stuff that makes up everything around us.

3. A push or pull that can change the motion of an object.

4. The branch of science that studies non-living systems and matter. (Two words)

5. The study of matter, its properties, and how substances interact and change.

6. A sudden event in nature that causes damage or loss of life, like earthquakes or hurricanes. Natural ----

8. Actions taken to preserve and care for the natural world. Environmental _____

10. The ability to do work or cause change in the world.

Introduction

1. Measurement is important because it helps us:
   - Understand and describe the world around us
   - Compare things
   - Make predictions
   - Solve problems

2. List three everyday activities that involve measurement:
   (Answers may vary, but could include:)
   a. Checking the weather   b. Cooking or baking
   c. Buying clothes

Units of Measurement

3. Units are like the alphabet of measurement. They give meaning to numbers.

4. Match the following quantities with their common units:
   - Length: inches, feet, meters
   - Weight: ounces, pounds, kilograms
   - Time: seconds, minutes, hours
   - Temperature: Fahrenheit, Celsius

5. Why is using the correct units important? Provide an example from the text:
   Using the correct units is important to avoid costly mistakes. For example, in 1999, NASA lost a $125 million Mars orbiter because one team used metric units while another used imperial units, causing the spacecraft to crash.

The Metric System

6. The metric system is based on powers of 10.

7. Complete the following metric conversions:
   - 1 kilometer =   1000 meters
   - 1 meter =   100 centimeters
   - 1 centimeter =   10 millimeters

8. Fill in the blanks for these metric prefixes:
   - Kilo means   1000 times bigger
   - Centi means   100 times smaller
   - Milli means   1000 times smaller

Scientific Notation

9. Scientific notation is used for numbers that are very big or very small.

10. Steps to write a number in scientific notation:
    a. Write the number as a decimal between 1 and 10
    b. Multiply it by 10 raised to a power

11. Convert the following numbers to scientific notation:
    - 5,000 = 5×10^3
    - 0.00025 = 2.5×10^{-4}

12. Why is scientific notation useful? Provide an example from the text:
    Scientific notation is useful for writing very large or small numbers in a more manageable way. For example, the mass of an electron (0.000000000000000000000000000000911 kg) can be written as 9.11×10^{-31} kg, which is much easier to write and understand.

Real-World Applications

13. List five reasons why understanding measurement, units, and scientific notation is important:
    a. Better understanding of the world
    b. Making smart decisions
    c. Preparing for the future
    d. Avoiding mistakes
    e. Appreciating science

14. Think of an example from your own life where you've used measurement concepts:
    (Answers will vary)

Reflection

15. What was the most interesting thing you learned from this lesson?
    (Answers will vary)

16. How might you use these concepts in your future studies or career?
    (Answers will vary)

Measurement, Units, & Scientific Notation

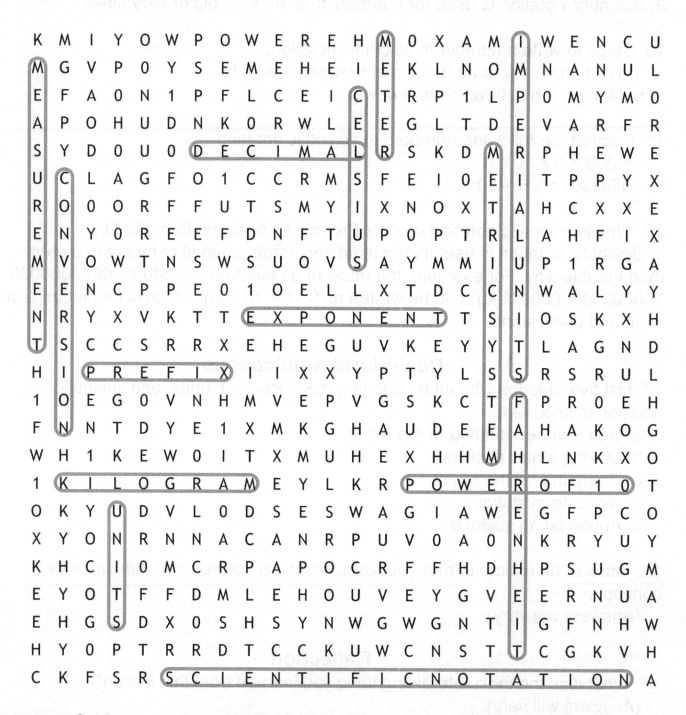

Power of 10

Scientific notation

Fahrenheit

Kilogram

Units

Imperial units

Exponent

Celsius

Prefix

Measurement

Metric system

Decimal

Meter

Conversion

Measurement, Units, & Scientific Notation

Across
3. The metric unit for measuring weight or mass.

4. The process of determining the size, amount, or degree of something using standard units.

7. The process of changing a measurement from one unit to another, like feet to meters.

9. The basic metric unit for measuring length or distance.

10. A number system based on 10, using a point to separate whole numbers from fractions.

11. A number that shows how many times a base number is multiplied by itself, often used in scientific notation.

13. A measurement system used in some countries, including the United States, with units like inches and pounds. _____ units

14. A temperature scale used in the metric system, where water freezes at 0° and boils at 100°.

Down
1. A temperature scale commonly used in the United States, where water freezes at 32° and boils at 212°.

2. Standard amounts used to express measurements, like inches for length or pounds for weight.

5. A measurement system based on powers of 10, used in most countries worldwide. ___ system

6. A number expressed as 10 multiplied by itself a certain number of times, used in scientific notation. _____ of 10

8. A way of writing very large or very small numbers using powers of 10. _____ notation

12. In the metric system, a word part added to the beginning of a unit to show size, such as "kilo-" or "milli-".

Chapter 2 Answer Key
GUIDED NOTES

What is Chemistry?

Chemistry is the study of matter, which makes up everything around us. It explores how different substances interact, combine, and change.

Think of chemistry as the science of building blocks. Like building with Lego bricks, chemists work with the tiniest particles of matter to understand our world and create new materials.

The Basics: Atoms and Molecules

1. Atoms are the tiny particles that make up everything.
2. When atoms join together, they form molecules.
3. Example: Water is a molecule made of 2 hydrogen atoms and 1 oxygen atom, written as H2O.

Why Chemistry Matters in Everyday Life

List five areas where chemistry plays a crucial role:

1. Food and Cooking
2. Personal Care and Cleaning
3. Medicine and Health
4. Technology
5. Environment

Chemistry in Action

Explain the chemistry behind these everyday phenomena:

1. Fizzy Drinks:
   Carbon dioxide gas is dissolved in the liquid under pressure. When opened, the gas is released, causing fizzing and bubbling.

2. Mood Rings:
   Liquid crystals in the ring react to body temperature, changing their structure and the way they reflect light, resulting in color changes.

3. Glow Sticks:
   Bending the stick breaks an inner glass tube, allowing two chemicals to mix. This creates a chemical reaction that produces light without heat.

Chemistry Careers

Match the chemistry career with its description:

Forensic Scientist	C. Use chemistry to solve crimes by analyzing evidence
Environmental Chemist|	D. Work on solutions to environmental problems
Food Scientist	A. Develop new foods or improve food safety
Pharmacist	E. Understand how medicines work and how to use them
Materials Scientist	B. Create new materials for technology or fashion

How to Learn More About Chemistry

List four ways to explore chemistry further:

1. Do simple experiments at home (e.g., making a volcano with baking soda and vinegar)
2. Watch online videos explaining chemistry concepts
3. Read science news, looking for chemistry-related stories
4. Ask teachers questions about chemistry topics that interest you

Reflection

In your own words, explain why understanding chemistry is important in our daily lives:

(Answers will vary, but should touch on how chemistry helps us understand the world around us, make informed decisions about products we use, appreciate technological advancements, and potentially contribute to solving global challenges. Students might mention specific examples from their own lives where chemistry knowledge is useful.)

Chemistry

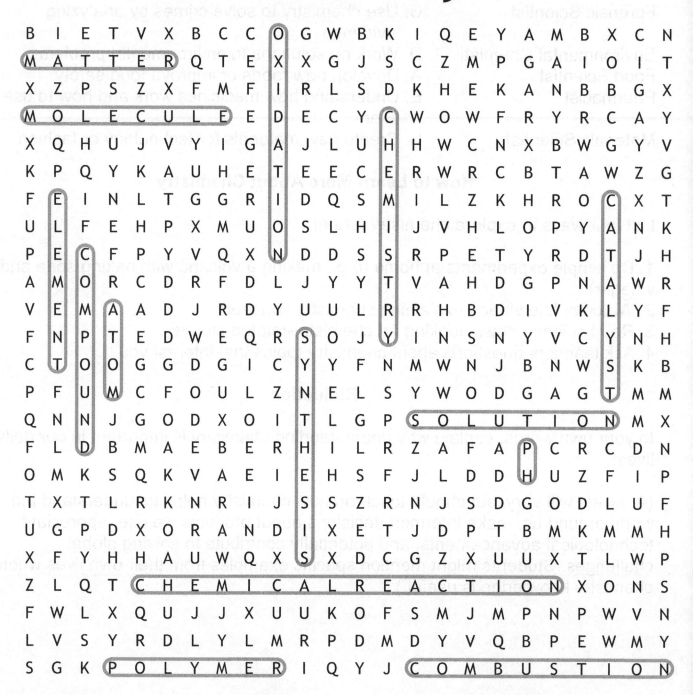

Synthesis

Polymer

Solution

Chemical reaction

Matter

Oxidation

pH

Element

Molecule

Chemistry

Combustion

Catalyst

Compound

Atom

Chemistry

Across

3. The smallest unit of matter, like a tiny building block of the universe.

5. A scale that measures how acidic or basic a substance is, from 0 (very acidic) to 14 (very basic)

8. The process of combining simpler substances to create a more complex substance.

9. When substances change into different substances through breaking and forming bonds. (Two words)

11. A mixture where one substance is dissolved evenly into another, like sugar in water.

12. The stuff that makes up everything around us, from tiny atoms to huge planets.

13. A substance made of two or more different elements chemically combined.

14. A large molecule made up of many repeated smaller units, like plastic or DNA.

Down

1. A substance that speeds up a chemical reaction without being used up itself.

2. A chemical reaction where a substance combines with oxygen, often producing heat and light.

4. The study of matter, its properties, and how substances interact and change.

6. A type of chemical reaction where a substance loses electrons, often when combining with oxygen.

7. A pure substance made of only one type of atom, like oxygen or gold.

10. Two or more atoms joined together, forming a specific substance.

Introduction

1. Matter is defined as anything that takes up space and has mass.
2. List three examples of matter from your everyday life:
   a. Water   b. Chair
   c. Air (or any other reasonable examples)

Properties of Matter

Physical Properties

1. Physical properties can be observed or measured without changing what the matter is made of.
2. Match the physical property with its description:
   a. Color   C How easily something can be scratched or dented
   b. Texture   F How much mass is packed into a certain volume
   c. Hardness   A The way matter looks to our eyes
   d. Melting point   B How something feels when you touch it
   e. Boiling point   D The temperature at which a solid turns into a liquid
   f. Density   E The temperature at which a liquid turns into a gas

Chemical Properties

1. Chemical properties describe how matter reacts with other substances or changes into different substances.
2. List three examples of chemical properties:
   a. Flammability   b. Reactivity
   c. Toxicity

States of Matter

1. Fill in the table with the characteristics of each state of matter:

State	Particle Arrangement	Shape	Volume	Example
Solid	Tightly packed	Fixed	Fixed	Ice cube
Liquid	Close together	Variable	Fixed	Water in glass
Gas	Far apart	Variable	Variable	Steam

2. What is the fourth state of matter mentioned in the article? Plasma
Where can you see it in everyday life? Lightning or neon signs

Changing States

1. Match the phase change with its description:
   a. Melting   C Gas to liquid
   b. Freezing   B Liquid to gas
   c. Evaporation   A Solid to liquid
   d. Condensation   D Liquid to solid

2. Provide an example for each phase change:
   a. Melting: Ice cream melting on a hot day
   b. Freezing: Water turning into ice cubes
   c. Evaporation: Puddles drying up after rain
   d. Condensation: Water droplets forming on a cold drink

Importance in Our Lives

Explain how understanding matter and its properties is important in each of the following areas:

1. Everyday decisions: Knowing melting points helps with food storage; understanding density explains why oil floats on water.
2. Safety: Learning about flammability and toxicity keeps us safe around household chemicals.
3. Cooking: Understanding phase changes helps in reducing sauces (evaporation) or making chocolate fondue (melting).
4. Technology: Smartphones use materials that change properties when electricity flows through them.
5. Environment: Understanding states of matter helps explain concepts like the water cycle and climate change.
6. Health: Knowledge of matter's behavior aids in developing new medicines and treatments.
7. Fun science experiments: Understanding matter allows for cool experiments like making slime or creating a lava lamp.

Properties & States Of Matter

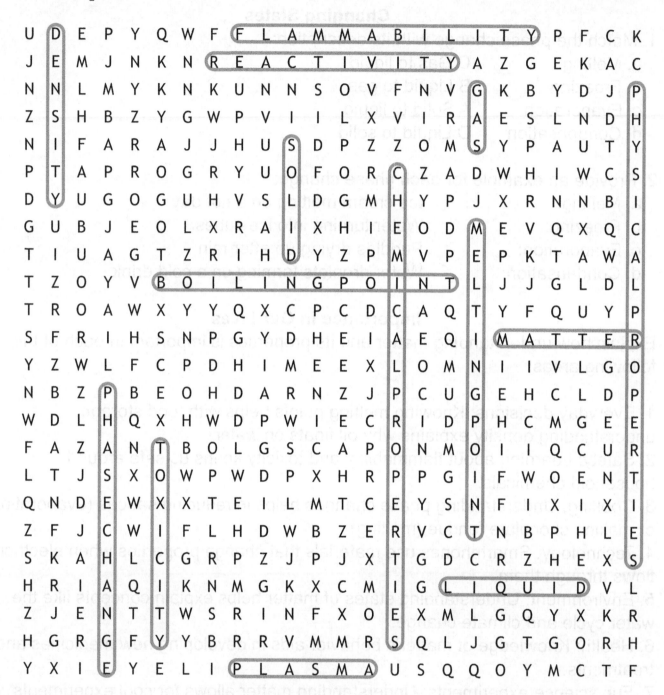

Phase change

Chemical properties

Gas

Toxicity

Density

Boiling point

Physical properties

Liquid

Reactivity

Matter

Melting point

Plasma

Solid

Flammability

Properties & States Of Matter

Across

2. Characteristics that describe how a substance reacts with or changes into other substances. ____ properties

4. A state of matter where particles are close together but can move around, with a fixed volume but no fixed shape.

6. A state of matter where particles are tightly packed and have a fixed shape and volume.

7. The amount of mass packed into a certain volume of a substance.

10. How easily a substance catches fire and burns.

12. A state of matter where particles are far apart and move freely, with no fixed shape or volume.

13. The temperature at which a liquid turns into a gas. ____ point

14. The temperature at which a solid turns into a liquid. ____ point

Down

1. How quickly or easily a substance interacts with other substances.

3. The process of matter changing from one state to another when energy is added or removed. ____ change

5. How poisonous or harmful a substance is to living things.

8. Observable characteristics of a substance that don't change its chemical makeup. ____ properties

9. A fourth state of matter, less common in everyday life, seen in things like lightning or neon signs.

11. Anything that takes up space and has mass.

What Is an Atom?

1. Atoms are the basic building blocks of all matter.
2. Everything in the universe is made up of atoms, including you.

Parts of an Atom

Fill in the table below with information about each part of an atom:

Part	Location	Charge	Function
Nucleus	Center of the atom	N/A	Contains most of the atom's mass
Protons	In the nucleus	Positive	Determines the element type
Neutrons	In the nucleus	Neutral	Helps keep the nucleus stable
Electrons	Around the nucleus in shells	Negative	Involved in chemical reactions and bonding

Why Atomic Structure Matters in Your Life

Match each application of atomic structure to its description:

1. D Chemistry in the Kitchen
2. C Electronics and Technology
3. E Medicine and Health
4. A Environmental Science
5. B Everyday Materials

A. Explains how carbon dioxide traps heat in the atmosphere
B. Allows for the creation of stronger, lighter, and more useful materials
C. Enables the function of smartphones and computers
D. Explains how cooking changes food at a molecular level
E. Helps in developing medicines and medical imaging techniques

The Building Blocks of You

True or False: The atoms in your body stay the same throughout your entire life.
Answer: False

Explain your answer: The atoms in your body are constantly changing. Almost all the atoms in your body are replaced with new ones every year.

Atomic Energy

1. Nuclear energy comes from two processes:
   a. Fission: splitting atoms
   b. Fusion: joining atoms together

2. Why is it important for everyone to have a basic understanding of atomic science?
   It helps us make informed decisions about how we use this knowledge, especially considering the power and potential risks associated with nuclear energy.

Looking to the Future

List three areas where our understanding of atomic structure is leading to new developments:

1. Nanotechnology: Building tiny machines atom by atom
2. New materials: Creating substances with amazing properties
3. Clean energy: Developing better ways to harness the power of atoms

Reflection

In your own words, explain why understanding atomic structure is important in our daily lives:

(Answers will vary, but should touch on some of the following points)

Understanding atomic structure is crucial because it explains the fundamental nature of everything around us. It helps us comprehend how materials behave, how chemical reactions occur, and how technologies work. This knowledge impacts various aspects of our lives, from the food we eat and the medicines we take to the gadgets we use and the environmental challenges we face. By understanding atoms, we can develop new technologies, create better materials, and find solutions to global problems. It gives us a deeper appreciation for the complexity of our world and empowers us to make informed decisions about scientific and technological advancements.

Atomic Structure

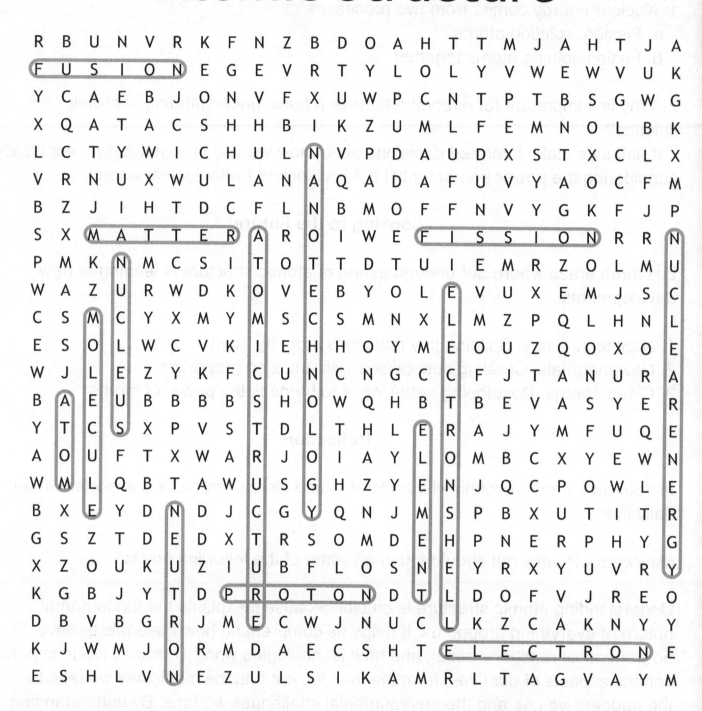

Nuclear energy   Atomic structure   Electron shell

Molecule   Matter   Nanotechnology

Fusion   Fission   Element

Electron   Neutron   Proton

Nucleus   Atom

Atomic Structure

Across
2. A positively charged particle found in the nucleus of an atom.
7. A group of atoms bonded together, forming the smallest unit of a compound.
8. Anything that takes up space and has mass, made up of atoms.
9. A negatively charged particle that moves around the nucleus of an atom.
10. The process of splitting atoms to release energy.
13. Power generated by changing the structure of atoms. _____ energy
14. The center part of an atom that contains most of its mass.

Down
1. The arrangement of parts within an atom. Atomic _____
3. The science of building extremely small machines at the atomic level.
4. A substance made up of atoms with the same number of protons.
5. The smallest unit of matter that makes up everything in the universe.
6. A particle with no electrical charge located in the nucleus of an atom.
11. An area around the nucleus where electrons move. Electron ___
12. The process of joining atoms together to create energy.

Introduction

1. elements

2. periodic table

What is the Periodic Table?

3. properties

4. a. name

   b. symbol

   c. atomic number

5. group

6. noble gases

Why is the Periodic Table Important?

7. It helps us understand the world

8. It predicts how elements behave

9. It organizes a lot of information

10. It guides scientific discoveries

How Does the Periodic Table Affect Your Life?

11. C. Contains elements needed for computer chips and batteries

12. D. Provides information on elements the body needs to function

13. A. Helps understand soil chemistry and create better fertilizers

14. B. Helps tackle pollution and develop cleaner energy

15. E. Includes elements used in everyday items like soda cans and toothpaste

Fun Facts About the Periodic Table

16. hydrogen, uranium

17. gold, silver

18. oganesson

19. helium

20. francium

Conclusion

21. world

22. chemical reactions, materials

The Periodic Table

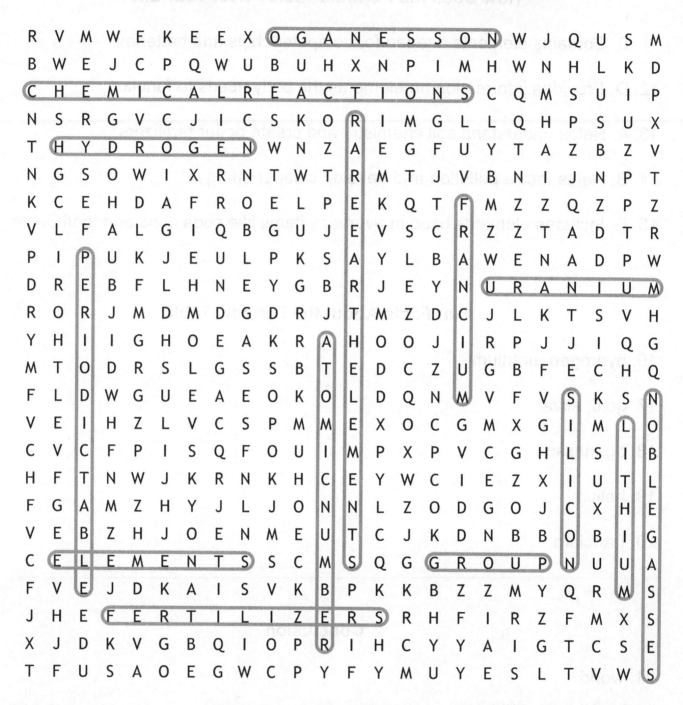

Noble gasses

Atomic number

Uranium

Lithium

Periodic table

Rare earth elements

Francium

Hydrogen

Silicon

Elements

Chemical reactions

Oganesson

Fertilizers

Group

The Periodic Table

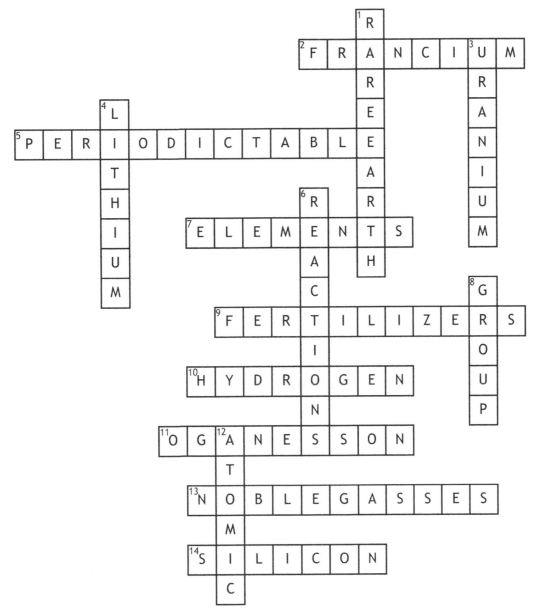

Across

2. An extremely rare and unstable element that exists in very small quantities on Earth.

5. A chart that organizes all known elements based on their properties. (Two words)

7. The basic building blocks of all matter in the universe.

9. Substances containing elements that help plants grow, used to improve soil quality.

10. The lightest element, found at the top left of the periodic table.

11. The most recently discovered element, named after a Russian physicist.

13. Elements in the far-right column of the periodic table that don't react easily with other elements. (Two words)

14. An element commonly used in computer chips and other electronic devices.

Down

1. A group of elements often used in technology, like headphones. ___ ___ elements

3. The heaviest naturally occurring element on Earth.

4. A light metal element used in rechargeable batteries.

6. Processes where elements or compounds interact to form new substances. Chemical ____

8. A column in the periodic table containing elements with similar characteristics.

12. A unique number assigned to each element, representing the number of protons in its nucleus. ____ number

Introduction

1. Chemical bonds are like glue that keeps molecules stuck together.

What Are Chemical Bonds?

2. The LEGO brick analogy:
   - Each brick represents an atom
   - The way bricks snap together represents chemical bonds

3. Chemical bonds form when atoms share or transfer electrons.

Types of Chemical Bonds

4. Fill in the table:

Bond Type	Description	Example
Covalent	Atoms share electrons to form strong bonds	Water (H_2O)
Ionic	One atom gives up an electron, another catches it, creating oppositely charged ions that attract	Table salt (NaCl)
Hydrogen	Weaker bonds, like a high-five between molecules	Important in water and DNA

Why Chemical Bonds Matter

5. List three areas where chemical bonds are important in our daily lives:
   a. The air we breathe   b. The water we drink
   c. The food we eat

   (Note: Any three from the list in the article are acceptable)

6. Explain how chemical bonds are important in each of the following:
   - Air: Oxygen molecules (O_2) are held together by covalent bonds, allowing oxygen to exist as a gas in our atmosphere.
   - Water: Hydrogen bonds between water molecules give water unique properties that make life possible, such as allowing ice to float and water to climb up plant stems.
   - Food: Bonds in sugar molecules give us energy when they break during digestion.

   - Our bodies: Chemical bonds determine the shape of proteins, which affects how they function in our bodies.
   - Clothes: Long chains of molecules held together by chemical bonds give clothes their strength and stretchiness.
   - Technology: Silicon chips in phones and computers rely on specific arrangements of chemical bonds to work properly.

Chemical Bonds in Action: A Day in Your Life
7. Match the daily activity with the role of chemical bonds:

a. Waking up and stretching	c Proteins in muscles allow movement
b. Eating cereal with milk	d Bonds in milk proteins and fats affect taste
c. Science class experiment	e New bonds form, creating carbon dioxide
d. Playing sports	a Bonds in rubber provide traction
e. Messaging friends	b Screen lights up due to special materials

The Future of Chemical Bonds
8. List two areas where scientists are working to use chemical bonds in new ways:
   a. New materials that are stronger and lighter than ever before
   b. Better ways to store energy, like improved batteries

   (Note: Developing new medicines is also an acceptable answer)

9. How might understanding chemical bonds help solve big problems? Give an example.
   Example answer: Understanding chemical bonds could help solve climate change by developing new materials for more efficient solar panels or better ways to capture and store carbon dioxide.

Reflection
10. In your own words, explain why chemical bonds are important in our everyday lives.
   Example answer: Chemical bonds are crucial in our everyday lives because they form the basis of everything around us. From the air we breathe and the water we drink to the food we eat and the technology we use, chemical bonds make it all possible. They determine the properties of materials and allow for chemical reactions that are essential for life and our modern world.

Chemical Bonds

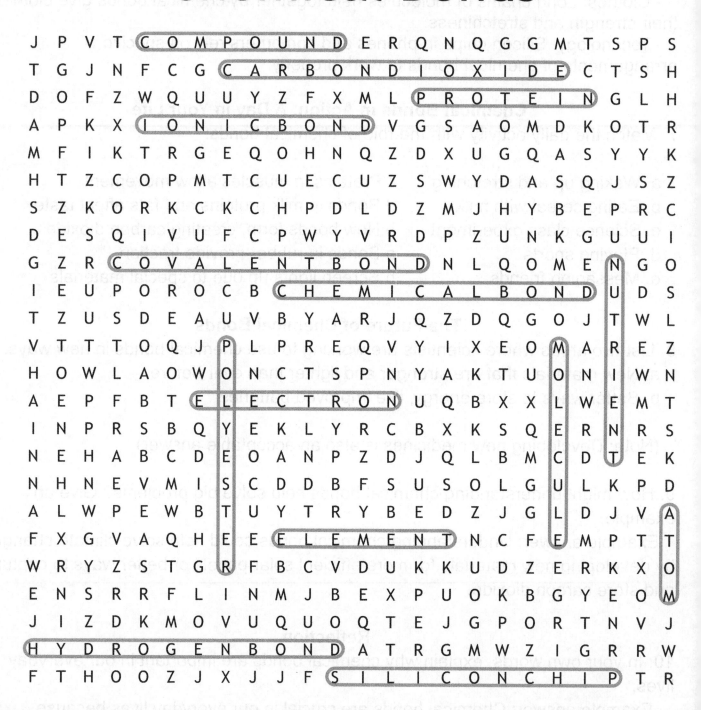

Silicon chip

Covalent bond

Polyester

Element

Atom

Hydrogen bond

Nutrient

Protein

Electron

Chemical bond

Ionic bond

Carbon dioxide

Compound

Molecule

Chemical Bonds

Across

3. A type of fabric made from long chains of molecules held together by chemical bonds.

5. A chemical bond formed when one atom gives up an electron to another, creating oppositely charged ions that attract each other. _____ bond

6. A type of chemical bond where atoms share electrons. _____ bond

8. A weak type of chemical bond, often found between water molecules. _____ bond

10. A substance made up of two or more different elements chemically bonded together.

12. The smallest unit of matter that keeps the properties of an element.

13. A large molecule made up of chains of amino acids, held together by chemical bonds.

14. A group of atoms held together by chemical bonds.

Down

1. A force that holds atoms together in molecules or compounds. (Two words)

2. A tiny, negatively charged particle that orbits the center of an atom.

4. A gas created when new bonds form during certain chemical reactions, like mixing baking soda and vinegar. (Two words)

7. A small piece of silicon used in electronics, relying on specific arrangements of chemical bonds to work. Silicon ___

9. A substance in food that provides energy or helps build and repair body tissues, often determined by chemical bonds.

11. A weak type of chemical bond, often found between water molecules.

Chapter 7 Answer Key

What Are Chemical Reactions?
Definition: A chemical reaction is a process where one or more substances change into different substances.

- Original substances are called: reactants
- New substances formed are called: products

Analogy: Chemical reactions are like building with LEGO bricks. You start with connected bricks (reactants), then rearrange them (products).

Signs of a Chemical Reaction
List five signs that indicate a chemical reaction is occurring:
1. Color changes
2. Temperature changes (it gets hot or cold)
3. Bubbles forming (gas being released)
4. Light being produced
5. A new solid forming (called a precipitate)

Example: When you mix baking soda and vinegar, you see bubbles form, which is a sign of a gas being released.

Importance of Chemical Reactions
Complete the table with examples of why chemical reactions are important:

Area	Importance
Human Body	Digestion, breathing, thinking; breaking down food into energy
Plants	Photosynthesis: turning sunlight, water, and CO_2 into food and oxygen
Manufacturing	Creating new materials like plastics
Household Activities	Cleaning (soap breaking down dirt), cooking (changing food structure)
Energy Production	Powering cars with gasoline, batteries in devices

Chemical Reactions in Everyday Life

Match the following everyday phenomena with the type of chemical reaction:

1. B Rusting
3. E Fireworks
5. D Batteries

2. C Baking a cake
4. A Glowsticks

A. Produces light through chemical reaction
B. Oxidation reaction
C. Multiple reactions creating texture and color
D. Chemical reactions between different materials produce power
E. Reactions producing colors and sounds in the air

Why Study Chemical Reactions?

List four reasons why studying chemical reactions is important:

1. Career opportunities (chef, doctor, environmental scientist, materials engineer)
2. Solving global challenges (cleaner energy, new medicines, environmental solutions)
3. Making informed everyday decisions (products, food, environmental impact)
4. Appreciating the complexity and wonder of the world

Reflection

(Answers will vary. Examples provided below.)

1. Name one chemical reaction you've observed today:
   Possible answers: Cooking breakfast, rust on a bicycle, leaves changing color

2. How might understanding chemical reactions help you in your future career or daily life?
   Possible answer: Understanding chemical reactions could help me choose safer cleaning products for my home, or it might be useful if I decide to pursue a career in medicine or environmental science.

Chemical Reactions

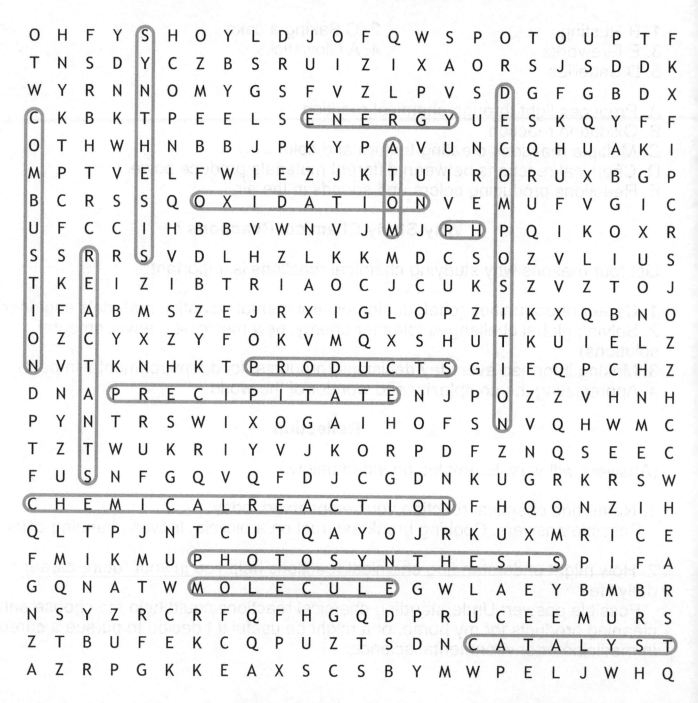

pH

Combustion

Atom

Oxidation

Reactants

Decomposition

Catalyst

Molecule

Precipitate

Chemical reaction

Synthesis

Energy

Photosynthesis

Products

Chemical Reactions

Across

2. A type of chemical reaction where a substance combines with oxygen, often resulting in rust formation on metals.

7. A process where one or more substances change into different substances. (Two words)

9. A chemical reaction used by plants to convert sunlight, water, and carbon dioxide into food and oxygen.

11. A substance that speeds up a chemical reaction without being consumed in the process.

12. The basic unit of matter, consisting of a dense nucleus surrounded by electrons.

13. A chemical reaction where a complex substance breaks down into simpler substances.

14. A chemical reaction where a substance combines with oxygen, often producing heat and light.

Down

1. A group of atoms bonded together, representing the smallest unit of a chemical compound.

3. The new substances formed as a result of a chemical reaction.

4. A new solid that forms and separates from a solution during a chemical reaction.

5. The original substances that undergo a change in a chemical reaction.

6. The capacity to do work or cause change, often released or absorbed during chemical reactions

8. A scale used to measure how acidic or basic a substance is, which can affect chemical reactions.

10. A type of chemical reaction where two or more simple substances combine to form a more complex substance.

Introduction

Solutions, acids, and bases are important chemical concepts that are present in our everyday lives. They help explain phenomena like:
- Why soda fizzes
- How soap cleans your hands

What Are Solutions?

Definition: A solution is a mixture where one substance (called the solute) is dissolved in another substance (called the solvent).

Common examples of solutions:
1. Sugar dissolved in water
2. The air we breathe (a solution of gases)
3. The ocean (a solution of salt and other minerals in water)
4. Blood (a complex solution carrying nutrients in our body)

Understanding solutions helps us:
- Make better drinks
- Create medicines
- Clean our homes more effectively

Acids

Definition: An acid is a substance that can give away hydrogen ions (H+) when dissolved in water.

Characteristics of acids:
- Taste: Sour
- Feel: Slippery

Everyday acids:
1. Citric acid in lemons and oranges
2. Acetic acid in vinegar
3. Carbonic acid in sodas

Important roles of acids:
- In digestion (stomach uses hydrochloric acid)
- Preserving foods
- In batteries that power our devices

Bases
Definition: Bases accept hydrogen ions (H+) or give away hydroxide ions (OH-) in water.

Characteristics of bases:
- Feel: Slippery
- Taste: Bitter (Note: Never taste chemicals in a lab!)

Common bases:
1. Sodium bicarbonate (baking soda)
2. Ammonia
3. Sodium hydroxide (used to make soap)

Important uses of bases:
- In cleaning products (they break down oils and grease)
- In antacids to neutralize stomach acid

Why This Matters to You
Understanding solutions, acids, and bases can help you in many ways:

1. Better cooking and baking:
   - Helps with mixing ingredients properly
   - Understanding acids and bases improves baking (e.g., baking soda reaction)

2. Safer cleaning:
   - Many cleaning products are basic
   - Never mix bleach (a base) with vinegar (an acid) – it creates dangerous fumes!

3. Health and medicine:
   - Understanding pH can help you make healthier choices
   - Example: Acid reflux and antacids

4. Environmental awareness:
   - Understanding acid rain and its effects on plants and animals

5. Future careers:
   - Chemistry is crucial in fields like medicine, environmental science, and food technology

6. Everyday problem-solving:
   - Example: Unclogging a drain using a mixture of baking soda (a base) and vinegar (an acid)

Solutions, Acids & Bases

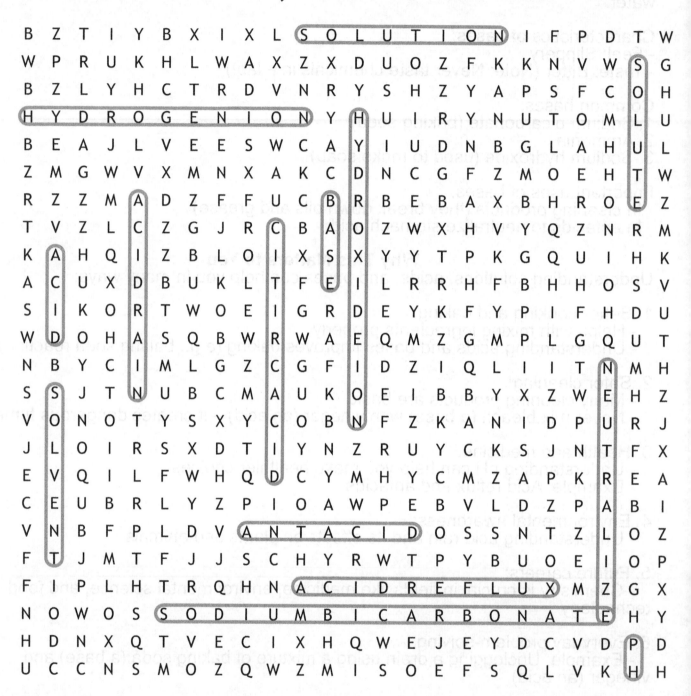

Citirc acid

Sodium bicarbonate

Antacid

Base

Solute

Hydroxide ion

Acid rain

Neutralize

Acid

Solution

Hydrogen ion

Acid reflux

pH

Solvent

Solutions, Acids & Bases

Across

2. A negatively charged particle (OH-) that bases release in water. _____ ion

3. Rainfall made acidic by pollution, which can harm plants and animals. (Two words)

9. A common acid found in citrus fruits like lemons and oranges. _____ acid

10. A positively charged particle (H+) that acids release in water. _____ ion

11. The substance that dissolves the solute in a solution.

12. A substance that accepts hydrogen ions (H+) or gives away hydroxide ions (OH-) in water, making it taste bitter.

13. A medicine that helps neutralize stomach acid to relieve heartburn.

14. To make an acid and base cancel each other out, resulting in a neutral solution.

Down

1. Another name for baking soda, a common base used in cooking and cleaning. (Two words)

4. A condition where stomach acid backs up into the esophagus, causing discomfort. (Two words)

5. A mixture where one substance (the solute) is dissolved in another substance (the solvent).

6. A substance that can give away hydrogen ions (H+) when dissolved in water, making it taste sour.

7. A measure of how acidic or basic a solution is.

8. The substance that is dissolved in a solution.

What is Organic Chemistry?

1. Organic chemistry is the study of compounds that contain __carbon__.

2. Why is carbon important in organic chemistry?
   - Carbon is the building block of life.
   - Almost everything in living things is made up of carbon-based compounds.

3. List two examples of things that contain organic compounds:
   a. _Plastic_
   b. _Gasoline_
   (Note: Medicines, living organisms, and many everyday materials are also correct answers)

Why is Carbon Special?

4. Carbon can form strong bonds with which elements? (List 3)
   - _Hydrogen_
   - _Oxygen_
   - _Nitrogen_

5. How is carbon similar to LEGO bricks?
   Just as you can build countless structures with LEGO, nature uses carbon to build an amazing array of molecules that make up living things and many useful materials.

Daily Organic Chemistry

6. Match the following areas of daily life with an example of organic chemistry:

Area of Life	Example of Organic Chemistry
Food	Carbohydrates, proteins, and fats
Clothes	Polyester, nylon, cotton, wool
Medicine	Aspirin, antibiotics
Fuels	Gasoline, natural gas
Plastics	Polymers used in packaging, phone cases
Cosmetics	Compounds in shampoos, lotions, makeup

Why Should You Care About Organic Chemistry?

7. List three reasons why organic chemistry matters (any three of the following):
   a. _Helps understand health and nutrition_
   b. _Increases environmental awareness_
   c. _Aids in making informed consumer choices_
   d. _Provides foundation for various career paths_
   e. _Improves problem-solving skills_

8. How can understanding organic chemistry help you make consumer choices?
   Understanding organic chemistry can help you choose cleaning products, decide what fabrics to wear, and make more informed decisions about the products you buy.

9. Name two career fields where organic chemistry is crucial:
   - _Medicine_
   - _Pharmaceuticals_
   (Note: Materials science and environmental science are also correct answers)

The Future of Organic Chemistry

10. List two areas where organic chemistry is being used for future developments:
    - _Developing new materials_
    - _Creating more efficient renewable energy sources_
    (Note: Designing better medicines is also a correct answer)

Reflection

11. What's one thing you learned about organic chemistry that surprised you?
    Answers will vary. Students might mention the prevalence of organic chemistry in daily life, the versatility of carbon, or specific applications of organic chemistry.

12. How do you think understanding organic chemistry could be useful in your daily life?
    Answers will vary. Students might discuss making informed choices about food, understanding how medicines work, or being more aware of environmental issues related to organic compounds.

Organic Chemistry

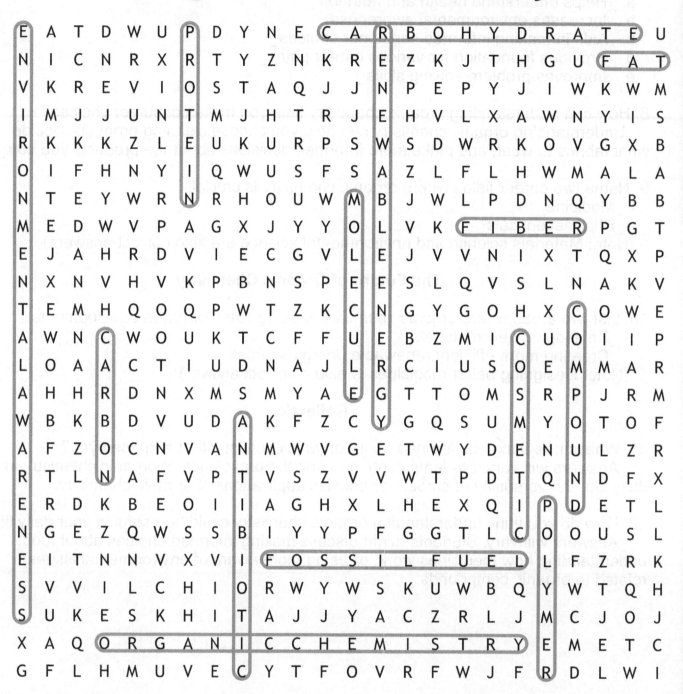

Renewable energy

Cosmetic

Fat

Polymer

Carbon

Environmental awareness

Fiber

Protein

Molecule

Organic chemistry

Fossil fuel

Antibiotic

Carbohydrate

Compound

Organic Chemistry

Across

4. A type of organic compound essential for building and repairing body tissues.

6. A medicine made from organic compounds that fights bacterial infections.

7. A group of atoms bonded together, forming the smallest unit of a chemical compound.

8. The study of compounds that contain carbon. (Two words)

10. A substance made up of two or more different elements joined together.

12. A fuel, like gasoline or natural gas, made from the remains of ancient plants and animals. _____ fuel

13. An organic compound used by the body for energy storage and insulation.

14. A chemical element that is the main building block of life and can form many different compounds.

Down

1. A product used to enhance appearance, often containing various organic compounds.

2. An organic compound found in foods that provides energy, like sugar and starch.

3. Understanding how human actions affect the natural world, including issues related to organic compounds. _____ awareness

5. A thread-like structure in fabrics, which can be made from natural or synthetic organic materials.

9. Energy from sources that are naturally replenished, which organic chemistry can help develop more efficiently. _____ energy

11. A large molecule made up of many repeated smaller units, often used to make plastics.

Chapter 10 Answer Key
GUIDED NOTES

Introduction

1. Nuclear chemistry explores changes in the nucleus of atoms.

2. The nucleus of an atom is incredibly small, but contains a lot of energy.

Basics of Atoms and Elements

3. List the four basic concepts mentioned in the article:

    a. Atoms are the building blocks of everything around us.

    b. The center of an atom is the nucleus, which contains protons and neutrons.

    c. Different elements have different numbers of protons in their nuclei.

    d. Isotopes are atoms of the same element with different numbers of neutrons.

Types of Nuclear Reactions

4. The two main types of nuclear reactions are:

    a. Fission: When a big atom splits into smaller ones.

    b. Fusion: When small atoms join to make bigger ones.

5. Both types of reactions release a lot of energy.

Applications of Nuclear Chemistry

6. Match the application to its description:

    a. Energy Production   2 Uses fission to generate electricity

    b. Medical Treatments   3 Diagnoses and treats diseases like cancer

    c. Food Safety   4 Kills harmful bacteria in food

    d. Archaeology   1 Helps determine the age of ancient objects

    e. Space Exploration   5 Powers spacecraft for long-distance travel

    f. Environmental Studies   6 Tracks pollutants in air and water

Pros and Cons of Nuclear Chemistry

7. List two positive aspects of nuclear chemistry (any two of the following):
   a. Clean energy production (no greenhouse gases)
   b. Advanced medical treatments
   c. Scientific research tools

8. List two negative aspects of nuclear chemistry (any two of the following):
   a. Potential for dangerous weapons
   b. Risk of accidents at nuclear plants
   c. Challenges in disposing of radioactive waste

Interesting Facts

9. True or False: The Sun's energy comes from nuclear fission. False (It comes from nuclear fusion)

10. Why are bananas slightly radioactive? Because of the potassium they contain

11. Who discovered radioactivity and won two Nobel Prizes for their work? Marie Curie

Future of Nuclear Chemistry

12. Scientists are working on developing:
   a. Safer and more efficient nuclear reactors.
   b. Ways to use nuclear fusion for energy production.

13. In medicine, researchers are exploring new treatments using radioactive materials to:
   Target cancer cells more precisely with fewer side effects

Conclusion

14. In your own words, explain why understanding nuclear chemistry is important:
   (Answers will vary, but should touch on its applications in energy, medicine, environmental studies, or other areas mentioned in the article)

Nuclear Chemistry

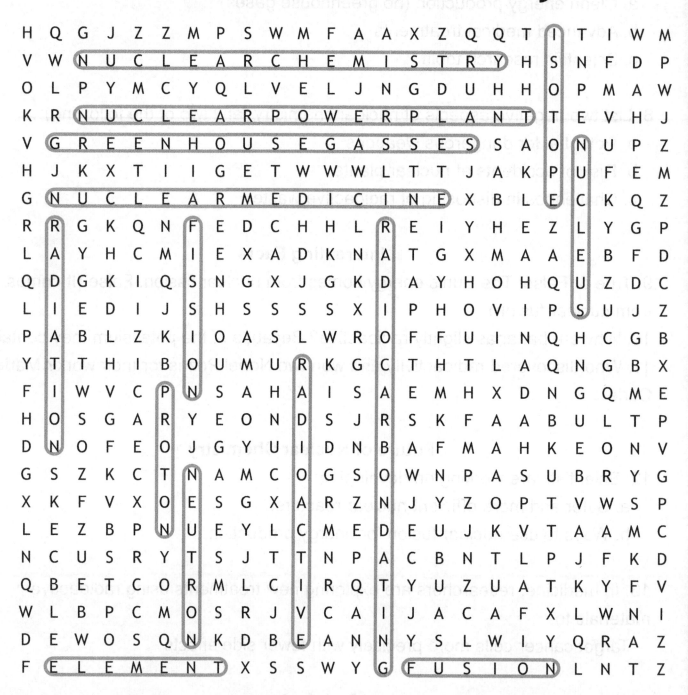

Greenhouse gasses

Nuclear power plant

Radioactive

Isotope

Nucleus

Radiocarbon dating

Element

Fusion

Neutron

Nuclear chemistry

Nuclear medicine

Radiation

Fission

Proton

Nuclear Chemistry

Across
2. A particle with no electric charge found in the nucleus of an atom.
5. A nuclear reaction where a large atom splits into smaller ones, releasing energy.
8. Describing materials that give off energy in the form of particles or waves.
9. A facility that uses nuclear reactions to generate electricity. Nuclear ____ ___
11. A substance made up of atoms with the same number of protons in their nuclei.

12. A nuclear reaction where small atoms join to form bigger ones, releasing energy.
13. Gasses that trap heat in Earth's atmosphere, contributing to climate change. ____ gasses
14. A method used to determine the age of ancient objects using radioactive carbon. ____ dating

Down
1. The use of radioactive materials to diagnose and treat diseases. Nuclear ___

3. The study of changes in the core of atoms and the energy they release. (Two words)
4. Energy released from atoms in the form of particles or waves.
6. The center of an atom, containing protons and neutrons.
7. Atoms of the same element with different numbers of neutrons.
10. A positively charged particle found in the nucleus of an atom.

What is Physics?

Physics is the study of matter, energy, and how they interact.

It helps us understand:
1. The basic rules that govern our universe
2. Why things happen the way they do in nature and technology

Why is Physics Important?

List 5 reasons why physics is important:
1. It explains how things work
2. It solves problems
3. It leads to new inventions
4. It prepares you for many careers
5. It helps you think critically

Key Physics Concepts

1. Gravity
Definition: The force that pulls everything towards the center of the Earth

Example in everyday life: It keeps us grounded when we jump

2. Energy
Definition: The ability to do work or cause change

Two forms of energy mentioned:
- Heat
- Light

3. Motion
Physics explains how things move and why.

Understanding motion helps us design:
1. Faster cars
2. More efficient airplanes
3. Predict the paths of comets

4. Electricity and Magnetism
These forces are behind many technologies we use daily.

Together, they form electromagnetism, which explains:
1. How light works
2. How we communicate wirelessly

5. Matter
Definition: Anything that takes up space and has mass

Physics explains:

- Why some materials are solid, liquid, or gas
- How they can change from one state to another

Physics in Your Everyday Life

Match the daily activity with the physics concept it demonstrates:

1. Alarm clock
2. Getting out of bed
3. Toasting bread
4. Writing with a pencil
5. Drinking through a straw

d. Electrical signals
e. Gravity and balanced forces
b. Chemical reaction and heat
a. Friction
c. Difference in air pressure

Benefits of Studying Physics

Complete the following statements:

1. You can understand how the world around you works.
2. It helps you develop problem-solving skills.
3. It prepares you for careers in science, technology, engineering, and math (STEM).
4. You can appreciate the beauty and complexity of nature.
5. It helps you make informed decisions about technology and environmental issues.

Reflection

In your own words, explain why physics is considered "more than formulas and equations":

Answers may vary, but should capture the idea that physics is a way of thinking that helps us understand and appreciate the world around us. It's not just about memorizing equations, but about developing a deeper understanding of how the universe works, from the tiniest particles to the largest galaxies. Physics encourages critical thinking, problem-solving, and a sense of wonder about the natural world.

Physics

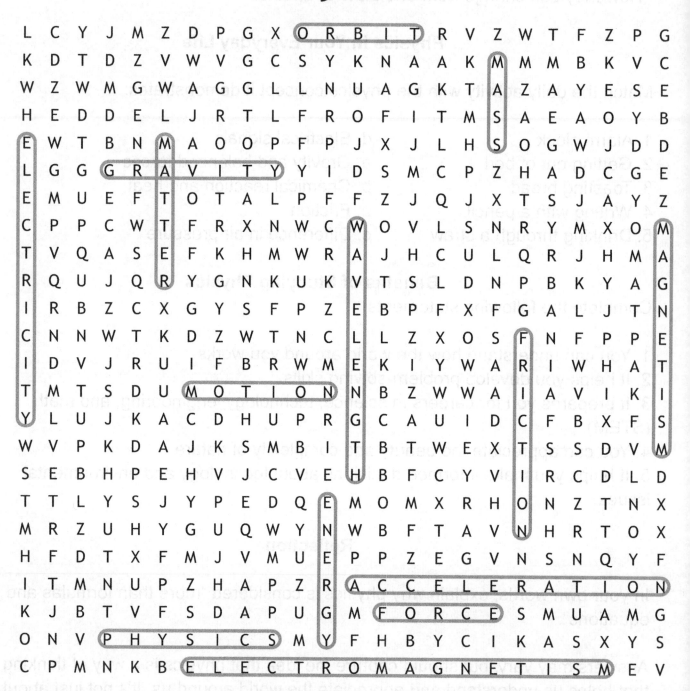

Orbit

Electromagnetism

Friction

Motion

Matter

Wavelength

Magnetism

Force

Gravity

Physics

Mass

Electricity

Acceleration

Energy

Physics

Across

4. A force that can attract or repel certain materials, like iron.

6. A push or pull that can change an object's motion or shape.

8. The ability to do work or cause change, existing in various forms like heat, light, and motion.

10. Anything that takes up space and has mass.

11. The path an object takes as it moves around another object in space, like planets around the Sun.

12. The act of an object changing its position over time.

13. The resistance that occurs when two surfaces rub against each other.

14. The study of matter, energy, and how they interact in the universe.

Down

1. The rate at which an object's speed or direction changes.

2. The amount of matter in an object.

3. The distance between two peaks of a wave, such as in light or sound.

5. The combination of electricity and magnetism, explaining how light works and enabling wireless communication.

7. A form of energy resulting from the flow of electric charge.

9. The force that pulls objects towards the center of the Earth and keeps planets in orbit.

Introduction

1. Motion is defined as: a change in position over time
2. A force is: a push or pull acting on an object

Newton's Laws

Fill in the blanks for Newton's three laws of motion:

1. Newton's First Law (Law of Inertia):
   Objects at rest stay at rest, and objects in motion stay in motion, unless acted on by an outside force.

2. Newton's Second Law:
   Force = mass × acceleration
   Write the equation: $F = ma$

3. Newton's Third Law:
   For every action, there's an equal and opposite reaction.

Importance of Forces and Motion

List five areas where understanding forces and motion is important:
1. Sports
2. Transportation
3. Safety
4. Technology
5. Nature

Everyday Examples

Explain how forces and motion apply in these situations:

1. Riding a Bike:
   - Force created by pedaling: Moves the bike forward
   - Role of friction: Helps you turn and stop
   - Effect of air resistance: Makes it harder to bike, especially into strong wind

2. Using a Seatbelt:
   Why do we move forward when a car stops suddenly? Due to inertia (Newton's First Law)
   How does a seatbelt prevent injury? It applies a force to keep you in your seat

3. Jumping on a Trampoline:
   Describe how this demonstrates Newton's Third Law: When you land, you exert a force on the trampoline, and it exerts an equal force back, pushing you up

Future Applications

Name three future technologies that rely on understanding forces and motion:
1. Magnetic levitation trains
2. Wind turbines for renewable energy
3. Space exploration technologies

Reflection

In your own words, explain why understanding forces and motion is important in everyday life:
(Sample answer) Understanding forces and motion is crucial in everyday life because it helps us make sense of the world around us. It explains why objects move the way they do, from simple actions like walking to complex systems like vehicles and machinery. This knowledge enhances our safety, improves technology, and even helps us appreciate sports and nature more deeply. By grasping these concepts, we can better interact with our environment and contribute to future technological advancements.

Forces & Motion

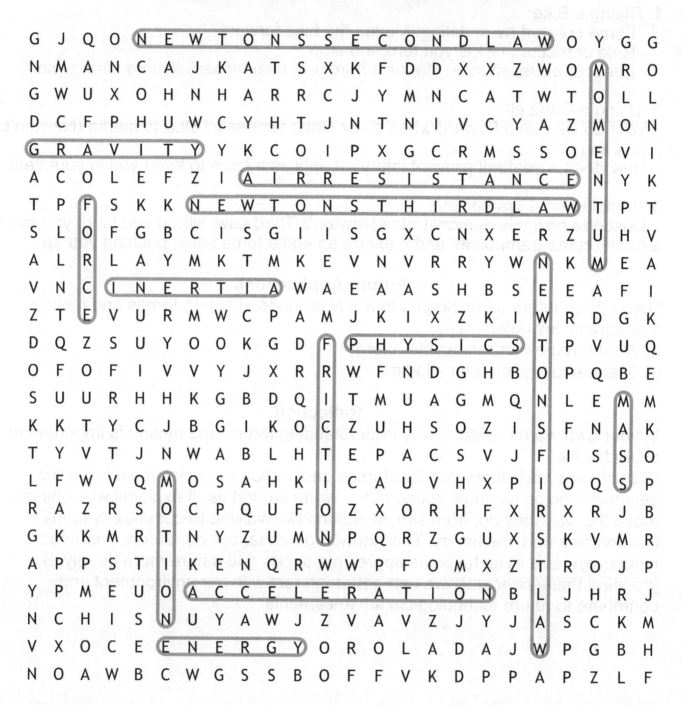

Air resistance

Newton's First Law

Momentum

Inertia

Gravity

Newton's Third Law

Physics

Acceleration

Force

Motion

Newton's Second Law

Energy

Mass

Friction

Forces & Motion

Across

2. The force that pulls objects towards the center of the Earth.

3. The product of an object's mass and velocity.

5. The principle that for every action, there's an equal and opposite reaction. Newton's ____ ____

7. The rate at which an object's speed or direction changes.

10. The principle that force equals mass times acceleration (F = ma). Newton's

11. The force of air pushing against a moving object, also known as drag. Air ____

13. The tendency of an object to resist changes in its motion.

14. The scientific study of matter, energy, and their interactions.

Down

1. The principle that objects at rest stay at rest, and objects in motion stay in motion, unless acted on by an outside force. Newton's ____ ____

4. The force that resists motion between two surfaces in contact.

6. A change in position over time.

8. The amount of matter in an object.

9. A push or pull acting on an object.

12. The capacity to do work or cause change.

Introduction

1. What three concepts does this lesson focus on?
   a. Work
   b. Power
   c. Machines

2. How do these concepts relate to our daily lives? (List two examples)
   - Possible answers: Smartphone charging, car engines, elevators, bicycles, can openers

What is Work?

3. In scientific terms, work occurs when:
   A force moves an object

4. Write the formula for work:
   Work = Force × Distance

5. According to this formula, how can you increase the amount of work done?
   - Increase the force applied
   - Increase the distance the object is moved

Understanding Power

6. How is power different from work?
   Power measures how quickly work is done

7. Write the formula for power:
   Power = Work ÷ Time

8. Why do we measure car engines in horsepower?
   It indicates how quickly the engine can perform work (accelerate the car)

Machines: Making Work Easier

9. List three ways machines help us do work:
   a. Increase the force we apply
   b. Change the direction of a force
   c. Increase the distance or speed of a motion

10. Name the six types of simple machines:
   1. Lever   4. Inclined plane
   2. Wheel and axle   5. Wedge
   3. Pulley   6. Screw

Real-Life Examples

11. Match the device with the concept it best demonstrates:
   a. Smartphone   C Uses pulleys and counterweights
   b. Car engine   B Converts chemical energy to mechanical energy
   c. Elevator   A Converts electrical energy to chemical energy
   d. Bicycle   D Uses wheels, axles, and gears
   e. Can opener   E Uses principles of lever and wedge

Why This Matters to You

12. List three ways understanding work, power, and machines can benefit you:
   1. Better problem-solving skills
   2. Increased energy awareness
   3. Preparation for future careers
   (Other acceptable answers: understanding sports/fitness, applying knowledge to everyday life)

The Big Picture

13. In your own words, explain why learning about work, power, and machines is important:
   Answer will vary. Should mention how these concepts help understand everyday devices, improve problem-solving, or relate to various aspects of life and potential careers.

14. Describe one way you might look at the world differently after learning these concepts:
   Answer will vary. Could mention seeing simple machines in everyday objects, understanding energy efficiency, or appreciating engineering in common devices.

Work, Power, & Machines

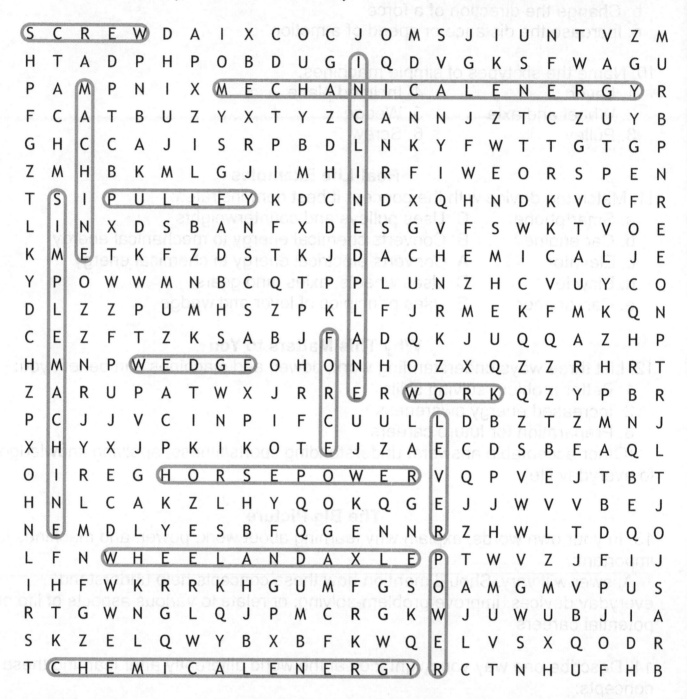

```
S C R E W D A I X C O C J O M S J I U N T V Z M
H T A D P H P O B D U G I Q D V G K S F W A G U
P A M P N I X M E C H A N I C A L E N E R G Y R
F C A T B U Z Y X T Y Z C A N N J Z T C Z U Y B
G H C C A J I S R P B D L N K Y F W T T G T G P
Z M H B K M L G J I M H I R F I W E O R S P E N
T S I P U L L E Y K D C N D X Q H N D K V C F R
L I N X D S B A N F X D E S G V F S W K T V O E
K M E T K F Z D S T K J D A C H E M I C A L J E
Y P O W W M N B C Q T P P L U N Z H C V U Y C O
D L Z Z P U M H S Z P K L F J R M E K F M K Q N
C E Z F T Z K S A B J F A D Q K J U Q Q A Z H P
H M N P W E D G E O H O N H O Z X Q Z Z R H R T
Z A R U P A T W X J R R E R W O R K Q Z Y P B R
P C J J V C I N P I F C U U L D B Z T Z M N J
X H Y X J P K I K O T E J Z A E C D S B E A Q L
O I R E G H O R S E P O W E R V Q P V E J T B T
H N L C A K Z L H Y Q O K Q G E J J W V B E J
N E M D L Y E S B F Q G E N N R Z H W L T D Q O
L F N W H E E L A N D A X L E P T W V Z J F I J
I H F W K R R K H G U M F G S O A M G M V P U S
R T G W Z N G L Q J P M C R G K W J U W U B J I A
S K Z E L Q W Y B X B F K W Q E L V S X Q O D R
T C H E M I C A L E N E R G Y R C T N H U F H B
```

Chemical energy — Mechanical energy — Wheel and axle

Simple machine — Horsepower — Screw

Wedge — Inclined plane — Pulley

Lever — Machine — Force

Power — Work

Work, Power, & Machines

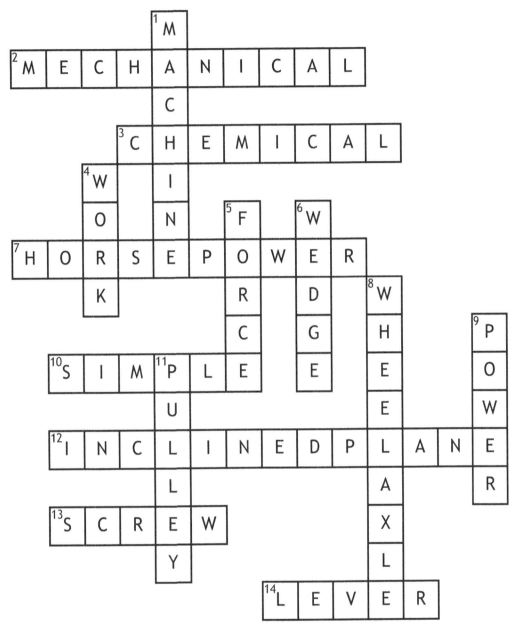

Across

2. Energy associated with the motion or position of an object. ____ energy

3. Energy stored in the bonds between atoms in a substance. ____ energy

7. A unit of power, often used to measure the output of engines.

10. A basic mechanical device that changes the direction or magnitude of a force. ____ machine

12. A flat surface set at an angle to reduce the force needed to move an object upwards. (Two words)

13. An inclined plane wrapped around a central cylinder, used to lift objects or hold things together.

14. A simple machine consisting of a rigid object used with a fulcrum to lift or move heavy loads.

Down

1. A device that makes work easier by changing the size or direction of a force.

4. The transfer of energy that occurs when a force moves an object over a distance.

5. A push or pull acting on an object.

6. A triangular-shaped tool used to separate objects or hold them in place.

8. A simple machine made of a wheel attached to a central rod, used to reduce friction in motion. ____ and ____

9. The rate at which work is done, measuring how quickly energy is transferred.

11. A wheel with a grooved rim around which a cord passes, used to change the direction of a force.

What is Energy?

Energy is defined as the ability to do work or cause change.

Types of Energy

There are two main categories of energy:

1. Potential Energy: This is stored energy.
   Examples:
   - A book on a high shelf (gravitational potential energy)
   - A stretched rubber band (elastic potential energy)
   - Food in your fridge (chemical potential energy)

2. Kinetic Energy: This is energy in motion.
   Examples:
   - A car driving down the road
   - A ball rolling down a hill
   - Heat from a fire

Energy in Our Daily Lives

List four areas where we encounter energy in everyday life:

1. At Home: Energy powers lights, heats homes, and runs appliances
2. Transportation: Cars, buses, and planes use energy to move
3. Food: The energy in food keeps us alive and active
4. Nature: The sun provides light, heat, and drives weather patterns

Why is Energy Important?

Complete the following reasons:

1. It keeps us alive
2. It powers our modern world
3. It drives economic growth
4. It affects our environment

The Energy Challenge

As our population grows, we need more energy. However, many current energy sources are:

- Non-renewable (meaning they'll eventually run out)
- Cause pollution and contribute to climate change

Renewable Energy Sources

List four clean, renewable energy sources:

1. Solar power: Using the sun's energy to generate electricity
2. Wind power: Using wind to turn turbines and generate electricity
3. Hydropower: Using flowing water to generate electricity
4. Geothermal energy: Using heat from inside the Earth

What Can You Do?

List four ways you can make a difference in energy use:

1. Be energy efficient (e.g., turn off lights and devices when not in use)
2. Walk, bike, or use public transportation when possible
3. Reduce, reuse, recycle to save energy used in making new products
4. Learn more about energy and its impacts

Reflection

In your own words, explain why understanding energy is important for our future:
Answers will vary, but should touch on points such as:
Understanding energy is crucial for our future because it affects every aspect of our lives, from powering our homes and technologies to driving our economy.
As we face challenges like climate change and the depletion of non-renewable resources, comprehending energy concepts will help us make informed decisions about energy use and development. It will also enable us to innovate and create sustainable solutions for our growing energy needs, ensuring a balance between technological progress and environmental protection.

Energy

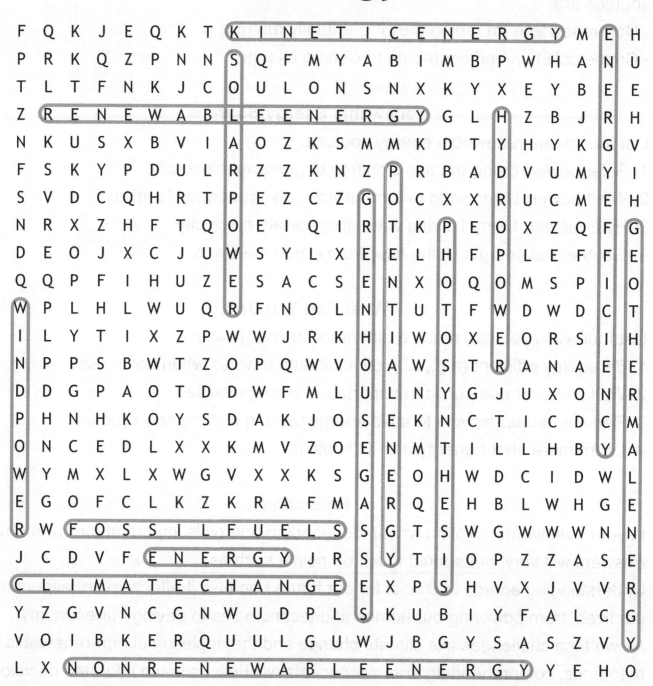

Energy efficiency

Wind power

Renewable energy

Photosynthesis

Fossil fuels

Greenhouse gasses

Solar power

Kinetic energy

Climate change

Energy

Geothermal energy

Non-renewable energy

Potential energy

Hydropower

Energy

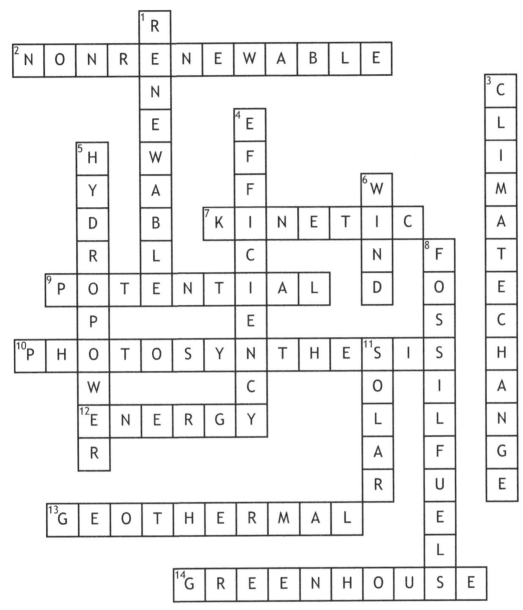

Across

2. Energy sources that will eventually run out, such as coal or oil. _____ energy

7. Energy of motion; energy that an object has due to its movement. _____ energy

9. Stored energy that has the potential to do work. _____ energy

10. The process by which plants use sunlight to make food and grow.

12. The ability to do work or cause change.

13. Heat energy from within the Earth. _____ energy

14. Gasses in the atmosphere that trap heat and contribute to climate change. ___ gasses

Down

1. Energy sources that can be naturally replenished, like solar or wind power. _____ energy

3. Long-term changes in global or regional climate patterns. (Two words)

4. Using less energy to perform the same task or produce the same result. Energy

5. Energy generated by the movement of water, often using dams.

6. Energy generated by the movement of air, typically using wind turbines. _____ power

8. Non-renewable energy sources formed from the remains of ancient plants and animals, like coal and oil. (Two words)

11. Energy generated from the sun's rays. _____ power

What Are Mechanical Waves?

Definition: Mechanical waves are disturbances that travel through a medium, transferring energy without moving the medium itself.

Example from the text: Ripples spreading out when a pebble is tossed into a lake

Types of mechanical waves:

1. Transverse waves: Medium moves perpendicular to the wave direction
   Example: Waves on a string
2. Longitudinal waves: Medium moves parallel to the wave direction
   Example: Sound waves in air
3. Surface waves: Combination of the above two types
   Example: Ocean waves

Sound: The Wave We Can Hear

Sound waves are a type of longitudinal wave that travels through air (or other mediums).

How sound works:
1. Something vibrates, like a guitar string or your vocal cords
2. This pushes air molecules together and apart
3. These compressions and rarefactions travel as a wave
4. When the wave reaches your ear, it makes your eardrum vibrate
5. Your brain interprets these vibrations as sound

Why Mechanical Waves and Sound Matter

List five areas where mechanical waves and sound are important:
1. Communication
2. Technology
3. Music
4. Safety
5. Nature

Careers That Use Waves and Sound

Match the career with its description:
1. Audio engineer   D. Works on recording albums and mixing sound
2. Seismologist   A. Studies earthquakes
3. Audiologist   B. Helps people with hearing problems
4. Acoustic engineer   C. Designs speakers and noise-canceling systems

Interesting Facts

Fill in the blanks:
1. Sound can't travel in space because there's no air to carry the waves.
2. The speed of sound in air is about 343 meters per second or 768 mph.
3. Whales can communicate over hundreds of miles using low-frequency sound waves in water.
4. The loudest sound ever recorded was the eruption of Krakatoa volcano in 1883.
5. Dogs can hear higher-pitched sounds than humans.

Reflection

1. What's one new thing you learned about mechanical waves or sound from this lesson?

   Answers will vary. Example: I learned that there are different types of mechanical waves, such as transverse, longitudinal, and surface waves.

2. How might understanding mechanical waves and sound be useful in your daily life?

   Answers will vary. Example: Understanding mechanical waves and sound could help me appreciate how my headphones work or why I can feel bass at a concert. It might also help me understand why I hear thunder after seeing lightning.

Mechanical Waves & Sound

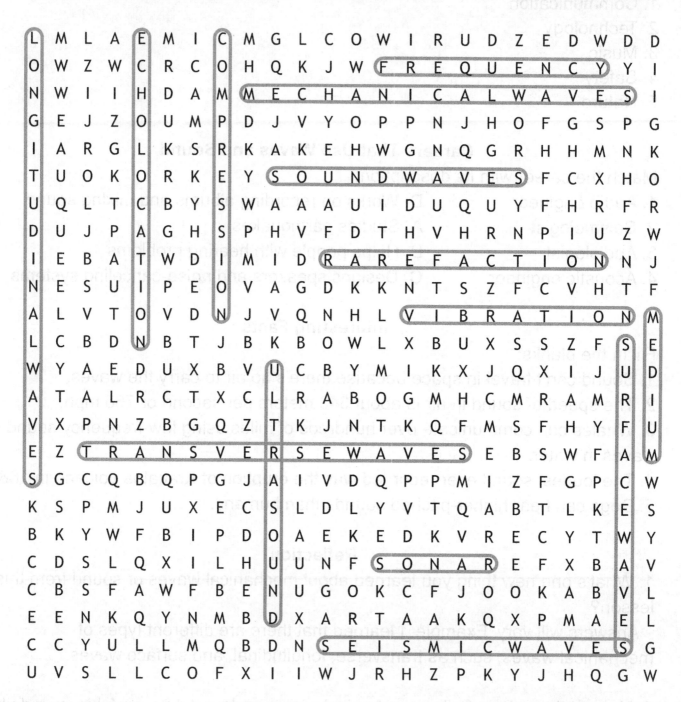

Seismic waves

Longitudinal waves

Frequency

Echolocation

Vibration

Sound waves

Transverse waves

Sonar

Rarefaction

Medium

Surface waves

Mechanical waves

Ultrasound

Compression

Mechanical Waves & Sound

Across
2. High-frequency sound waves used in medical imaging and other technologies.

8. A combination of transverse and longitudinal waves, such as ocean waves. _____ waves

9. The substance or material through which a wave travels, such as water, air, or solid objects.

11. A rapid back-and-forth movement that creates sound waves.

12. A system that uses sound waves to navigate and detect objects underwater.

13. The part of a longitudinal wave where particles are pushed closer together.

Down
1. Waves where the medium moves parallel to the direction of the wave, like sound waves in air. _____ waves

3. Waves where the medium moves perpendicular to the direction of the wave, like waves on a string. _____ waves

4. The number of wave cycles that pass a fixed point in a given time, which determines the pitch of a sound.

5. Disturbances that travel through a medium, transferring energy without moving the medium itself. _____ waves

6. The use of sound waves to locate objects, as used by bats and dolphins.

7. The part of a longitudinal wave where particles are spread farther apart.

10. Mechanical waves that travel through the Earth, often caused by earthquakes. _____ waves

14. Longitudinal waves that travel through air or other mediums and can be detected by our ears. _____ waves

Introduction

1. What are two examples of how we use the electromagnetic spectrum in everyday life?
   a) Sending text messages
   b) Seeing inside the body without surgery (medical imaging)

What is the Electromagnetic Spectrum?

2. The electromagnetic spectrum is all the different types of energy that travel through space as waves.

3. List the seven types of waves in the electromagnetic spectrum:
   a) Radio waves   b) Microwaves
   c) Infrared light   d) Visible light
   e) Ultraviolet light   f) X-rays
   g) Gamma rays

Visible Light

4. Visible light is the part of the spectrum that our eyes can detect.

5. List the colors of visible light in order from longest to shortest wavelength:
   Red, Orange, Yellow, Green, Blue, Indigo, Violet

6. What mnemonic device can help you remember these colors? ROY G. BIV

Importance of the Electromagnetic Spectrum

7. Match each type of wave with its application:
   a) Radio waves   D Carrying text messages
   b) Microwaves   A Heating food
   c) Infrared light   B TV remotes
   d) Ultraviolet light   E Tanning (and sunburns)
   e) X-rays   C X-ray imaging

8. How do gamma rays help scientists? They help scientists learn about distant stars and galaxies.

The Electromagnetic Spectrum in Action

9. Fill in the blanks:
   a) Wi-Fi uses radio waves to send data.
   b) Thermal cameras detect infrared light to see heat.
   c) Sunscreen protects your skin by blocking harmful ultraviolet light.
   d) Night vision goggles amplify infrared light.
   e) Airport security uses X-rays to scan luggage.

The Future of Light Technology

10. Name three potential future applications of the electromagnetic spectrum:
    a) 5G Networks
    b) Light-based computers
    c) Terahertz waves for medical imaging or ultra-fast wireless communication

Reflection

11. In your own words, explain why the electromagnetic spectrum is important in our daily lives:

   (Answers will vary, but should touch on some of the following points)

   The electromagnetic spectrum is crucial in our daily lives because it enables many of the technologies we rely on. It allows us to communicate wirelessly through radio and microwaves, see the world around us with visible light, cook food quickly with microwaves, and perform medical imaging with X-rays. It also helps us understand our universe through the study of different types of radiation from space. Without our understanding and use of the electromagnetic spectrum, many modern conveniences and scientific advancements would not be possible.

Electromagnetic Spectrum & Light

```
A  F  G  T  5  B  F  V  O  M  M  H  A  Y  M  H  H  V  L  E  B  5  W  C
E  N  H  H  W  G  Y  K  T  E  R  A  H  E  R  T  Z  W  A  V  E  S  H  Z
L  T  P  X  D  A  S  K  5  G  N  E  T  W  O  R  K  S  O  I  5  L  K  A
E  U  L  T  R  A  V  I  O  L  E  T  L  I  G  H  T  Y  S  S  G  B  R  R
C  W  N  N  A  N  I  K  H  I  N  R  R  U  X  S  C  P  G  I  H  M  A  U
T  B  Y  R  P  A  O  R  O  V  H  O  H  M  Y  W  X  R  U  B  R  U  D  F
R  H  E  X  X  D  P  C  X  K  5  Y  X  X  K  T  C  B  C  L  M  P  I  K
O  U  U  S  G  Z  H  P  X  5  X  G  M  F  5  T  E  X  W  E  X  E  O  O
M  P  O  L  G  D  S  W  R  Y  P  B  G  U  F  G  K  W  X  L  A  C  W  A
A  W  Z  T  F  G  M  N  A  Y  O  I  H  S  Y  R  V  A  D  I  V  R  A  Z
G  D  P  H  C  T  5  R  Y  T  A  V  E  T  C  G  L  V  G  G  C  Y  V  A
N  Y  5  B  U  F  Y  V  S  N  E  B  T  D  D  V  Z  E  I  H  A  F  E  N
E  O  Z  T  H  E  R  M  A  L  C  A  M  E  R  A  M  L  Y  T  N  K  S  I
T  F  M  O  U  W  F  G  E  B  E  N  T  P  X  S  M  E  N  K  W  X  T  L
I  X  Z  B  O  O  U  B  S  R  H  E  U  5  C  S  O  N  O  K  S  T  L  A
C  T  B  V  G  M  R  Z  5  E  N  D  H  E  V  K  Z  G  A  T  A  Y  A  Z
S  I  Z  Y  A  H  D  S  T  F  G  O  Z  P  S  W  X  T  Y  E  S  I  N  P
P  L  R  F  M  G  N  P  B  Z  M  E  N  A  P  Z  X  H  U  F  I  U  Z  D
E  Z  X  E  M  N  G  P  H  R  I  N  F  R  A  R  E  D  L  I  G  H  T  U
C  O  W  W  A  P  R  N  D  G  F  G  Y  X  W  U  W  D  D  V  U  R  D  P
T  5  I  H  R  S  U  L  W  I  F  I  R  T  G  D  F  L  Z  B  H  Y  V  X
R  F  G  P  A  U  K  V  U  F  P  Y  M  H  Y  B  S  T  5  5  E  E  N  H
U  U  Y  U  Y  D  E  G  F  D  M  N  P  H  M  I  C  R  O  W  A  V  E  S
M  Z  H  F  S  I  I  I  F  U  B  I  5  5  S  X  K  S  G  D  M  X  M  P
```

Terahertz waves	5G networks	Thermal camera
Ultraviolet light	Visible light	Infrared light
Radio waves	Electromagnetic spectrum	Wi-Fi
ROY G. BIV	Gamma rays	X-rays
Microwaves	Wavelength	

Electromagnetic Spectrum & Light

Across

4. The distance between two peaks of a wave in the electromagnetic spectrum.

7. Electromagnetic waves between microwaves and infrared, with potential uses in medicine and communication. ___ waves

10. The part of the electromagnetic spectrum that our eyes can see, including all the colors of the rainbow. ____ light

11. A type of electromagnetic radiation that we feel as heat, used in thermal imaging. ____ light

12. High-energy electromagnetic waves that can pass through soft tissue, used in medical imaging.

13. A technology that uses radio waves to connect devices to the internet wirelessly.

14. A memory aid for the colors of the visible light spectrum.

Down

1. The highest-energy waves in the electromagnetic spectrum, used to study space and in some medical treatments. (Two words)

2. The latest generation of cellular networks using high-frequency radio waves for faster data transmission. __ networks

3. A device that detects infrared radiation to create images of heat. ____ camera

5. The full range of all types of electromagnetic radiation, from radio waves to gamma rays. Electromagnetic ____

6. Long wavelength electromagnetic waves used for communication, like in cell phones and radios. ____ waves

8. Invisible electromagnetic waves from the sun that can cause sunburns and are blocked by sunscreen. ____ light

9. Electromagnetic waves that can heat food and are used in some communication devices.

Introduction

1. Imagine a morning where nothing in your house works.
2. Electricity is woven into our daily lives.

What is Electricity?

3. Electricity is a form of energy caused by the movement of tiny particles called electrons.
4. When electrons move from one atom to another, they create an electric current.
5. Analogy: Electricity is like water flowing through a pipe.
   - Electrons are like the water.
   - Wires are like the pipes.

How Do We Make Electricity?

6. List three methods power plants use to generate electricity:
   a) Burning fossil fuels (coal or natural gas)
   b) Using nuclear reactions
   c) Harnessing renewable sources (wind, solar, or hydroelectric power)

7. The complex network that delivers electricity is called the power grid.

Why is Electricity Important?

8. Match the following aspects of modern life with how electricity powers them:

   a) Lighting   F Illuminates streets and screens
   b) Communication   E Connects phones and internet
   c) Entertainment   G Powers video games and TV
   d) Health Care   B Powers medical devices
   e) Education   C Enables online learning
   f) Transportation   D Runs traffic lights
   g) Food Storage   A Keeps food fresh and safe

The Future of Electricity

9. Many countries are moving towards renewable energy sources like solar and wind power.

10. Electric cars are becoming more common to reduce pollution.

11. Scientists are working on new ways to store electricity, like advanced batteries.

Electricity Safety

12. List four important safety tips related to electricity:

    a) Never put metal objects in electrical outlets

    b) Keep electrical devices away from water

    c) Don't overload outlets with too many plugs

    d) Stay away from fallen power lines and call for help

Reflection

13. In your own words, explain why electricity is essential in our modern world:

    Answers will vary, but should touch on how electricity powers essential aspects of modern life such as communication, healthcare, education, transportation, and daily conveniences.

14. Describe two ways you use electricity in your daily life that you might take for granted:

    Answers will vary, but might include:

    a) Charging and using smartphones

    b) Using lights and appliances at home

    c) Watching TV or using computers

    d) Using air conditioning or heating

    e) Storing food in refrigerators

Electricity

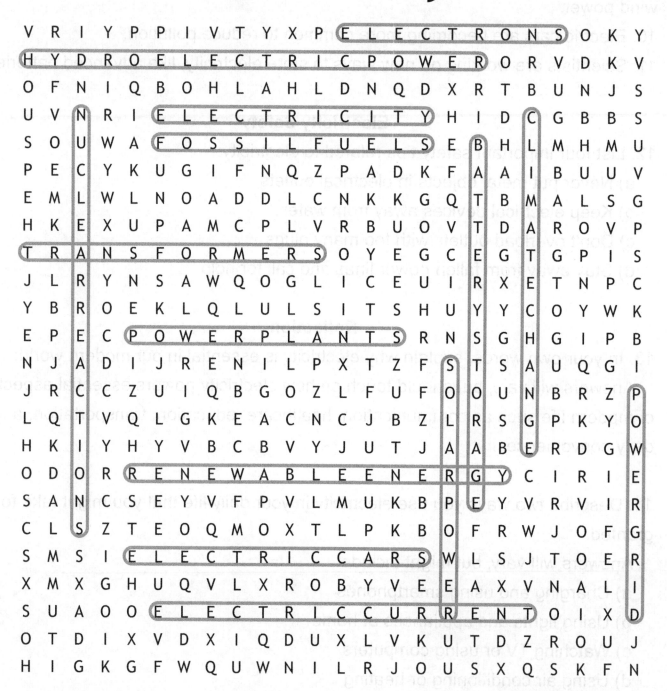

Battery storage
Power plants
Renewable energy
Electric cars
Electrons

Solar power
Climate change
Electric current
Fossil fuels
Electricity

Hydroelectric power
Nuclear reactions
Transformers
Power grid

Electricity

Across

3. Facilities where electricity is generated using various methods like burning fossil fuels or harnessing renewable sources. ___ plants

5. Vehicles that run on electricity stored in batteries instead of gasoline, helping to reduce pollution. (Two words)

9. A renewable energy source that converts sunlight into electricity using solar panels. ___ power

10. Sources of power that can be naturally replenished, such as wind, solar, or hydroelectric power. ___ energy

11. Devices in the power grid that change the voltage of electricity for safe transmission and use.

12. A process used in some power plants to generate electricity by splitting atoms. ___ reactions

13. Long-term changes in the Earth's weather patterns, often linked to human activities like burning fossil fuels. ___ change

14. Tiny particles that are part of atoms and create electric current when they move.

Down

1. Technology used to store electrical energy for later use, important for making renewable energy more reliable. ___ storage

2. Natural resources like coal and natural gas that are burned to generate electricity. (Two words)

4. The flow of electrons from one place to another, which creates electricity. Electric ___

6. A complex network of wires and transformers that delivers electricity to homes, schools, and businesses. (Two words)

7. A form of energy caused by the movement of electrons, used to power devices and machines.

8. A form of renewable energy that generates electricity using the force of flowing water. ___ power

Introduction
1. Magnetism is an invisible force that plays a huge role in our daily lives.

What is Magnetism?
2. Magnetism is created by the movement of electrons inside atoms.
3. A magnetic field is created when many atoms have their electrons lined up in the same direction.
4. Three common magnetic materials are:
   a. Iron
   b. Nickel
   c. Cobalt

The Earth as a Magnet
5. The Earth's core is mostly made of iron, creating a magnetic field around the planet.
6. This magnetic field protects us from harmful radiation from space.
7. A compass works because the needle aligns with the Earth's magnetic field.

Electromagnetism
8. Electromagnetism is the relationship between electricity and magnetism.
9. List three technologies that use electromagnetism:
   (Any three of the following)
   a. Electric motors
   b. Generators
   c. Speakers/headphones
   d. Computer hard drives
   e. MRI machines

Magnetism in Nature
10. Name two animals that use the Earth's magnetic field for navigation:
    (Any two of the following)
    a. Birds
    b. Sea turtles
    c. Some bacteria

The Future of Magnetism

11. Maglev trains use powerful magnets to float above the tracks.
12. Scientists are researching how to use magnetism for fusion energy and quantum computing.

Why Magnetism Matters

13. List three ways magnetism impacts your daily life:
   (Any three of the following)
   a. Powers devices like smartphones and video game consoles
   b. Helps in medical diagnostics (e.g., MRI machines)
   c. Generates electricity for homes and devices
   d. Potential for developing clean energy sources
   e. Enables navigation tools like compasses

Reflection

14. Answers will vary. Students should provide a personal response explaining what they found interesting and why.

15. Answers will vary. Possible examples could include:
   - Refrigerator magnets
   - Magnetic clasps on jewelry or bags
   - Magnetic strips on credit cards
   - Magnetic locks on doors
   - Magnetic name tags or badges

Magnetism

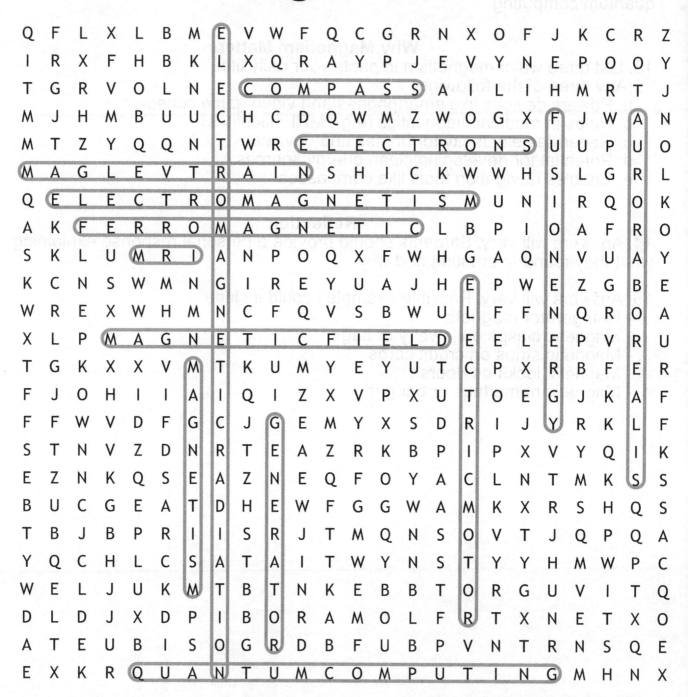

Electromagnetic radiation

Fusion energy

Compass

Electromagnetism

Electrons

Aurora borealis

Maglev train

MRI

Ferromagnetic

Magnetism

Quantum computing

Electric motor

Generator

Magnetic field

Magnetism

Across

5. The relationship between electricity and magnetism, where moving electric charges create magnetic fields and changing magnetic fields create electric currents.

6. A force that can attract or repel certain materials.

9. A type of advanced computing that sometimes uses magnetic fields to manipulate individual atoms. _____ computing

10. Tiny particles inside atoms that create magnetism when they move.

11. A super-fast train that uses strong magnets to float above the

12. A potential future energy source that uses powerful magnets to contain superheated plasma. _____ energy

14. Energy that travels through space as waves, including harmful types that the Earth's magnetic field protects us from. Electromagnetic _____

Down

1. Also known as the Northern Lights, a natural light display in the sky caused by the Earth's magnetic field. _____ borealis

2. A navigation tool with a magnetic needle that always points toward the Earth's magnetic north pole.

3. aterials that can be attracted to magnets, like iron, nickel, and cobalt.

4. An invisible area around a magnet where its force can be felt. (Two words)

7. A medical imaging tool that uses powerful electromagnets to create detailed pictures of the inside of the body.

8. A machine that converts motion into electricity, the opposite of an electric motor.

13. A device that uses electromagnets to convert electrical energy into motion. Electric _____

Introduction

Earth Sciences, also known as geosciences, is the study of our planet Earth. It helps us understand:

1. Why earthquakes happen
2. How mountains form
3. Where our drinking water comes from
4. Why the weather changes

What are Earth Sciences?

Earth Sciences is like putting together a giant puzzle to figure out how our world works.

Earth scientists study four main parts of our planet:

1. The solid Earth: rocks, soil, mountains
2. The water on Earth: oceans, rivers, glaciers
3. The air around us: atmosphere
4. Living things on Earth: plants, animals, humans

Earth Sciences combines knowledge from other subjects like physics, chemistry, and biology.

Major Areas of Earth Sciences

Fill in the definition for each area:

1. Geology: The study of rocks, minerals, and the processes that shape the Earth's surface
2. Meteorology: The study of the atmosphere and weather patterns
3. Oceanography: The study of the oceans and their processes
4. Environmental Science: The study of how living things interact with their environment
5. Climate Science: The study of long-term weather patterns and how they change over time

Why Earth Sciences Matter in Our Lives
For each area, briefly explain how Earth Sciences impacts our daily lives:

1. Natural Disasters: Help predict and prepare for earthquakes, volcanic eruptions, and hurricanes
2. Water Resources: Study groundwater and help find and manage clean water sources
3. Energy Resources: Help find resources like oil and gas, and develop cleaner energy sources
4. Climate Change: Study how our planet's climate is changing and its effects on our lives
5. Weather Forecasting: Predict weather to help us plan daily activities and prepare for severe weather
6. Agriculture: Help farmers understand soil types, weather patterns, and water availability
7. Building and Construction: Study ground stability to ensure safe building of structures

Earth Sciences and Your Future
List three potential career paths related to Earth Sciences:
1. Environmental consultant
2. Meteorologist
3. Geologist

(Note: Other acceptable answers include oceanographer, urban planner, science teacher, natural resource manager)

Reflection
In 2-3 sentences, explain why understanding Earth Sciences is important for everyone, even if they don't become Earth scientists:

Understanding Earth Sciences helps us make informed decisions about important issues like energy use, water conservation, and climate change. It gives us a better appreciation of our planet and how its systems work. This knowledge allows us to be more responsible citizens and contribute to solving global challenges related to our environment and natural resources.

Earth Sciences

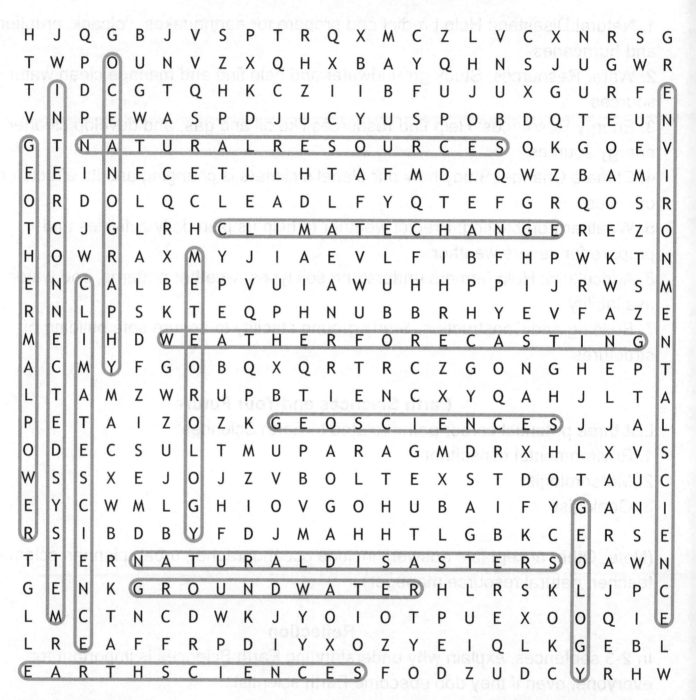

Climate change

Weather forecasting

Climate science

Oceanography

Geosciences

Interconnected system

Geothermal power

Environmental science

Meteorology

Earth sciences

Natural resources

Natural disasters

Groundwater

Geology

Earth Sciences

Across

2. The study of oceans and their processes.

3. The study of rocks, minerals, and the processes that shape Earth's surface.

8. Another name for Earth Sciences.

10. Predicting what the weather will be like in the near future. Weather ____

11. Long-term changes in Earth's weather patterns and average temperatures. ____ change

13. Water found underground in spaces between rocks and soil.

14. The study of our planet, including its rocks, water, air, and living things. (Two words)

Down

1. Materials found in nature that are useful to humans, like water, oil, or minerals. Natural ____

4. A group of parts that work together and affect each other, like Earth's different environments. ____ system

5. The study of how living things interact with their surroundings. ____ science

6. The science of studying the atmosphere and weather patterns.

7. A clean energy source that uses heat from inside the Earth. ____ power

9. Dangerous events caused by nature, like earthquakes, hurricanes, or volcanic eruptions. Natural ____

12. The study of long-term weather patterns and how they change over time. ____ science

Introduction

What's deep under our feet? Earth is like a giant onion, made up of different layers.

The Crust: Our Home Sweet Home

1. The crust is the outermost layer of the Earth.

2. Thickness of the crust: 5 to 70 kilometers

3. The crust makes up less than 1% of Earth's total radius.

4. Two types of crust:
   a) Continental crust: This is the land we live on. It's thicker and lighter.
   b) Oceanic crust: This is under the oceans. It's thinner and heavier.

5. Why the crust matters: (List two reasons)
   - Provides resources we need to survive (soil for growing food, materials for building)
   - Helps us find important minerals and manage natural disasters like earthquakes

The Mantle: Earth's Muscle

1. The mantle is located just below the crust.

2. It makes up about 84% of the planet's volume.

3. The mantle is divided into two parts:
   a) Upper mantle: This part is rigid and forms the bottom of tectonic plates.
   b) Lower mantle: This part is hotter and can flow, driving plate tectonics.

4. Why the mantle matters: Its slow movement causes plate tectonics, which shapes our planet's surface, creating mountains, volcanoes, and earthquakes

The Core: Earth's Powerhouse

1. The core is split into two parts:
   a) Outer core: This layer is liquid metal, mostly iron and nickel.
   b) Inner core: This is a solid ball of metal at the very center of the Earth.

2. Temperature of the inner core: About as hot as the surface of the Sun

3. Why the core matters: The spinning outer core creates Earth's magnetic field, which protects us from harmful radiation and helps animals navigate

Why Earth's Layers Matter

Match each aspect to its importance:

1. Natural resources   B
2. Natural disasters   A
3. Climate   D
4. Navigation   E
5. Life itself   C

a) Helps predict and prepare for events like earthquakes and tsunamis
b) Provides materials we use daily, like metals and fossil fuels
c) Creates conditions necessary for life, including temperature regulation
d) Affects global temperatures through processes like volcanic eruptions
e) Makes compasses work through the Earth's magnetic field

Reflection

In your own words, explain why understanding Earth's layers is important for our daily lives:

(Example answer) Understanding Earth's layers is crucial for our daily lives because it helps us manage our resources, prepare for natural disasters, and protect our environment. By knowing how the Earth works, we can better predict events like earthquakes and volcanic eruptions, potentially saving lives. It also helps us find and responsibly use natural resources that we depend on every day. Moreover, this knowledge allows us to better understand and address long-term issues like climate change, ensuring a safer and more sustainable future for everyone.

Earth's Layers

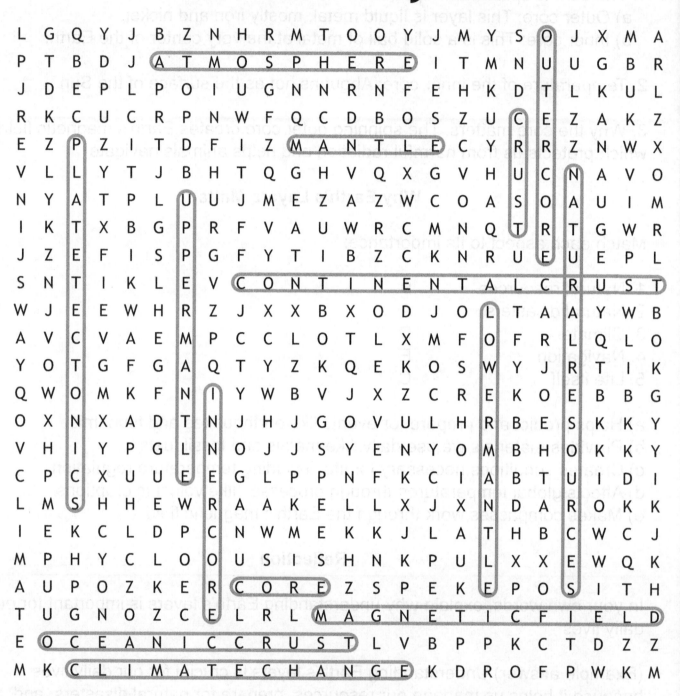

Climate change

Natural resources

Magnetic field

Inner core

Outer core

Lower mantle

Upper mantle

Oceanic crust

Continental crust

Atmosphere

Plate tectonics

Core

Mantle

Crust

Earth's Layers

Across
3. The typical weather patterns in an area over a long period of time.
5. The hotter, flowing part of the mantle that drives plate tectonics. ____ mantle
7. The layer of gasses surrounding the Earth, providing air for us to breathe.
9. The solid metal center of the Earth, extremely hot and dense. ____ core
10. The thinner, heavier part of the Earth's crust found under the oceans. ____ crust

12. Materials from the Earth, like metals and fossil fuels, that we use in daily life. ____ resources
13. The outermost layer of the Earth where we live and build our cities.
14. The rigid top part of the mantle that forms the bottom of tectonic plates. ____ mantle

Down
1. The largest layer of the Earth, located between the crust and the core.

2. The movement of large sections of the Earth's crust, driven by the mantle. (Two words)
4. The thicker, lighter part of the Earth's crust that forms land masses. ____ crust
6. The center part of the Earth, divided into outer and inner sections.
8. An invisible force created by the Earth's spinning outer core that protects us from harmful space radiation. ____ field
11. The liquid metal layer of the Earth's core, mostly made of iron and nickel. ____ core

Introduction
1. Geology is the science that studies:
   - The Earth
   - Its structure
   - The processes that shape it

What is Geology?
2. Geologists are like detectives for the Earth. They use clues from:
   - Rocks
   - Mountains
   - Volcanoes
   - Earthquakes

The Building Blocks: Rocks and Minerals
3. Complete the table about the three main types of rocks:

Rock Type	How It Forms
Igneous	Forms when hot, molten rock (magma or lava) cools and hardens
Sedimentary	Forms when bits of other rocks, plants, or animals get squeezed and cemented together over time
Metamorphic	Starts as other rocks but changes when exposed to extreme heat or pressure deep in the Earth

4. Minerals are:
   - Naturally occurring substances
   - With a specific chemical makeup

5. List three common minerals mentioned in the text:
   - Quartz
   - Feldspar
   - Mica

Earth's Dynamic Surface

6. Define the following terms:
   - Plate tectonics: The theory that explains how pieces of the Earth's crust move around, causing earthquakes, forming mountains, and creating volcanoes
   - Erosion: How wind, water, and ice wear away rocks and land over time, shaping landscapes
   - Deposition: When eroded materials get dropped off in new places, forming new landforms

Why Geology Matters in Your Life

7. Match each application of geology to its description:

   a) Natural Hazards   C Predicts earthquakes and volcanic eruptions
   b) Resources   A Helps find resources for electronics
   c) Environmental Protection E Tracks pollutant movement in soil and rock
   d) Climate Change   D Studies past climate patterns
   e) Building and Construction B Ensures ground stability for construction

Geology in Your Backyard

8. List three ways you can explore geology in your everyday life:
   - Look at the rocks in your yard or a nearby park. Spot different colors, shapes, or patterns.
   - Notice how water flows when it rains. Observe where it collects and if it's changing the land.
   - If you live near mountains or a beach, observe how the landscape changes over time.
   - Check out buildings in your town. Notice what materials they're made of and consider their geological origins.

The Big Picture

9. How old is the Earth? 4.6 billion years

10. Why is studying geology important for our future? (Answers may vary, but should include ideas such as:)
    Studying geology helps us understand and predict natural hazards, manage our natural resources sustainably, protect our environment, understand climate change, and ensure safe construction practices. It gives us insight into Earth's history and helps us make informed decisions about how to care for our planet in the future.

Geology

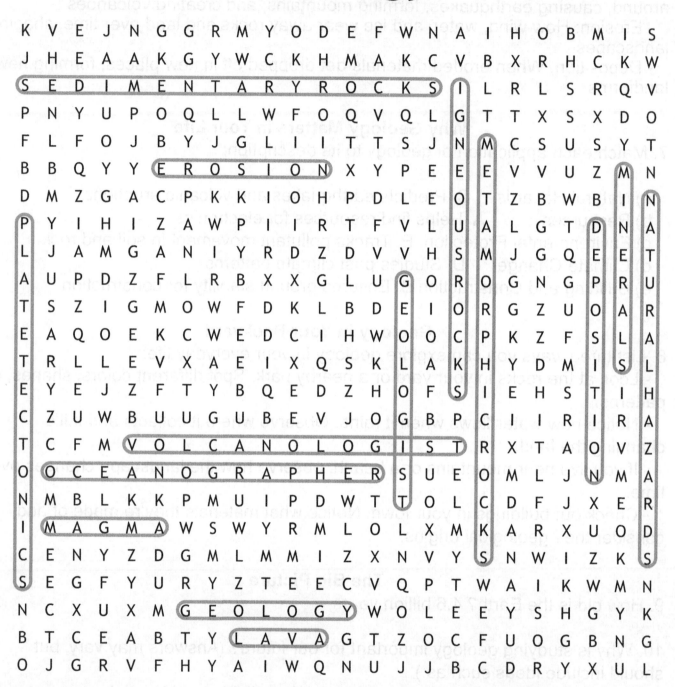

Natural hazards

Igneous rocks

Lava

Erosion

Geologist

Metamorphic rocks

Oceanographer

Magma

Plate tectonics

Geology

Sedimentary rocks

Volcanologist

Deposition

Minerals

Geology

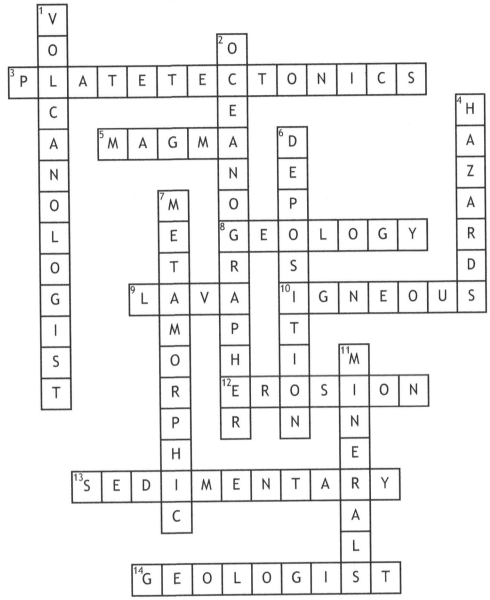

Across

3. The theory that explains how pieces of the Earth's crust move around, causing earthquakes, forming mountains, and creating volcanoes. (Two words)

5. Hot, molten rock beneath the Earth's surface.

8. The science that studies the Earth, its structure, and the processes that shape it.

9. Hot, molten rock that has erupted onto the Earth's surface.

10. Rocks formed when hot, molten rock (magma or lava) cools and hardens. ____ rocks

12. The process of wind, water, and ice wearing away rocks and land over time, shaping landscapes.

13. Rocks formed when bits of other rocks, plants, or animals get squeezed and cemented together over time. ____ rocks

14. A scientist who studies the Earth's structure and processes.

Down

1. A scientist who studies volcanoes and their behavior.

2. A scientist who studies the oceans and their processes.

4. Dangerous natural events like earthquakes, volcanic eruptions, landslides, and tsunamis that geologists help predict and prepare for. Natural ____

6. When eroded materials get dropped off in new places, forming new landforms.

7. Rocks that start as other types of rocks but change when exposed to extreme heat or pressure deep in the Earth. ____ rocks

11. Naturally occurring substances with a specific chemical makeup that make up rocks.

Introduction

1. What percentage of Earth's surface is covered by water? 71%

Definitions

2. Oceanography is the study of the world's oceans.

3. Hydrology is the study of fresh water on land.

Importance of Oceanography and Hydrology

List four reasons why these fields are important:

4. Weather and climate prediction

5. Food source management

6. Transportation safety and efficiency

7. Clean water supply

(Note: Students may also mention natural disaster prediction or recreation safety)

Impact on Daily Life

Explain how oceanography and hydrology affect each area:

8. Weather and Climate: Oceans store and distribute heat, affecting daily temperatures and long-term climate patterns.

9. Food: Help protect important food sources from the sea and assist farmers in using water efficiently for crops.

10. Transportation: Understanding ocean currents and weather patterns makes shipping safer and more efficient.

11. Clean Water: Study how pollutants move through water systems and how to clean them up, ensuring safe drinking water.

Fascinating Facts

Fill in the blanks:

12. The deepest part of the ocean is called Challenger Deep and it's approximately 7 miles deep.

13. The world's longest river is the Nile River, measuring about 4,132 miles long.

14. The Great Lakes contain approximately 20% of the world's fresh surface water.

15. True or False: The ocean's blue color is due to the water itself. False

Getting Involved

List three ways you can help protect water systems:

16. Use less plastic

17. Don't waste water

18. Participate in beach or river clean-ups

(Note: Students may also mention learning about local water sources or sharing knowledge with others)

Reflection

19. Why do you think it's important for everyone, not just scientists, to understand oceanography and hydrology?

   Answers may vary. Example: It's important for everyone to understand these fields because water affects all aspects of our lives, from the food we eat to the weather we experience. Understanding water systems helps us make better decisions about resource use and conservation.

20. What's one new thing you learned from this lesson that surprised you?

   Answers will vary based on individual student experiences and prior knowledge.

Oceanography & Hydrology

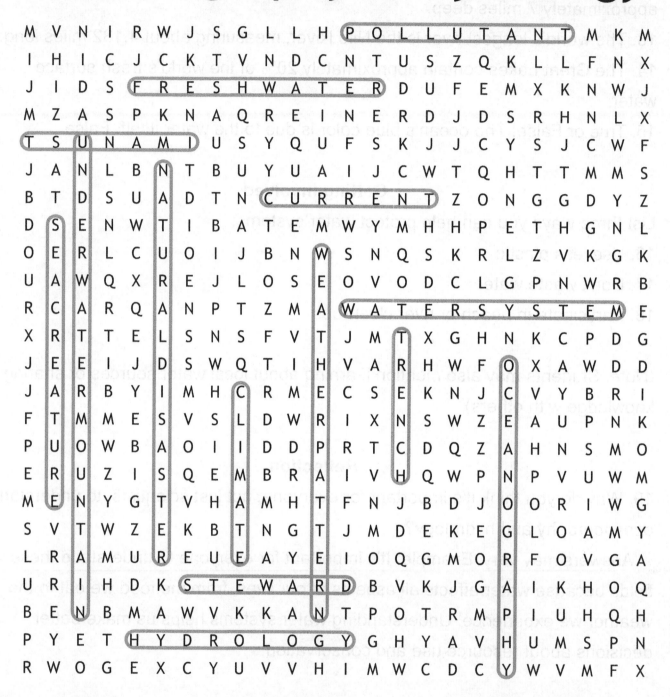

Water system

Fresh water

Sea creature

Pollutant

Hydrology

Natural disaster

Underwater mountain

Steward

Current

Oceanography

Weather pattern

Trench

Tsunami

Climate

Oceanography & Hydrology

Across

3. A substance that contaminates water, air, or soil, making it harmful to living things.

5. The typical way weather behaves in a specific area. Weather ____

7. A major event caused by nature that can harm people and damage property. Natural ____

11. Any animal that lives in the ocean. (Two words)

13. The study of fresh water on land, including rivers, lakes, and underground water.

14. A steady flow of water in a particular direction within a larger body of water.

Down

1. The typical weather patterns in an area over a long period of time.

2. A large raised area on the ocean floor, also known as a seamount. ____ mountain

4. The study of the world's oceans, including their physical and biological features.

6. A giant ocean wave usually caused by an underwater earthquake or volcanic eruption.

8. Water that contains little or no salt, like in rivers and lakes. ____ water

9. Someone who takes care of and protects something, like the environment.

10. A long, narrow, deep depression in the ocean floor.

12. The network of water sources and how they connect and interact with each other. Water ____

Introduction

1. atmosphere
2. Sun's

What is the Atmosphere?

3. blanket
4.

Gas	Percentage
Nitrogen	78%
Oxygen	21%
Other gases (e.g., argon, carbon dioxide, water vapor)	1%

5. thinner

Layers of the Atmosphere

6. Match each layer with its correct description:

   a) Troposphere   - Where we live and breathe
   b) Stratosphere   - Contains the ozone layer
   c) Mesosphere   - Where meteors burn up
   d) Thermosphere   - Where auroras occur
   e) Exosphere   - Outermost layer

Why is the Atmosphere Important?

7. List five crucial roles of the atmosphere:
   a) Provides the air we breathe
   b) Regulates temperature
   c) Protects us from harmful radiation
   d) Creates weather and climate
   e) Shields us from space debris

8. oxygen

9. It acts like a greenhouse, trapping heat from the Sun and keeping Earth warm.

10. harmful ultraviolet (UV) radiation

11. As the Sun heats the Earth unevenly, it creates air currents, which lead to wind, clouds, and precipitation.

The Atmosphere in Our Daily Lives

12. Give four examples of how the atmosphere affects our daily lives:
   a) Weather forecasts are predictions about atmospheric conditions
   b) The blue sky is caused by sunlight scattering in the atmosphere
   c) Air pollution occurs when harmful substances enter the atmosphere
   d) Climate change is largely due to changes in the atmosphere's composition

Caring for Our Atmosphere

13. Burning fossil fuels

14. List three ways we can help protect our atmosphere:
   a) Use energy-efficient appliances and vehicles
   b) Reduce, reuse, and recycle to lower our carbon footprint
   c) Support clean energy sources like solar and wind power
   (Note: Planting trees is also an acceptable answer)

Earth's Atmosphere

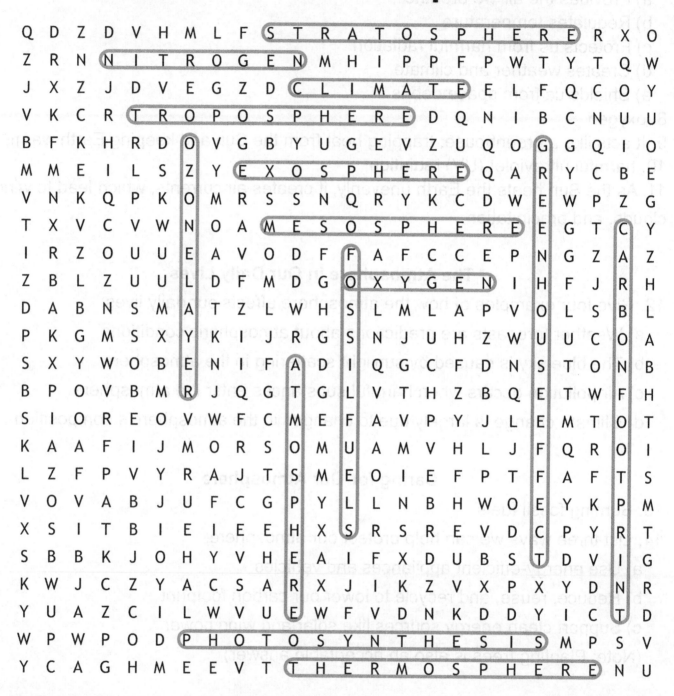

Fossil fuels	Carbon footprint	Greenhouse effect
Photosynthesis	Climate	Exosphere
Thermosphere	Mesosphere	Ozone layer
Stratosphere	Troposphere	Oxygen
Nitrogen	Atmosphere	

Earth's Atmosphere

Across

4. The amount of carbon dioxide released into the atmosphere as a result of human activities. Carbon ____

10. The typical weather patterns in an area over a long period of time.

11. The fourth layer of the atmosphere where auroras (like the Northern Lights) happen.

12. The lowest layer of the atmosphere where we live and most weather occurs.

14. The third layer of the atmosphere where most meteors burn up.

Down

1. The process by which plants and some bacteria produce oxygen using sunlight, water, and carbon dioxide.

2. A part of the stratosphere that blocks most of the Sun's harmful ultraviolet radiation.

3. The second layer of the atmosphere, containing the ozone layer that protects us from harmful UV rays.

5. Energy sources like coal, oil, and natural gas that release greenhouse gasses when burned. ____ fuels

6. The process by which the atmosphere traps heat from the Sun, keeping Earth warm. ____ effect

7. The most abundant gas in Earth's atmosphere, making up 78% of its composition.

8. The layer of gasses surrounding Earth that makes life possible.

9. The outermost layer of the atmosphere that gradually fades into space.

13. The second most common gas in the atmosphere, essential for breathing and making up 21% of its composition.

Introduction

1. Astronomy is the science that studies everything in space.

2. Why should we care about astronomy? It connects to our everyday life in many ways, from technology to understanding our place in the universe.

What is Astronomy?

3. Definition: The study of objects and events outside of Earth's atmosphere.

4. Tools astronomers use:
   - Telescopes
   - Satellites
   - Computers

The Building Blocks of Life

5. The elements in our bodies were created inside stars billions of years ago.

6. How did these elements reach Earth? Through exploding stars that scattered elements across space.

Astronomy's Impact on Technology

7. List three technologies influenced by astronomy and explain their connection:
   a. Wireless internet: Radio astronomy techniques helped develop Wi-Fi.
   b. GPS: Understanding how gravity affects satellite orbits makes GPS possible.
   c. Digital cameras: Technology first used in space telescopes is now in phone cameras.

Solving Earth's Challenges

8. How does studying Venus help us understand Earth's changing climate?

9. Astronomy contributes to better weather prediction on Earth.

10. Research on stars could lead to improvements in clean energy on Earth.

Inspiration and Perspective

11. How does astronomy inspire innovation? It pushes us to ask big questions and solve complex problems.

12. Explain how astronomy gives us perspective on our place in the universe:
    It shows that Earth is just one small planet in a vast universe, making our daily problems seem smaller and reminding us of our shared humanity.

Astronomy in Everyday Life

13. List four ways astronomy affects our daily lives:
    a. The Moon's phases affect ocean tides.
    b. Earth's tilt and orbit around the Sun cause seasons.
    c. Solar particles interacting with Earth's magnetic field create the Northern lights.
    d. Meteorites teach us about the early solar system.

The Future of Astronomy

14. Four areas of future exploration in astronomy:
    a. Space exploration: Planning missions to Mars and beyond.
    b. Finding other habitable planets that could support life.
    c. Developing ways to detect and deflect potentially dangerous asteroids.
    d. Studying dark matter, black holes, and the early universe with new telescopes and missions.

Getting Involved in Astronomy

15. List five ways you can explore astronomy without expensive equipment:
    a. Stargazing: Find a dark spot on a clear night and look up.
    b. Use free astronomy apps to identify stars and planets.
    c. Attend local astronomy club events or stargazing gatherings.
    d. Use online resources from NASA and other space agencies.
    e. Choose astronomy topics for school projects or science fairs.

Reflection

16. In your own words, explain why studying astronomy is important:
    (Answers will vary, but should touch on themes like understanding our place in the universe, driving technological innovation, helping solve Earth's problems, or inspiring curiosity and wonder about the cosmos.)

Astronomy

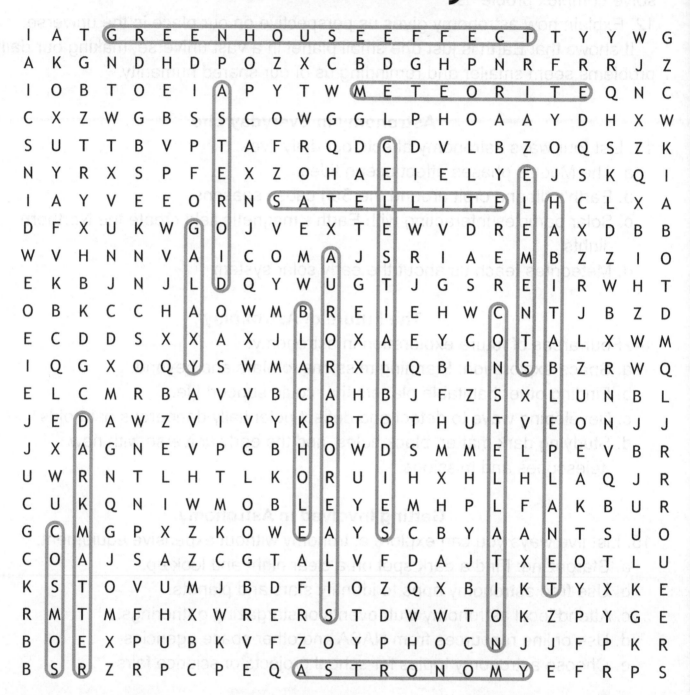

Habitable planet
Greenhouse effect
Asteroid
Constellation
Cosmos

Dark matter
Celestial bodies
Black hole
Satellite
Astronomy

Aurora borealis
Galaxy
Meteorite
Elements

Astronomy

Across

4. The warming of a planet's surface due to gasses in its atmosphere trapping heat. _____ effect

8. An object that orbits around a planet or star, either natural (like moons) or artificial (made by humans).

11. A group of stars that form a pattern in the night sky.

12. A mysterious substance in space that can't be seen directly but affects the motion of visible matter. _____ matter

13. A vast collection of stars, gas, dust, and dark matter held together by gravity, like our Milky Way.

14. A piece of rock from space that survives falling through Earth's atmosphere and lands on the surface.

Down

1. An extremely dense region of space with gravity so strong that nothing, not even light, can escape it. (Two words)

2. A small, rocky object that orbits the Sun, typically found between Mars and Jupiter.

3. Also called the Northern Lights; colorful light displays in the sky caused by solar particles interacting with Earth's magnetic field. _____ borealis

5. The basic building blocks of matter, like carbon, oxygen, and iron.

6. The scientific study of objects and events beyond Earth's atmosphere.

7. Natural objects visible in the sky, such as stars, planets, and moons. _____ bodies

9. Another word for the universe, including all of space and everything in it.

10. A world with conditions that could potentially support life as we know it. _____ planet

What are Environmental Sciences?

Environmental sciences is a field that studies how living things interact with the world around them.

Environmental scientists study:
1. The air we breathe
2. The water in our rivers and oceans
3. The soil where our food grows
4. The plants and animals in our ecosystems
5. The weather and climate patterns

Why Should You Care?

List five reasons why environmental sciences are important for your life:

1. It affects your health:
   Explanation: Environmental scientists work to keep air and water resources clean and safe.

2. It shapes your future:
   Explanation: Understanding environmental issues helps us find solutions to challenges like climate change and pollution.

3. It creates job opportunities:
   Explanation: There's a growing need for people who understand environmental sciences, leading to exciting career paths.

4. It helps you make informed choices:
   Explanation: Knowledge about environmental issues helps in making better decisions in daily life.

5. It connects you to the world:
   Explanation: Learning about the environment helps you appreciate the natural world and understand your place in it.

Real-Life Examples

Match the environmental science application to its description:

1. Weather forecasts   (B)   A. Helps farmers grow food
2. Food production   (A)   B. Predicts storms and heatwaves
3. Clean energy   (D)   C. Protects endangered species
4. Wildlife conservation   (C)   D. Develops solar and wind power
5. Urban planning   (E)   E. Designs parks and manages waste

How You Can Get Involved

List five ways you can get involved in environmental sciences now:

1. Join environmental clubs
2. Start recycling
3. Do a science fair project on an environmental topic
4. Volunteer for environmental activities
5. Stay informed about environmental news

Looking to the Future

How does your physical science class connect to environmental sciences? Concepts like energy, matter, and chemical reactions are key to understanding environmental processes.

Name three areas of study that can connect to environmental sciences:
1. Technology
2. Biology
3. Chemistry
(Note: Social studies was also mentioned in the text as a possible area)

Reflection

Write two sentences about why you think environmental sciences are important for your future:
(Answers will vary, but should reflect understanding of the importance of environmental sciences for health, career opportunities, decision-making, or global issues.)

Environmental Sciences

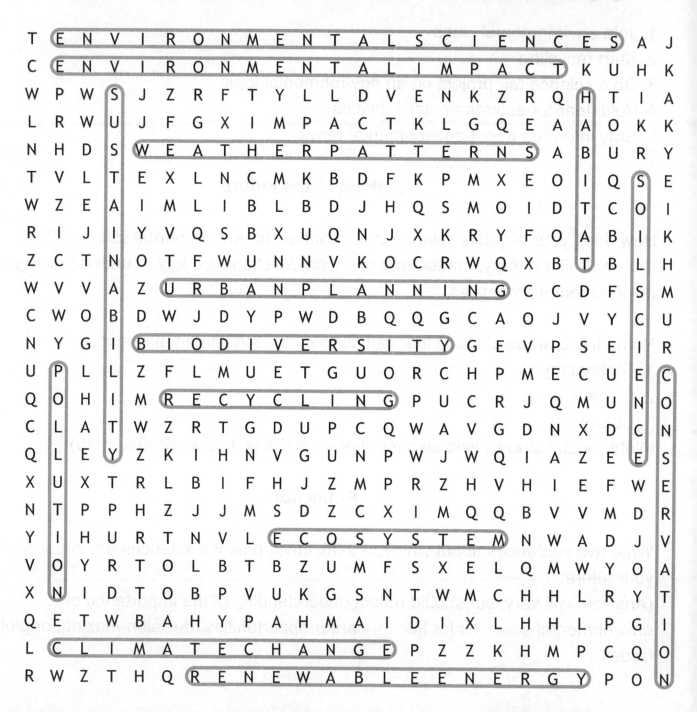

Environmental impact

Renewable energy

Recycling

Sustainability

Biodiversity

Soil science

Environmental sciences

Urban planning

Conservation

Ecosystem

Weather patterns

Habitat

Pollution

Climate change

Environmental Sciences

Across
2. Energy from sources that are naturally replenished, like sunlight or wind. _____ energy

3. The effect of human activities on the natural environment. Environmental _____

7. A community of living things and their environment, working together as a system.

8. The process of designing and organizing cities and towns for efficient and sustainable living. (Two words)

9. The recurring characteristics of weather in a particular area. Weather _____

12. The study of the mixture of minerals and organic matter as a natural resource, including its formation, classification, and mapping. _____ science

13. Meeting our current needs without compromising the ability of future generations to meet their needs.

14. Long-term changes in temperature and weather patterns on Earth. (Two words)

Down
1. The study of how living things interact with the world around them. _____ sciences

4. The protection and careful management of natural resources and the environment.

5. The variety of plant and animal life in a particular habitat or on Earth as a whole.

6. The introduction of harmful substances into the environment.

10. The process of converting waste materials into new materials and objects.

11. The natural home or environment of an animal, plant, or other organism.

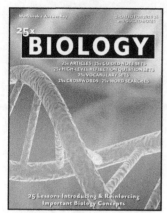
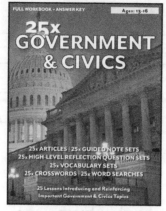
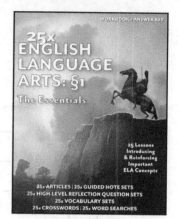

Inspired Educators Reflection Journal, Now Available On Amazon

Introducing - Inspired Educators K-12 Professional Development (PD Credit Available)

Empower teachers with the resources to nurture resilience and longevity.

Introducing the *Inspired Educators K-12 Professional Development Series!* Designed for educators, this unique program offers five 60-90 minute sessions that focus on nurturing teacher mental and emotional well-being.

Join us for engaging sessions delivered through Zoom, in-person, or via our convenient online course system. By completing the optional reflection journal, educators can earn one professional development credit.

The Five Sessions Are: 1. The Importance of Self-Care, 2. The Importance of Letting Go, 3. Raising Self-Awareness as an Educator, 4. Maintaining a Positive Mindset, and 5. Maintaining a Growth Mindset

Introducing - Let It Go: 7-Steps to Keeping Your Cool for High School Stu dents!

This comprehensive workbook is written specifically for grades 9-12 and contains 10 complete lessons for students looking to improve their social emotional learning.

Let It Go teaches students to take back control from their Defense Cascade (fight-flight-freeze response) and remain calm, cool, and collected when facing any situation. The program is designed with real solutions that teach students how to regulate their emotions, build self-awareness, and maintain a positive mindset. Not only does this program give students the skills they need to manage difficult situations in life but also gives them practical solutions to help them live their very best lives.

Let It Go: 7-Steps To Keeping Your Cool Workbook for High School Students. TPT & Amazon

Our Lessons On:
TeachersPayTeachers (TPT)
https://www.teacherspayteachers.com/store/3andb

Our Workbooks On:
Amazon
https://amzn.to/3ygpsvk

To learn more about our resources visit our website: 3andB.com

Made in the USA
Las Vegas, NV
15 November 2024

11861946R00203